Vegetarian Gourmet Cookery

REVISED EDITION
BY ALAN HOOKER

Drawings By
Sara Raffetto

101 Productions

Dedicated to vegetarians everywhere

Revised Edition

Cover design: Gary Hespenheide
Cover photography: Chuck Undersee

Printed and bound in the U.S.A.
Published by 101 Productions and distributed by Ortho Information Services, Box 5047, San Ramon, CA 94583

Library of Congress Catalog Card Number 88-71965
ISBN 0-89721-179-0

contents

ACKNOWLEDGMENTS

The success of the Ranch House as well as this book would not have been possible without the help of several people. I particularly want to thank Ranch House manager and chef David Skaggs, executive chef David Del Nagro, public relations director and hostess Nancy Adams, head waitress May Morse, head baker Tom Mooney and my wife Helen. All of them have been very patient, and with their honest criticisms have been most helpful.

introduction

"There's no sauce in the world like hunger." —Cervantes

At the moment of birth a problem is created that has to be faced every day as long as one lives. That problem is one's relationship to the environment. The infant solves the problem by feeding and thus conditions himself from the beginning with the idea that when one is in trouble—or in a strange situation—and can think of nothing else to do, one eats. In one form or another this idea haunts us all the days of our lives.

Some people use other than physical food to assuage their hunger—money, sex, social status, etc.—but still the simplest comfort is palatable food. There may be such a thing as going beyond this eternal sense of hunger to another level of our being that does not hunger, but this journey is not taken by many people.

Rather than just eating something to satisfy the pangs of hunger, we can become more perceptive about food. This may have unanticipated repercussions, for such sensitivity means a deepening of our awareness of all that surrounds us, thus providing more satisfaction from the environment.

When people come together who have not previously met they are a bit reserved, but when food is introduced there is an immediate change in the atmosphere. The power of the festive table begins to operate, bringing a feeling of gentleness and warmth. What I am trying to convey is that we have to begin somewhere to relate to the environment. How better than with food?

Why one decides no longer to eat meat is sometimes difficult to state. Every argument for a vegetarian diet can be met with an equally logical argument against. Years ago I read a book by Max Heindel in which he talked about the "oneness of all life." It made such sense to me that I stopped eating meat—for the first time.

But gradually this philosophy slipped away. It was the time of the hectic twenties, I was a traveling musician, and it was just too difficult to maintain a vegetarian diet.

After this period I lived for a time in Ohio and did the cooking for a communal group where I lived. There was a market where chickens were killed for you as you waited. One day I stood there waiting for my chicken to be killed. Perhaps I was in a relaxed and receptive state, for when the chicken squawked for its life on being caught something within me screamed just as hard for my life. The man handed me a wrapped-up dead chicken. I took it home and put it into the cooking pot. I served it on a platter, this dead chicken; but for me the transition to the word "meat" never took place. One cannot eat a "dead chicken" so, again I was not eating meat.

My wife Helen and I moved to the Ojai Valley in California and opened a boarding house where most of us were strict vegetarians. It became my job to invent new meatless entrées that would satisfy the non-vegetarian guests of the boarders. These new friends in turn invited their friends, and soon we were in real financial trouble. We had a begging bowl on the mantle, but found that the tradition of the bowl is not an American one, for it never contained enough money to pay our bills.

Eventually we opened The Ranch House Restaurant. Although the restaurant did have a menu, guests began to ask, "Where is the meat?" In those days there were not enough patrons interested in a vegetarian diet to support us. The restaurant began to lose money, and so to survive (perhaps following nature's first law), I started experimenting with meat recipes and soon we were serving *toutes les viandes* at the Ranch House. The nightmares I had when I first began this transition are too horrible to recount.

During these years I have devised several hundred recipes, both vegetarian and meat dishes, continually working to create something new. It is in the process of discovery that the fun of life comes, more than in what is discovered.

Personally I have again returned to a vegetarian diet. I think it is important to act in such a manner that guilt is not part of one's life. To eat meat and feel guilty is a horror, as I know only too well. To try and rationalize it is equally miserable. At any rate, once again I am a vegetarian, and though the Ranch House serves meat, it doesn't seem to bother me.

Perhaps interest is the key to the whole thing, I don't know; but I do know that the garden where we live is rife with things that excite me—new plants, new vegetables, new ways of making them happy in the garden, new ways of preparing them.

I hope this book will help you who use it and you who merely read it to provide for yourselves and others an adequate diet so you can live full vital lives, as you seek a better way to live in the world without having to resort to any type of violence—not even mental or emotional violence.

A sensitive approach to food may extend sensitivity almost without effort on our part, into other areas of our lives. Not only will our appreciation of the arts increase, but also we may be aided in practicing the most difficult and greatest art—that of friendly relationship to others. The art of getting along amicably with neighbors and friends requires true sensitivity, an awareness of all of man's hungers.

During the twelve years since the first publication of this book, my wife Helen and I have traveled extensively in Europe and Asia, eating in the finest restaurants we could find. This is the best teaching experience I know. Though one does not need to imitate exactly what others are doing, it sparks the imagination to discover something new that is delightful. Thus, the new recipes in this book have nearly all been "invented" through experiences such as these.

In considering the problems encountered in producing excellent food, one thing seems to be the most important and that is the method one uses in the preparation. This includes "liking" the closeness of food.

One must touch it and feel happy about the contact. If for one reason or another there is not this feeling (which should be an everlasting one), then the caring that is necessary in preparation leaves the food without the flavor and texture content that is required for excellent food.

Flavor and texture are especially important in cooking vegetarian food, for much of the attention in preparation has focused on these qualities in the meat-eating diet. In changing to a meatless diet, people often miss that place on the plate where meat once was placed. Vegetarian food purveyors have attempted to fill this spot with all manner of look-alike foods, mostly made of wheat gluten or soy or peanut meal. This has always struck me as the wrong approach to the problem. Why is it necessary to substitute something formal? Why not merely put something on the plate that tastes excellent and the absence of meat will not be noticed. This is done in other cultures, where bean curd, cheese, eggs, nuts and grains are used as sources of protein.

So what is necessary is loving fingers and a sensitive palate. In this way, experiments become a marvelous source of pleasure. Even when the desired result is not achieved, one learns something.

What constitutes a good vegetarian meal? Bread, it seems to me, is basic, the foundation of a good meal. Soup is not too difficult when one's interest is going full tilt. There are so many combinations possible, if one takes the time to consider what can be done. Vegetable broths are easy with vegetable cubes, and with the addition of various vegetables or grains and a judicious addition of herb blends, soup can take on an important meaning in the meal. There is a bounty of fresh vegetables for the dinner plate, and these same vegetables or seasonal fruits can be combined for a beautiful salad. Properly cooked rice and other grains, noodles and potatoes grace any plate. Finally, there is the entrée, and this book provides many choices, or you can create a new one on your own, always keeping in mind the importance of texture and flavor.

Though I have stressed flavor and texture so far, eye appeal must also be considered. Nancy Adams, our hostess at the Ranch House, was recently on a panel of judges for a food contest. She was told that eye appeal should count for 50 percent of her judgment about a dish. This attitude is one of the things wrong with food preparation today. In actuality, eye appeal should account for no more than 25 percent of any consideration about the success of a dish. Taste and texture are much more important, for one does have to *eat* the food, not simply look at it, and when the preparation is a good one, there is automatically wonderful eye appeal.

Some years ago when I managed a pie bakery, I made a test that successfully questioned the notion of eye appeal. I told the young woman whose job it was to put a butter chip on top of each pie before she put on the top layer to double the amount, adding two butter chips instead of one. I said nothing to anyone else about this. Within two weeks, one of the pie salesmen came to me and said, "A very funny thing has been happening. The apple pie business has doubled." I said nothing to him, but for me it proved that the subconscious is always at work. When one eats, something is recorded, like the taste of a good slice of apple pie. Even when one is talking and a waitress says, "What will you have for dessert," a little voice unconsciously says, "I'll have apple pie." You've remembered the wonderful flavor.

On another occasion, I was sitting at a restaurant counter. The man next to me was reading the menu and said, "I'll have some apple pie." In front of us stood one of those tall pie cases with cut pieces. They looked horrible and I said, "But you are going to have that piece in the case, aren't you?" Here eye appeal would have told the story, but it was not at work for this customer. You cannot deceive a baker's eye, however, because fresh eggs, butter, and cream create a "bloom." Without these, the bloom is absent.

You always remember the last taste of anything you eat, and the last bite should leave you with a very happy memory. I do hope you discover many happy memories when using this book. I have a "love affair" with food, thank goodness.

And so I think it useful to present this volume of vegetarian recipes that have been invented or adapted here at the Ranch House. Experimenting with them may bring out new facets of your understanding of food and people, and spur you on to do some inventing yourself. At least I hope so. Bon voyage on your food journeys!

Alan Hooker
Ojai, California
January 1982

herbs

HERBS HAVE A SPECIAL MAGIC

When one forgoes the meat-based stock pot as a source of flavoring, the herb garden acquires new meaning. A judicious use of herbs can change a dull dish into something of tongue-clicking interest. A new world of flavors opens with the use of those little leaves and plants. To the cook making a dietary change and worrying about missing the solid flavors of the flesh, combining herbs can be a challenge. So be creative and experiment. In fact, now the vegetable world takes on an entirely new aspect. The care that should always have been present when merely boiling a carrot, now becomes worthwhile because of the magic ingredient of new flavor. And see what herbs can do to ordinary cabbage, corn and tomatoes!

Let it be stated with emphasis that you should eliminate now from your cooking vocabulary two unfortunate terms: success and failure. There is no place for either of them in true experimentation. You cannot perform an experiment, if you are really interested in it, without learning something. I have been cooking for years and hardly a cooking day passes that I don't discover something new. Perhaps half of the things I try are not worth repeating, but from every experiment I learn more about what will or won't work.

I keep a notebook in which I write down what I have done, *after* I have done it. There is something about trying to record what you are doing while the experiment is going on that chokes off the fun and flow of creativity. Even if you forget one of the ingredients, when you come to the same stage again usually it will pop into your head. It is something like walking down a road and seeing landmarks as you go along.

One additional thought: Many people have asked me what defines an herb and what defines a spice. According to the dictionary, herbs are "flowering plants whose stems above ground do not become woody and persistent . . ." The same book defines spices as "any class of pungent or aromatic substances of vegetable origin, such as pepper, cinnamon, cloves and the like, used as seasonings or preservatives . . ." The most obvious difference, however, is that herbs are usually soft, leafy plants, while spices are most often hard and seldom found growing in this country.

ONIONS AND GARLIC

"A good cook begins with an onion," it is said. So let us begin our adventures with herbs the way a good cook should. One of the reasons, apart from flavor, for using any of the *Allium* family is the power of penetration inherent in it. All the parts of a good dish need one central substance to bind them together, and the onion is most frequently used for this purpose. The onions in common use are Spanish, yellow and white, garlic, leeks, chives, shallots and scallions.

For most cooked dishes, onions are chopped fine and then cleared by cooking them in butter or oil. This is important, for just this much cooking makes the catalyst that binds the flavors. When clearing onions and/or garlic, the herbs you plan to use with them should be added only *after* the clearing. The heat would drive off some of the essential oils in the herbs, leaving what I call a hole in the flavor.

Used raw, onions keep more of their own particular characteristics and do not have this catalytic ability. They season like an herb, which is, of course, what they are.

Garlic If the common onion is the most important seasoning (if such a distinction may be made), garlic is second. Many people use a garlic press, but I think this releases too much of the essential oils, which then evaporate. Garlic should be minced and cleared by cooking it in butter in a small covered pan until it looks transparent, but not browned. This may seem to be making a big thing out of something relatively unimportant, but I think you will find that it improves the flavor to treat the garlic in this way. Another good way to prepare the garlic cloves for seasoning is to pound them with salt in a mortar with a pestle.

Scallions These are little green onions and are for foods that require a light flavoring. There is a multiplier onion that I grow to use as scallions, which is excellent for this purpose. It grows like garlic, in clusters. It can be taken up and the buds separated, one of them replanted, and the process of growth begins again. This onion is easy to obtain from the nursery. Shallots grow in a similar manner.

Shallots These French bulbous onions have a sweeter flavor than scallions and the two are not interchangeable. Béarnaise sauce, for instance, demands shallots as well as fresh French tarragon.

Leeks These are like giant green onions and very sweet in flavor.

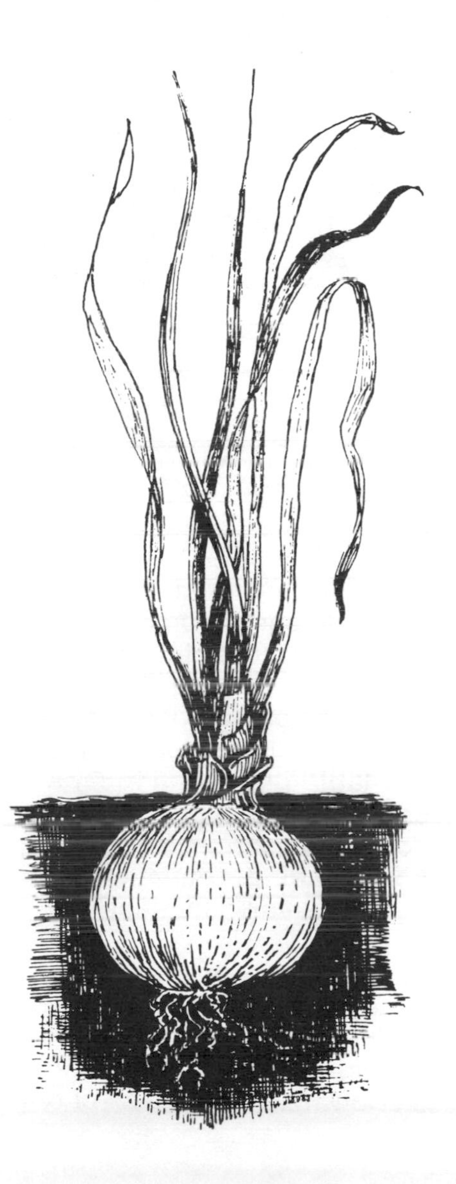

HERB COOKING MADE EASY

Now, about other herbs, those mysterious, often feared bits that hold such promise if only "someone would tell me how to use them!" Here's good news—it's easy! If one lacks the space to grow herbs, they are available packaged in most stores. However, dried herbs do lose flavor from the evaporation of their essential oils. Buy them in small quantities.

In herb cooking, it is quite necessary to have a mortar and pestle. There are many types available—wood, glass and stoneware. We grind all of our herbs in this way at the Ranch House.

First, let's divide herbs into some simple classifications for convenience: sweet herbs, bitter herbs, fragrant herbs, tart herbs and peppery herbs. What do you want to flavor? And in what way? This will determine the herb combinations you will use. You need only to understand the properties of the important ones.

Sweet Herbs
Celery Yes, it is an herb, and chervil is its strong brother.
Onion Garlic is its strong brother.
Summer Savory Winter savory is its strong brother.
Marjoram Oregano is wild marjoram.
Basil Anise is its strong brother.
Parsley Coriander, also called Spanish parsley, Chinese parsley or cilantro, is the strong brother.

Bitter Herbs Perhaps pungent is the better term. These include oregano, rosemary, thyme and sage.

Fragrant Herbs Mint and peppermint, lemon verbena, costmary (delicate mint), tarragon (the sister to fennel).

Tart Herbs French sorrel, sour grass.

Peppery Herb Watercress (the variety grown on dry ground is called overland cress).

HERB BLENDS

There is no rule about herb mixtures. Herbs should be blended according to the individual preference for certain flavors imparted. Variety in dishes is obtained by varying the given amounts in any blend. However, some foods almost demand certain herbs: Tomato or cheese demands basil and eggs demand tarragon. Vegetables such as peas need only marjoram or mint, or both. Corn can nicely use thyme.

The two simplest combinations of herbs are, of course, onions and garlic, and celery and parsley. Marjoram or thyme, when added to onion and a touch of garlic, form the perfect combination for a sweet herb blend.

The two classic methods of adding herbs to a dish are:

Aux Fines Herbes Finely chopped dried or fresh herbs added directly to the food and mixed throughout it.

Herb Bouquet (bouquet garni)
Literally, a bouquet of fresh herbs tied together and immersed in a sauce or dish, and then removed before serving. (If dried herbs are used, tie them in a cheesecloth bag.) This is done to add the herb flavor without the herbs showing in the finished preparation.

At the Ranch House, we have developed some *fines herbes* mixtures that are called for in various recipes in this book. These are given in proportions so that they can be made up ahead of time and stored for use as needed.

All the combinations are for dry herbs. They must not be portioned out by weight. "Part" refers to the size of the unit of measurement you are using: one tablespoon, one teaspoon, etc. Put the amount of salt or herb salt and the herbs you are going to use for your dish into a mortar and grind them together. The flavors will blend nicely and this mixture then can be added to the dish.

Omelet Herb Blend
3 parts parsley
1 part each: chervil, marjoram, tarragon, basil, chives

Salad Herb Blend
4 parts each: marjoram, basil, tarragon, parsley, chervil, celery leaves, chives
1 part each: lemon thyme, summer savory, costmary

Soup Herb Blend
2 parts each: thyme or summer savory, parsley, chervil, basil, marjoram, celery or lovage leaves
1 part each: sage, rosemary, ground dried lemon peel

Vegetable Herb Blend
1 part each: marjoram, basil, chervil, parsley, chives
Pinch of: summer savory, thyme

Savory Herb Blend
1 part each: basil, marjoram, celery leaves, parsley, costmary, tarragon
Pinch of: summer savory, thyme

Tomato Herb Blend
3 parts each: basil, parsley
1 part oregano
1/2 part each: summer savory, thyme, dill, celery leaves

Herb Salt
There are several varieties of blended herb salt on the market. Our own herb salt and herb blends, which have become quite famous, are available from The Ranch House, P.O. Box 458, 102 Besant Road, Ojai, California 93023.

THE HERB GARDEN

A three- by three-foot plot of ground at the kitchen door, or a box with eight pots, is most adequate for the usual kitchen "bouquet garni."
Here is the scheme:
Marjoram Thyme
Oregano Sage Mint Basil
Summer Savory Tarragon
The herbs shown above are partly perennials, partly annuals. Basil and summer savory are the annuals and, to keep them growing instead of going to seed, they must be constantly cut back to about eight inches in height. All blossoms and seeds must be picked off. The cuttings of leaves and blossoms may be laid on waxed paper on a flat surface and dried for winter use.

In the culture of your herb garden, experiment to see how much sun the plants need. In coastal areas they need full sun, especially tarragon, marjoram and thyme. Inland, a little shade is acceptable. Good drainage and fairly rich humus soil speed growth. Keep the plants picked back to encourage branching.

sauces

THE SAUCE IS THE MELODY

"Sauces are to cookery what grammar is to language and melody is to music."
—Careme and Soyer,
Master Chefs

Home cooks are apt to think that making many of the gourmet sauces, such as the famous béchamel, require a great number of ingredients, most of which will be found only in the kitchens of the famous restaurants of the world. Our kitchen at the Ranch House is a small one and we do not always have at hand this array of ingredients. In vegetarian cooking, I have often had to improvise in order to get the flavor and texture desired.

In my culinary thinking, the ingredients are often blended in my mind, much as a pianist practices his concert silently, away from the piano. If you who read this have never tried mentally to concoct a dish, you may be surprised to discover you have the same ability. To experiment, go where you won't be interrupted and think of the food you want to prepare, and what you can do to improve its flavor and texture.

I'd like to give you an example of a simple sauce I made. I visualized a small whole carrot, steamed just enough to remove the raw taste. Then I imagined a crunchy texture and to get it I chose poppy seed, sesame seed, onion salt and fresh peppercorns. I wanted these flavors to blend together more than they would when they were whole, and I wanted an accompanying flavor that would marry with all the other ingredients. This was celery seed. Then I went into the kitchen and began mixing the ingredients, always remembering the intensity of each separate one to achieve a proper balance.

On the supermarket shelves today are substitutes for things that had to be made from scratch not too long ago. If a vegetable broth is desired, a vegetable cube can be dissolved to prepare it. Granted these cubes are not as good as the real thing, but they are a passable substitute and they can broaden the scope of any home cook. Also, modern equipment such as a blender or food processor makes it possible to prepare a smooth sauce with so little effort that there should be no hesitance at all in attempting even a complicated recipe.

Most of the sauces given here are simple ones, although some of them are well known in the cuisines of famous chefs. This cookbook is for ordinary people like myself and I hope you do not mind being included in this category. Even though I love cooking I do not want to spend endless hours in the preparation process just to follow some recipe devised long before many of the present-day gadgets were invented.

RANCH HOUSE BÉCHAMEL SAUCE

Scald in a copper-bottom pan so the milk will not scorch:
4 cups milk
1 bay leaf
Discard the bay leaf when the milk is hot.
In a small saucepan, melt:
6 tablespoons butter
Add and cook, stirring constantly, for 3 minutes:
9-1/2 tablespoons unbleached flour
2-1/2 tablespoons herb salt
1/16 teaspoon freshly ground white pepper
Add the butter-flour mixture to the hot milk and stir constantly with a wire whisk until the mixture thickens.
Add and cook 1 minute, or until thickened:
1 egg yolk, mixed with 1/4 cup half-and-half cream
Remove from the heat and add:
3 tablespoons sherry (not dry type)
Put on top of sauce to prevent a skin from forming before using:
Small bits of butter
Use immediately, or let cool, cover and refrigerate. Reheat in a double boiler.
Makes approximately 4 cups

RICH CREAM SAUCE

Use this sauce in any recipe calling for a good cream sauce. It is wonderful thinned slightly and used to prepare creamed asparagus, peas, green beans or baby lima beans.

Scald in a copper-bottom pan so the milk will not scorch:
2 cups milk
In a small saucepan, melt:
3 tablespoons butter
Add and cook, stirring constantly, for 3 minutes:
4-1/2 tablespoons all-purpose flour
1-1/4 teaspoons herb salt
Dash white pepper
Add the butter-flour mixture to to the hot milk and stir constantly with a wire whisk until the mixture thickens. Then add and stir in well:
1 tablespoon heavy cream or evaporated milk
Makes approximately 2 cups

MORNAY SAUCE

The secret of this sauce is the quality and age of the cheese. It must be a very strong variety, such as a good cheddar, and well aged so that it will melt. The aging process breaks down the protein and makes it possible for the cheese to melt without becoming stringy. Kraft has a very good sharp cheddar, packaged in a red-foil wrapper, that is available in most markets.

This sauce is good for so many uses that it is a wise idea to make a large amount. It can be stored in the refrigerator in an airtight container for one week. Reheat it in a double boiler.

Scald in a copper-bottom pan so the milk will not scorch:
4 cups milk
1 bay leaf
Discard the bay leaf when the milk is hot.
In a small saucepan, melt:
6 tablespoons butter
Add and cook, stirring constantly, for 3 minutes:
9-1/2 tablespoons all-purpose flour
2-1/2 teaspoons herb salt
Good dash white pepper
Add the butter-flour mixture to the hot milk and stir constantly with a wire whisk until the mixture thickens. Add and cook 1 minute, or until thickened:
1 egg yolk, mixed with 1/4 cup half-and-half cream
Then stir in, mixing thoroughly:
2-1/2 tablespoons sherry
3 ounces sharp cheddar cheese, finely grated (3/4 cup)
1/4 teaspoon Worcestershire sauce
Dash cayenne pepper
Reheat, stirring to blend flavors.
Makes approximately 4 cups

FRESH MUSHROOM SAUCE

Serve over omelets or add to cooked rice.

Cook until very soft in:
2 tablespoons butter
1 clove garlic, minced
1/2 cup sliced onion
When onion starts to brown, add and cook until tender:
1/2 pound mushrooms, sliced
1 tablespoon all-purpose flour, mixed in 1/2 cup water
1/2 teaspoon fresh lemon or lime juice
Makes approximately 1-1/2 cups

Variation Omit flour and lemon or lime juice. When mushrooms are tender, stir in 1/2 cup sour cream. The mushrooms should be cooked down to a good consistency for this, or the addition of the sour cream will make the mixture too thin.

SAUCE ZOIA

In a saucepan, cook until clear in:
1/4 pound butter
3 cups thinly sliced onion
Add and cook for 2 to 3 minutes:
1 pound mushrooms, thinly sliced
Grind in a mortar:
1/2 teaspoon herb salt
1/2 teaspoon Vegetable Herb Blend
Add to skillet and stir in:
1 tablespoon Marmite
Mortar mixture
Mix together, then add and stir in well:
1/2 cup milk, or to taste
1 cup Ranch House Béchamel Sauce (page 15) or any white sauce
1-1/2 cups sour cream
1/2 teaspoon Kitchen Bouquet
Heat to serving temperature; do not boil or sauce will curdle.
Makes approximately 6 cups

MUSHROOM GRAVY WITH SAVITA

In a saucepan, melt:
2 tablespoons butter
Add and cook 2 minutes over medium heat:
1/2 pound mushrooms, sliced
1/2 teaspoon herb salt
1/2 teaspoon Savory Herb Blend
Add and cook until thickened:
1 tablespoon Savita, or 3 vegetable bouillon cubes, dissolved in 3 cups boiling water
2 tablespoons cornstarch, dissolved in 3 tablespoons cold water
Makes approximately 1-1/2 cups

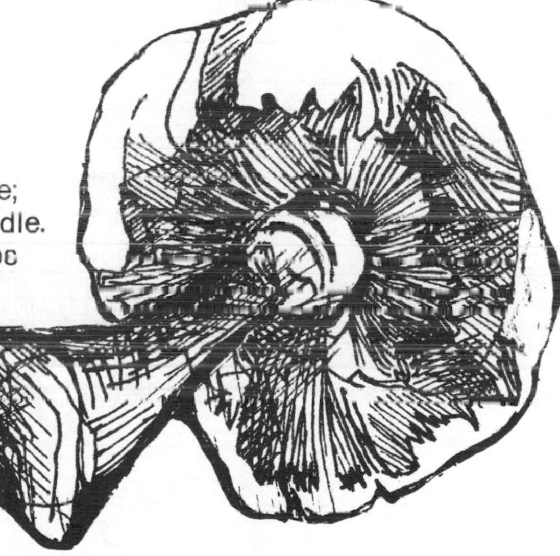

MUSHROOM SAUCE FOR SPAGHETTI

In a kettle, cook until golden in:
1/2 cup olive oil
3 onions, thickly sliced
Add and cook about 30 minutes:
3/4 pound mushrooms, chopped
4 bay leaves
2 tablespoons chopped fresh oregano
1 tablespoon chopped fresh thyme
1 tablespoon chopped fresh basil
1 teaspoon ground cumin
1/2 teaspoon freshly ground black pepper
4 vegetable bouillon cubes, crushed
Add and simmer, covered, for 3 hours:
1 cup water
1 tablespoon Savita
Discard bay leaves and store, refrigerated, in a tightly covered container, or freeze, removing small amounts as needed.
Makes approximately 4 cups

SPANISH SAUCE

In a large saucepan or kettle, cook, covered, until tender but not mushy:

4 cups coarsely chopped onion
3 cups sliced celery
1 cup coarsely chopped green bell pepper
1 cup sliced mushrooms (optional)
1 (3-1/2-ounce) can black olives, drained and chopped
1 cup canned tomatoes, mashed
2 vegetable bouillon cubes, crushed
1/2 teaspoon salt
1 bay leaf
1 clove garlic, minced
1/2 teaspoon Tomato Herb Blend

When vegetables are cooked, add and simmer 15 minutes:

3 (6-ounce) cans tomato paste
1 (4-ounce) can pimientos, drained and chopped

Discard bay leaf and store, refrigerated, in a tightly covered container, or freeze, removing small amounts as needed.

Makes approximately 2-1/2 quarts

ITALIAN SAUCE

In a kettle, cook until clear in:

1/4 cup olive oil
2 cups finely chopped onion
4 cloves garlic, minced

Add and boil slowly for 15 minutes:

2 large green bell peppers, seeded and finely chopped
4 bay leaves
4 vegetable bouillon cubes, crushed
1 (46-ounce) can tomato juice

Grind in a mortar and add to kettle:

1/2 teaspoon dried rosemary
1/2 teaspoon dried thyme
1 teaspoon dried oregano
1 teaspoon dried basil

When vegetables are tender, add and simmer for 30 minutes:

3 (6-ounce) cans tomato paste

Discard bay leaves and store, refrigerated, in a tightly covered container, or freeze, removing small amounts as needed.

Makes approximately 2 quarts

ITALIAN SPAGHETTI SAUCE

In a kettle or large saucepan, cook until clear in:
1/3 cup olive oil
2 cups minced onion
4 cloves garlic, minced
Add and cook over low heat to blend well:
1 (15-ounce) can Italian-style tomatoes
5 (6-ounce) cans tomato paste
2 ounces dried Italian mushrooms, soaked in water to soften, or
1/2 pound fresh mushrooms, sliced
1 cup minced parsley
1 tablespoon granulated white sugar
10 vegetable cubes, crushed
Grind in a mortar and add to kettle:
1 teaspoon salt
1 teaspoon dried basil
1 teaspoon dried rosemary
1 teaspoon dried thyme
1 teaspoon freshly ground black pepper
1 teaspoon cumin seeds
Simmer very gently, covered, for at least 2 hours; longer, if possible. Serve over spaghetti or store, refrigerated, in a tightly covered container. This sauce may also be frozen and removed in small amounts as needed.
Makes approximately 6 cups

LOW-CALORIE SAUCE FOR VEGETABLES

Serve over steamed broccoli or Swiss chard.

In a saucepan, combine and heat:
1 cup buttermilk
1/2 cup plain yogurt
Grind in a mortar:
1 teaspoon dried thyme
1 teaspoon herb salt
1/2 teaspoon ground turmeric
Add to saucepan:
Mortar mixture
1 teaspoon capers
Then add and cook, stirring constantly, until thickened:
1 tablespoon cornstarch, dissolved in a little water
Makes approximately 1-1/2 cups

ANOTHER LOW-CALORIE SAUCE FOR VEGETABLES

In a saucepan, heat together until thickened, stirring constantly:
2 cups buttermilk
1/4 cup plain yogurt
1/4 cup cornstarch
Grind in a mortar:
1/2 teaspoon herb salt
1/2 teaspoon dried winter savory
Add to saucepan:
Mortar mixture
1-1/2 tablespoons capers
1 teaspoon ground turmeric
Heat just until flavors are blended.
Makes approximately 2-1/4 cups

LIGHT TOMATO SAUCE

This sauce is delicious served with Deep-fried Pimiento Relleno. Dip the pimiento into the sauce and let it absorb some of the tomato fragrance.

In a large saucepan, bring to a boil:
1 (46-ounce) can tomato juice
1 vegetable bouillon cube, crushed
1 bay leaf
1/2 teaspoon herb salt
1/2 teaspoon crumbled dried basil
1/2 teaspoon crumbled dried marjoram
Discard bay leaf and store, refrigerated, in a tightly covered container, or freeze, removing small amounts as needed.
Makes approximately 5-1/2 cups

SAUCE OLIVOS

This sauce is extraordinarily delicious. Serve on steamed Swiss chard, broccoli or cauliflower.

In a saucepan, heat just to serving temperature:
1/2 pound butter
2 tablespoons Bakon yeast
2 tablespoons capers, mashed with a little of the bottling liquid
1/3 cup chopped black olives
Do not let this sauce boil or it will curdle.
Makes approximately 1-1/4 cups

SEED SAUCE FOR CARROTS

In a blender or food processor, mix for 2 minutes:
1 tablespoon celery seeds
1 tablespoon poppy seeds
1 tablespoon sesame seeds
1 teaspoon onion salt
1/4 teaspoon black peppercorns
5 gratings fresh nutmeg
In a small saucepan, melt:
3/4 pound butter
Add seed mixture to butter.
This sauce may be stored, refrigerated, in a tightly covered container for 1 to 2 weeks.
Makes approximately 1-1/2 cups

BUTTERMILK SAUCE FOR ASPARAGUS

This sauce is also good on steamed broccoli and cauliflower

In a saucepan, combine and heat:
1 cup Rich Cream Sauce (page 16)
1/3 cup buttermilk
1 teaspoon fresh lemon juice
1/8 teaspoon herb salt
Large pinch ground turmeric
Dash cayenne pepper
In a skillet, cook until clear in:
2 tablespoons butter
1 shallot or green onion and top, finely chopped
Add to cream sauce mixture.
Then stir in:
1 tablespoon cornstarch, dissolved in a little water
Cook, stirring constantly, until thickened.
Makes approximately 1-1/4 cups

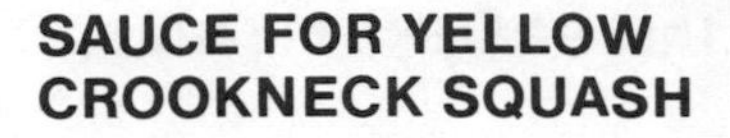

SAUCE FOR YELLOW CROOKNECK SQUASH

In a small saucepan, combine and heat:
1/4 pound butter
1/4 cup fresh lemon juice
Grind in a mortar and add to saucepan:
1/2 teaspoon herb salt
4 sprigs lemon thyme, or 1/4 teaspoon dried thyme
Transfer mixture to a blender container or food processor and mix to blend thoroughly.
Makes approximately 2/3 cup

PIQUANT SAUCE FOR GREENS

Grind in a mortar:
1/2 teaspoon dried lemon thyme
1 teaspoon herb salt
1/2 teaspoon ground turmeric
In a saucepan, combine and heat to boiling point:
Mortar mixture
1/4 pound butter
Juice of 1 lemon
Add and cook, stirring constantly, until thickened:
1 teaspoon cornstarch, dissolved in 1/2 cup water
Makes approximately 1 cup

SWEET PEPPER BUTTER

Steam until soft, then seed and finely chop:
1 green bell pepper
Whip until light and fluffy:
1/2 pound butter, at room temperature
Add to butter, folding in well:
1/2 teaspoon herb salt
Chopped green bell pepper
1 (4-ounce) can pimientos, drained and finely chopped
Makes approximately 2 cups

GREEN ONION BUTTER

This sauce is excellent on baked, boiled or mashed potatoes, or steamed rice.

In a covered pan, cook until tender but not browned in:
2 tablespoons butter
2 tablespoons minced onion
In a blender or food processor, mix for 1 minute:
Cooked onion
3 green onion tops, chopped
2 tablespoons water
Whip until light and fluffy:
1/2 pound butter, at room temperature
Add the onion mixture to the butter and mix until well blended.
Makes approximately 2 cups

GARLIC BUTTER

Delicious on steamed zucchini.

In a covered pan, cook until tender but not browned in:
2 teaspoons butter
3 cloves garlic, minced
In a blender or food processor, mix for 1 minute:
Cooked garlic
1 teaspoon garlic salt
1/2 teaspoon herb salt
Whip until light and fluffy:
1/4 pound butter, at room temperature
Add the garlic mixture and mix until well blended.
Makes approximately 1-1/2 cups

QUICK-AND-EASY HOLLANDAISE SAUCE

In a saucepan, melt:
1/2 pound butter
Add and bring to a boil:
1/4 cup fresh lemon or lime juice, mixed with water to make 2/3 cup
Heat a blender container by rinsing it in hot water. While the container is still hot, add:
3 egg yolks, at room temperature
Dash cayenne pepper
Dash herb salt
Dash crumbled dried chervil
When the butter mixture reaches a boil, start the blender motor and add the butter mixture immediately. Blend for about 10 seconds, no more. Once sauce has set, additional blending will thin it. Keep the sauce warm in the top pan of a double boiler until ready to serve.
Makes approximately 2 cups

RANCH HOUSE MAYONNAISE

In a blender, break:
1 egg, at room temperature
In a very slow, steady stream, add with blender running at low speed and blend for 20 seconds:
1 cup safflower oil or oil of choice
Add and blend for 20 seconds:
1/2 teaspoon herb salt
1/2 teaspoon Salad Herb Blend
1/2 teaspoon dry mustard
2 teaspoons prepared sharp horseradish
1/8 teaspoon white pepper
1 tablespoon fresh lemon or lime juice
Turn off blender immediately or mayonnaise will set too much to handle.
Makes approximately 1-1/2 cups

soups

SOUP—THE GOOD START

Because I am a self-taught cook, I have been able to embark on a journey of flavors not conditioned by the traditions of *haute cuisine.* Being a vegetarian, there were no meat-based stock pots to draw on. Herb seasonings are of the utmost importance in vegetarian cookery and these were the bulwark and foundation of my knowledge. When the basis of flavoring rests on beef, fowl and fish, the possibilities for variety in flavoring are altogether too limited. In all my experiments I have tried to branch out as much as possible, using the efficacy of fresh herbs. Such a variety of flavors is possible and thus the inventive spirit can begin to flower.

The dominant feature of a soup is the liquid and this liquid takes its character from one or a combination of vegetables. With the help of various herbs and spices, the panorama of flavors is further extended. Some soups accumulate; others are always made from scratch. All juices from cooked vegetables should be faithfully saved and stored in the refrigerator; all scraps of vegetables that are still fresh should likewise be saved and stored in a plastic bag or humidifier. Some soups are served with no thickening at all; others need a little binding, the addition of various forms of *roux.* So, the chance to employ the full scope of one's imagination is almost unlimited.

Are you intrigued by now? I hope so, for in experimenting with this marvelous old menu standby, many of the secrets you learn will be found useful in all your other cooking.

VICHYSSOISE

In a skillet, cook until clear but not brown in:
2 tablespoons butter
4 large leeks (white part only), minced
1/2 cup minced onion
Cook until tender in:
Boiling salted water
6 large potatoes
Drain and cool until they can be handled, then peel. Crush the potatoes with a fork and mix with the cooked leeks. Transfer to a saucepan and add:
4 vegetable bouillon cubes, dissolved in
6 cups hot water
Boil gently for 10 minutes, being careful that the mixture does not stick to the bottom or the flavor will be ruined. Put through a Foley mill (or sieve) and then briefly run in a blender or food processor. (Do not blend too much or it will become slimy.) Chill overnight. The next day, add to the potato mixture:
2 cups half-and-half cream
2-1/2 cups heavy cream
When well mixed, blend thoroughly with a wire whisk. Season to taste with:
Few dashes ground nutmeg
Serve in chilled bowls, garnished with:
Finely chopped chives
Makes 10 servings

CHILLED CUCUMBER CREAM SOUP

Cook in a pressure cooker for 3 minutes at 15 pounds pressure:

3 cucumbers, peeled and quartered
1/2 cup chopped green onion (white part only)
1 cup water
1/2 teaspoon crumbled dried chervil
1 teaspoon salt
1 tablespoon herb salt
Good dash white pepper

Add to cooked cucumber mixture and simmer gently for 2 minutes, stirring constantly, to thicken:

2 tablespoons all-purpose flour, mixed in 1/4 cup water

Purée cucumber mixture in a blender or food processor and strain into a bowl. In a blender or food processor, purée:

1 cup half-and-half cream
1 cucumber, peeled and halved

Strain this into the bowl holding the cucumber mixture and add:

2 cups heavy cream

Stir together well with a wire whisk, then chill, preferably overnight.

Makes 4 servings

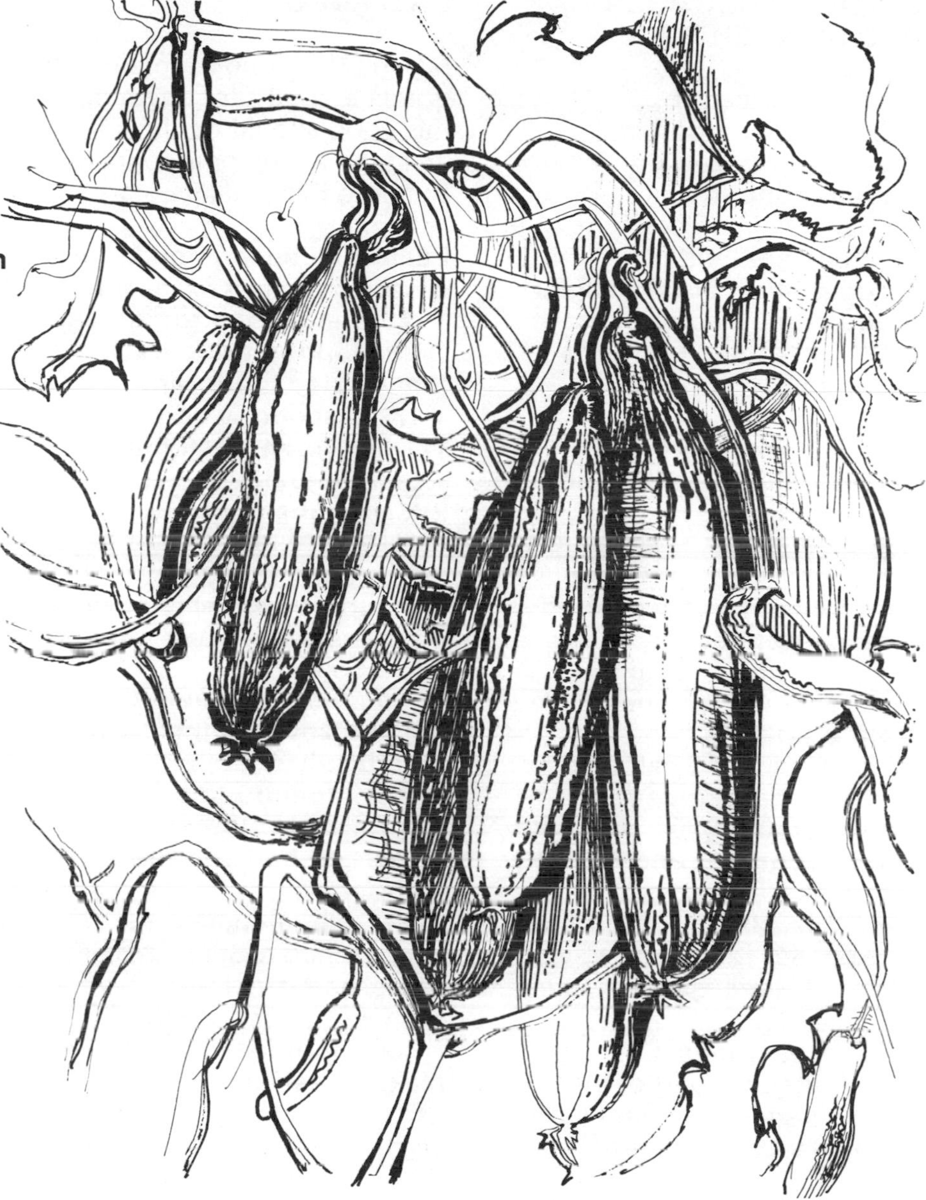

CHILLED CUCUMBER AND SPINACH SOUP

Cook until clear in:
4 tablespoons butter
2 bunches green onions and tops, minced
Add and simmer, covered, until potatoes are tender:
1 cup peeled potato slices
8 cups diced cucumber
1 bunch spinach (2 cups chopped), cooked
6 cups water
1 tablespoon herb salt
3 vegetable bouillon cubes, crushed
6 tablespoons fresh lemon juice
Good dash freshly ground black pepper
Purée in a blender or food processor in 2 batches:
Potato mixture
4 cups half-and-half cream
2 cucumbers, diced
Chill thoroughly. Garnish with:
Thin cucumber and radish slices
Tiny threads of green onion tops
Makes 8 servings

Note Heavy cream may be substituted for part or all of the half-and-half cream if a thicker soup is desired.

GAZPACHO

Making this soup is so easy it is almost a pity, for anything this good should be difficult and take a long time to make. But here it is in all its glory.

Put in a blender or food processor and mix for 1 minute:
1 (15-ounce) can tomatoes
1/2 teaspoon dried basil
Pinch dried marjoram
1-1/2 teaspoons herb salt
1/2 teaspoon fresh lemon or lime juice
2 teaspoons fresh coriander leaves
Add and mix 30 seconds:
1/4 cup good-quality olive oil
Strain tomato mixture and put into a bowl. Add:
1/3 cucumber, peeled, diced and sprinkled with herb salt
1 small tomato, diced and sprinkled with herb salt
1/2 green bell pepper, finely chopped
Cover and refrigerate for at least 24 hours. Serve in chilled bowls, garnished with:
Finely chopped fresh coriander leaves or chives
Makes 4 servings

Note A guest at the Ranch House, who had just returned from South America, told me of another way to serve gazpacho—as a midday meal, very elaborately prepared with many chopped vegetables and other things. The soup is served in large, individual, chilled bowls. The garnishes, which are anything that will go well with the soup's tomato flavor such as the cucumber, tomato and green pepper mentioned in the recipe, plus chopped green onions, sliced hard-cooked eggs, green and black olives, thinly sliced celery, are served in small bowls from which the diner makes his own selection.

FRENCH SORREL SOUP

At the Ranch House we grow our own sorrel and can therefore serve a chilled sorrel soup just as it is made in France. We had grown sorrel for salads ever since we first had the restaurant up on the hill, but I had never heard of sorrel soup until someone exclaimed about our having fresh sorrel and said she had had a most delicious chilled sorrel soup in France. And so we now have it.

My wife, Helen, and I were going on vacation, leaving the restaurant in charge of Marjorie Smith and a young fellow by the name of King Hutchinson. I suggested to him that he try to concoct a soup out of the sorrel we had growing. He had not done much cooking, but he seemed to have a flair for it, and did succeed in making the soup, so I cannot claim credit for the basic recipe, though I did refine it somewhat. The main thing is to have enough fresh sorrel so that its tartness is imparted to the soup. The addition of carrots gives a bit of sweetness, and this can be adjusted if one does not care to have a very tart soup. Carrots will sweeten it without adding sugar.

We do the whole soup in a kettle and then purée and strain it. At first, when the soup has just been made, it may seem to lack flavor, but letting it stand twenty-four hours will bring out all the hidden flavor. It should be put into a covered stainless steel pot or glass vessel and kept overnight in the refrigerator. Sometimes people ask what kind of cheese we put in it, probably because of the combination of tartness and the sour cream garnish.

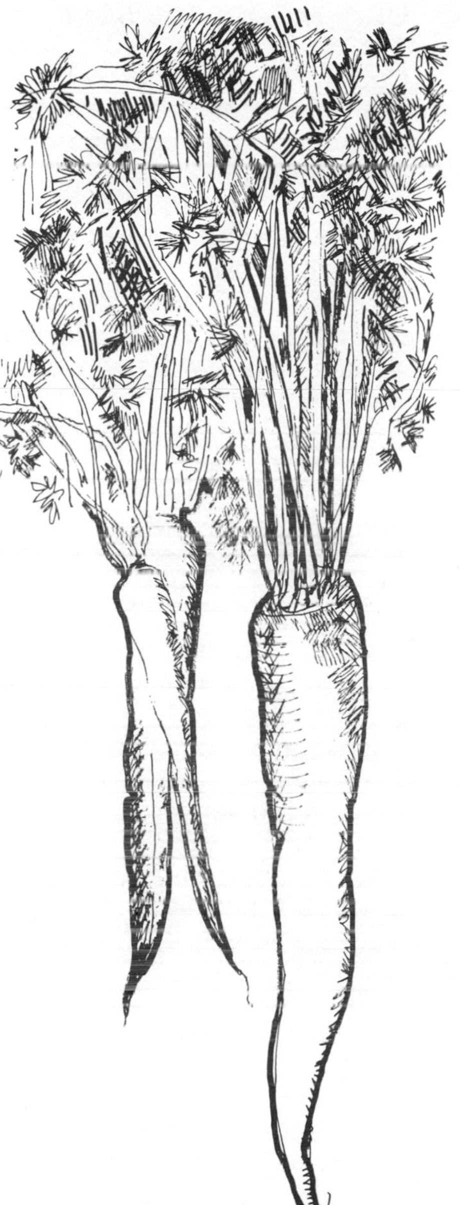

Cook in a pressure cooker for 10 minutes at 15 pounds pressure:

7 cups water
1 large carrot, finely chopped
2 stalks celery, finely chopped
1/2 small cucumber, finely chopped
1 medium onion, finely chopped
2 large leaves cabbage, chopped
1/2 teaspoon Soup Herb Blend
5 vegetable bouillon cubes, crushed
1/4 cup chopped parsley

In a small saucepan, cook slowly for 5 minutes:

6 large fresh sorrel leaves and stems
1/4 cup water

Combine all ingredients, purée in a blender or food processor and strain. Add:

1 tablespoon fresh lemon juice

Chill for 24 hours and serve, garnished with:

Sour cream

Makes 8 servings

GREEN BEAN BISQUE

Cook in a pressure cooker for 1 minute at 15 pounds pressure:

1-1/3 pounds green beans (4 cups)
1/2 cup water

In a blender or food processor, purée in 2 batches:

Cooked green beans
4 cups milk, scalded
1 tablespoon herb salt
Pinch fresh thyme leaves
1/8 teaspoon fresh marjoram leaves
1/8 teaspoon fresh basil leaves
Dash celery seeds
Dash freshly ground black pepper
1 tablespoon granulated white sugar

Transfer to a double boiler or saucepan and adjust seasoning with:

Onion salt

Then add:

1-1/2 teaspoons sherry

Heat just to serving temperature. Garnish with:

Toasted thinly sliced almonds

If the almonds are sliced very thin, they will float on the surface of the soup.
Makes 6 servings

GREEN GODDESS SOUP

Cook until just tender in:

1/4 cup water
1 small bunch asparagus, trimmed

Heat together, but do not boil:

4 cups shelled green peas
1/4 cup water

In a blender or food processor, purée the asparagus and peas. Strain into a vessel containing:

6 cups milk
1/4 teaspoon fresh marjoram leaves
2 fresh mint leaves
Pinch fresh thyme leaves
1-1/4 tablespoons herb salt

In a blender or food processor, purée in 2 batches the milk mixture. (Do not strain.) Transfer to a double boiler or saucepan and add:

1 large avocado, cubed
2 cups milk

Heat just to serving temperature. Garnish with:

Unsweetened whipped cream
Chopped parsley

Makes 8 servings

Note A good idea, when there is fresh asparagus available, is to save the stalks of a couple of bunches for this soup and use the tips as a vegetable dish. It is important that the peas be only heated and not boiled, as this retains their fresh flavor. Equally important is not to boil the soup after the avocado has been added, because overheating creates a strong acid flavor. This has been an extremely popular soup at the Ranch House and many people have been unable to identify the ingredients. It should be light in color when served.

FRESH CORN BISQUE

Select:

3 ears corn

Stand each ear on end and, with a sharp knife, cut each row of kernels down the center, then scrape the cob with the back of the knife blade to get all of the milk out. Combine and cook over low heat for 7 minutes:

Corn from ears
1/2 cup water
1/2 teaspoon fresh thyme leaves
3/4 teaspoon herb salt
Dash celery seeds
Dash freshly ground black pepper
Pinch fresh marjoram leaves
Pinch fresh basil leaves
3 vegetable bouillon cubes, crushed

In a blender or food processor, purée corn mixture in 2 batches with:

2 quarts milk, scalded

Strain into a double boiler or saucepan and return to stove. Add:

1 tablespoon butter
1 tablespoon granulated white sugar, or to taste
1 teaspoon salt

Heat to serving temperature and add:

1-1/2 teaspoons sherry

Serve, garnished with:

Dollop unsweetened whipped cream
Minced parsley

Makes 6 to 8 servings

Note Some corn is sweeter than others, and the amount of sugar used should be governed by this. You may find that you will have to double the amount given in the recipe, or use less if the corn is very fresh and unusually sweet. Many times the growers have allowed their soil to be depleted and when its minerals are exhausted, corn cannot manufacture its sugar. Also, the sugar changes to starch in about 4 hours, so most corn from the market has already gone through this stage.

CREAM OF ONION SOUP

In a covered saucepan, cook for 12 minutes:

1 tablespoon butter
2 cups sliced onion
1/4 green bell pepper, chopped
1/4 bunch parsley stems, minced
1/2 stalk celery, finely chopped
1/2 teaspoon Soup Herb Blend
8 vegetable bouillon cubes, crushed

In a separate saucepan, heat, stirring constantly, until thickened:

2 quarts milk, or 6 cups milk and 2 cups half-and-half cream
2 tablespoons cornstarch, dissolved in a little of the cold milk

Combine onion mixture and milk in a double boiler and heat just to serving temperature. Garnish with:

Croutons
Grated Parmesan cheese

Makes 6 to 8 servings

CREAM OF ALMOND SOUP

Toast in a 350°F oven for 10 minutes:

1 cup blanched whole almonds

Grind in a blender until very fine, then set aside.

Cook until clear in:

4 tablespoons butter
1 small onion, minced

Add and cook, stirring constantly, for 3 minutes:

4 tablespoons all-purpose flour

Add and cook, stirring, until thickened:

4 cups water
4 vegetable bouillon cubes, crushed
1 teaspoon curry powder
1/4 teaspoon white pepper
1/2 teaspoon herb salt
1 teaspoon fresh lime juice

Add the reserved ground almonds and cook very slowly for 10 minutes. Purée in a blender or food processor in 2 batches, then strain and repeat process, returning the pulp to the blender with a little additional water. Strain again.

Return soup to pot and stir in:

1 cup heavy cream

Reheat to serving temperature.

Garnish with:

Toasted sliced blanched almonds, lightly seasoned with herb salt
Dash paprika

Makes 4 to 6 servings

CREAM OF CELERY AND PIMIENTO SOUP

In a saucepan, cook until clear in:

1 tablespoon butter
1/2 onion, minced
2 cups minced celery
1/2 clove garlic, minced

Grind in a mortar:

1/2 teaspoon herb salt
1/2 teaspoon Soup Herb Blend

Add to the onion mixture in a double boiler or saucepan:

Mortar mixture
6 cups milk
5 vegetable bouillon cubes, crushed

Heat and stir in:

3 tablespoons cornstarch, dissolved in
2 tablespoons milk

Cook, stirring constantly, until thickened. Stir in:

1 (4-ounce) can diced pimientos, drained

Heat to serving temperature.
Garnish as desired.
Makes 8 servings

CREAM OF BROCCOLI SOUP

Here is a fine way to use the stalks of broccoli, especially when they are too tough to serve as a vegetable. In fact, the flavor is better in the stalk than the top because it contains more sugar.

Cook in a pressure cooker without a cap for 2 minutes:

2 heads broccoli, or 4 large broccoli stalks
1/2 cup water

Drain and set broccoli aside.

In a saucepan, melt:

6 tablespoons butter

Add and cook, stirring constantly, for 3 minutes:

6 tablespoons all-purpose flour

Add and cook, stirring, until thickened:

2 cups milk
2 cups half-and-half cream
1 bay leaf
1-1/2 teaspoons herb salt
2 vegetable bouillon cubes, crushed

Combine the broccoli and sauce and purée in a blender or food processor in 2 batches. If only stalks are used, the mixture should be strained after puréeing, as the stalks sometimes are too tough and will not purée completely. Return mixture to a double boiler or saucepan and heat just to serving temperature. (If necessary, add additional milk to create proper consistency.) Garnish with:

Sliced pimiento-stuffed olives

The olive slices should float on top, revealing their red centers.

Makes 4 servings

CREAM OF PARSLEY SOUP

In a blender or food processor, purée in 2 batches:

4 cups milk
2 cups half-and-half cream
5 vegetable bouillon cubes, crushed
1/2 teaspoon Soup Herb Blend
1/2 teaspoon herb salt
1 bunch parsley, stems trimmed and discarded

Transfer to a double boiler or saucepan and heat to serving temperature. Garnish with:

Paprika
Avocado cubes (optional)

Makes 6 servings

Note This soup must not be heated too much as it tends to curdle. If it should curdle, return it to the blender and mix until smooth.

CREAM OF GREEN PEA SOUP

Either fresh or frozen peas may be used for this soup. Many times the frozen ones have more flavor, for they are frozen quickly after having been picked, when they contain the most sugar. In stores, the peas you purchase may be at least two days old, therefore they have lost much of their flavor from aging.

In a blender or food processor, purée for 1 minute:
3 cups warm milk
1 (10-ounce) package frozen green peas, thawed, or 2 cups shelled fresh green peas
1/2 teaspoon dried marjoram, or 3 sprigs marjoram
Pinch dried thyme, or 1 sprig thyme
1 fresh mint leaf
1-1/2 teaspoons onion salt
1/2 teaspoon garlic salt
1-1/2 teaspoons granulated white sugar
Strain. Return the pulp to the blender and blend again. Strain. Put in a double boiler or saucepan and heat to serving temperature. Serve garnished with:
Dollop unsweetened whipped cream
Makes 4 servings

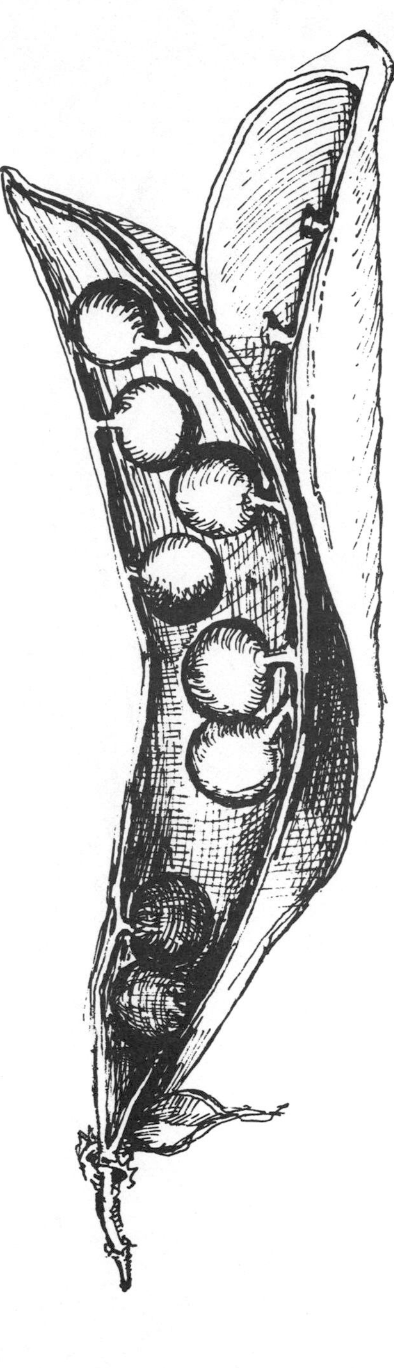

Note This is one of the most popular blender soups at the Ranch House. The important thing in getting the flavor of the soup just right is in not cooking the peas. This also preserves their lovely green color.

CREAM OF POTATO SOUP

Cook in a pressure cooker for 10 minutes at 15 pounds pressure:
4 large potatoes, peeled and quartered
1 cup water
In a skillet, cook until clear but not brown:
2 large leeks, finely chopped, or 1 very large onion, minced
1/2 cup water
1 tablespoon herb salt
1/2 teaspoon Soup Herb Blend
1/2 teaspoon garlic salt
Combine:
Cooked potatoes
Cooked leek mixture
6 cups milk, scalded
2 cups half-and-half cream, scalded

In a blender or food processor, purée the potato mixture in 2 batches. Transfer to a double boiler or saucepan and heat to serving temperature. When hot, stir in:

4 tablespoons butter

Serve immediately, garnished with:

Croutons dusted with paprika
Finely chopped parsley

Makes 6 servings

Note This soup is best when made with leeks rather than onions, since they have a higher sugar content.

CREAM OF FRESH SPINACH SOUP

Boil for 3 minutes in:

1 cup water
3 bunches spinach, trimmed
2 sprigs summer savory
2 sprigs marjoram
2 sprigs thyme
2 fresh costmary or mint leaves
1 tablespoon herb salt
5 vegetable bouillon cubes, crushed
2 turns of the pepper mill

In a blender or food processor, purée in 2 batches:

Spinach mixture
4 cups milk, scalded
4 cups half-and-half cream, scalded

Transfer to a double boiler or saucepan and reheat to serving temperature. Then stir in:

2 tablespoons butter

Makes 8 servings

Note An interesting appetizer can be made from the stems trimmed from the spinach leaves used to make this soup. Blanch the stems just until tender, being sure not to overcook them or they will become mushy. Drain and cool thoroughly. Add just enough French Olive Oil Dressing (page 48) to coat them well and chill for at least 1 hour. Drain the stems and lay them on a lettuce-lined salad plate. Garnish with canned pimiento strips or halved cherry tomatoes.

CREAM OF WATERCRESS SOUP

If you have a stream running through your garden as there is here at the Ranch House, watercress will grow easily along its banks and you will indeed be lucky. Gather the watercress without taking the seedpods or flowers, so more will be produced. If you do not have the advantage of such a stream, you will have to use the "store-bought" variety. Regardless of the source, here is a delicious soup to make with it.

Cook in a pressure cooker for 10 minutes at 15 pounds pressure:

3 potatoes, peeled and cut into thirds
1 cup water

In a skillet, cook until clear in:

2 tablespoons butter
1/2 cup chopped shallots or white part of leek

In a blender or food processor, purée in 2 batches:

Cooked drained potatoes
Cooked shallots
4 cups milk, scalded

Strain the potato purée through a sieve and put in a double boiler or saucepan; set aside. Remove tops from:

1 bunch watercress

In a blender or food processor, purée:

Watercress stems
3 vegetable bouillon cubes, crushed
1/2 teaspoon herb salt

Strain the watercress purée through a sieve and add to potato purée. Add and heat to serving temperature:

Reserved watercress tops, chopped

If desired, a small amount of the watercress tops can be reserved for garnish.

Makes 4 to 6 servings

AVOCADO SOUP

For each serving, heat in a saucepan but do not boil:
1 cup milk
1 teaspoon butter
1/8 teaspoon onion salt
Dash garlic salt
Add:
1/2 very ripe avocado, mashed (not too fine)
Beat constantly with rotary beater until soup is very hot. Garnish with:
Dash paprika or diced canned pimiento
This soup is wonderful if you have lovely fresh, ripe avocados on hand. It is a simple soup, the main thing being to have the milk very hot, but of course not boiling, before adding the other ingredients. Whipping the soup as it heats gives it a frothy texture that is nice; and you have a chance to use your imagination in garnishing it. Do not try to keep it hot very long before serving, or it will develop an acid taste.
Makes 1 serving

SNOW-WHITE SOUP

Cook in a pressure cooker without a cap for 2 minutes:
1 medium head cauliflower, cut into eighths
1/2 cup water
Drain and set cauliflower aside. In a saucepan, melt:
6 tablespoons butter
Add and cook, stirring constantly, for 3 minutes, being careful not to brown:
6 tablespoons all-purpose flour
Combine half of the cauliflower and the sauce and purée in a blender or food processor in 2 batches, adding:
2 cups half-and-half cream or milk
1-1/2 teaspoons herb salt
2 vegetable bouillon cubes, crushed
Transfer the mixture to a double boiler or saucepan. Finely chop the remaining cauliflower and add to the soup. Heat to serving temperature. Serve, garnished with:
Shredded sharp cheddar cheese
The cheese is very important. This is a wonderful soup for a first course at a formal meal.
Makes 4 servings

FRESH TOMATO SOUP

This is a very good, old-fashioned soup, but its success depends on the use of vine-ripened tomatoes.

Cook until clear in:
2 tablespoons butter
1 clove garlic, minced
1/2 red onion, thinly sliced
Add and cook, stirring constantly, for 3 minutes:
2 tablespoons all-purpose flour
Add and continue to cook very slowly until thickened and tomatoes are cooked:
2 cups milk
1/2 teaspoon Soup Herb Blend
1/2 teaspoon herb salt
2 vegetable bouillon cubes, crushed
4 very ripe, very large tomatoes, chopped
Purée in a blender or food processor in batches, then strain, return to stove top and reheat to serving temperature. If desired, garnish with:
Croutons or grated cheddar cheese
Makes 6 servings

FRESH TOMATO AND CORN SOUP

Core but do not peel:
3 pounds tomatoes
In a pressure cooker, cook for 2 minutes at 15 pounds pressure:
Cored tomatoes
2 cups water
Cut from the cob without scoring them, kernels from:
2 ears corn
In a saucepan, cook for 7 minutes:
Corn kernels
2 tablespoons butter
1/2 cup water
1 bay leaf
Pinch crumbled dried thyme
1/4 teaspoon crumbled dried marjoram
1/4 teaspoon crumbled dried basil
2 turns of the pepper mill
5 vegetable bouillon cubes, crushed
Put cooked tomatoes through a sieve (or Foley mill, if you have one), and add to the corn mixture when it is done. Heat for 10 minutes to blend flavors before serving.
Makes 6 servings

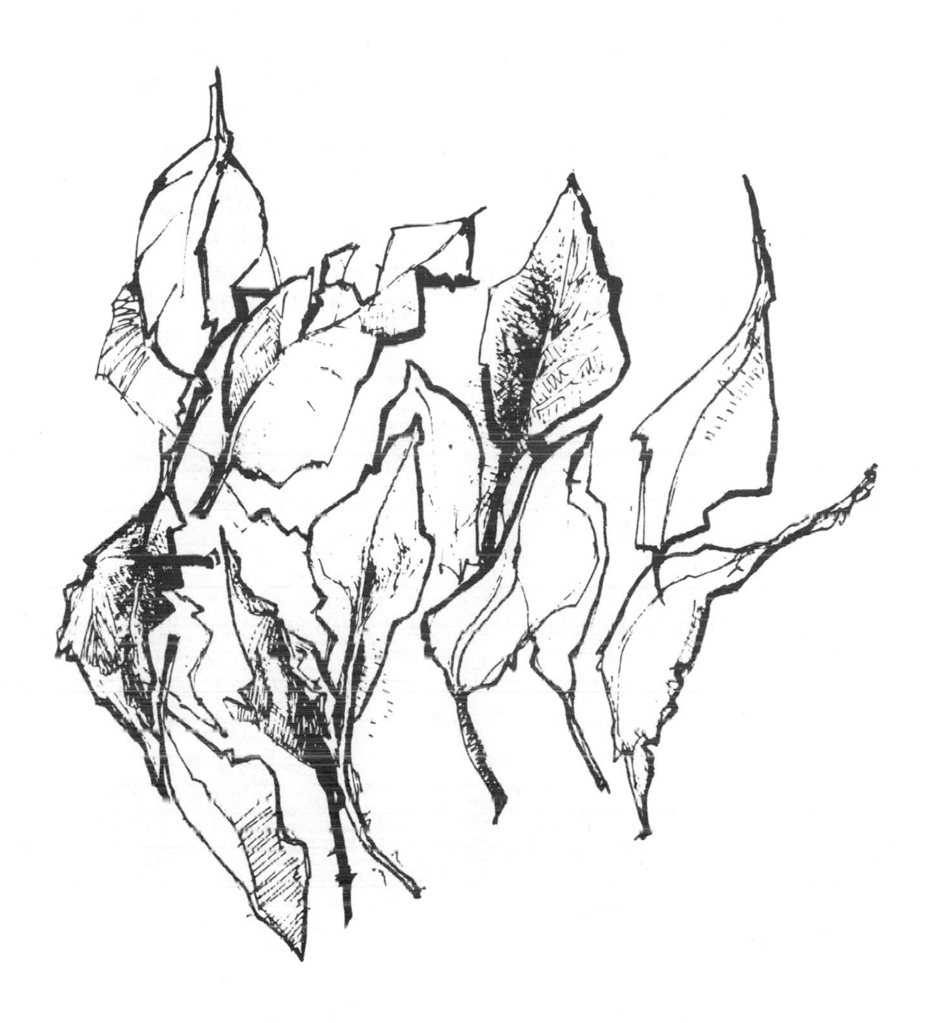

FRENCH ONION SOUP

A man I talked to in the office of the French Consul in New Orleans told me that the trick of getting the real "brown" flavor for French onion soup, especially without meat stock, is to simmer the onions very, very slowly in butter until they turn dark brown. This develops the delicious brown flavor and gives the soup a body that it should have.

Slice as thinly as possible:
6 large, strongly flavored onions
In a large skillet, melt:
3 tablespoons butter
Add half of the onion slices and cook, covered, over very low heat until brown. If cooked too fast, the onions will scorch and the flavor will be wrong. The onions should be cooked to a mush. Repeat with an equal amount of butter and the remaining onions. In a large kettle, put:
8 vegetable bouillon cubes, dissolved in
6 cups boiling water
8 fresh sorrel leaves, finely chopped
Browned onion
Simmer, covered, for at least 1 hour over very low heat.
Serve with:
Sourdough croutons
Grated Parmesan cheese
Makes 8 servings

MINESTRONE

Soak overnight in:
4 cups water
1 cup garbanzo beans
The next day, put the beans and their soaking water in a pressure cooker and cook for 20 minutes at 15 pounds pressure. In a saucepan, cook until tender in:
2 cups water
2 small onions, finely chopped
2 stalks celery, finely chopped
1 (15-ounce) can tomatoes, mashed
2 zucchini, thinly sliced
1 carrot, finely chopped
1/2 green bell pepper, finely chopped
1 bay leaf
Pinch minced fresh thyme
Pinch minced fresh summer savory
1/8 teaspoon minced fresh marjoram
1/8 teaspoon minced fresh basil
1/8 teaspoon minced fresh rosemary
In a skillet, cook until clear in:
1 tablespoon olive oil
2 cloves garlic, chopped
Dissolve in:
6 cups hot water
12 vegetable bouillon cubes

Combine all of the ingredients, discarding the bay leaf, and heat to boiling. Serve, topped with plenty of:
Grated Parmesan cheese
Makes 8 servings

GREEN SPLIT PEA SOUP

Cook in a pressure cooker for 15 minutes at 15 pounds pressure:
2 cups green split peas
2-1/2 quarts water
5 vegetable bouillon cubes, crushed
1/8 teaspoon freshly ground black pepper
1 teaspoon herb salt
1 teaspoon Soup Herb Blend
1 bay leaf
Cook for 2 minutes without pressure cap, then add to cooked split peas:
1/2 green bell pepper, finely chopped
1/2 large carrot, finely chopped
1/2 cup finely chopped celery
1/2 large onion, finely chopped
1/2 cup water
Discard bay leaf and reheat to serving temperature.
Makes 8 servings

SEVEN BEAN SOUP

What a marvelous soup this is! It has nutritional value, excellent flavor and good, hearty body. Don't let the list of ingredients throw you off the track. Just plunge ahead and the final taste will be worth any extra trouble it takes to prepare. Some markets carry a package containing many varieties of beans—just enough for this recipe.

Soak overnight in:
6 cups water
1/4 cup each: yellow split peas, green split peas, red kidney beans, Great Northern (small white) beans, garbanzos, lima beans, pinto beans
The next day, cook the beans in their soaking water in a pressure cooker for 20 minutes at 15 pounds pressure.
Combine and cook until tender:
1 cup finely chopped onion
1 cup finely chopped green bell pepper
1/2 cup finely chopped celery
1/2 cup finely chopped carrot
1/2 cup finely chopped parsley
1 clove garlic, finely chopped
2 tablespoons butter
5 cups water
Combine the cooked beans and vegetables and add:
2 bay leaves
1/4 teaspoon crumbled dried marjoram
1/4 teaspoon crumbled dried basil
Pinch crumbled dried summer savory
Pinch crumbled dried thyme
12 vegetable bouillon cubes, crushed
1 cup chopped ripe tomato
Simmer for 20 minutes to blend flavors. Discard bay leaves and serve.
Makes 8 servings

EASY LENTIL SOUP

Cook in a pressure cooker for 20 minutes at 15 pounds pressure:
1 cup lentils
6 vegetable bouillon cubes, dissolved in 4 cups hot water
2 large onions, sliced
2 zucchini, sliced
2 teaspoons Soup Herb Blend
Garnish with:
Dollop plain yogurt
Makes 6 servings

KIDNEY BEAN SOUP

Soak overnight in:
2 quarts water
1-1/2 pounds red kidney beans
Drain the beans and combine in a pressure cooker with:
4 cups hot water
3 stalks celery, finely chopped
2 cups finely chopped onion
1 green bell pepper, seeded and finely chopped
1/4 teaspoon freshly ground black pepper
8 vegetable bouillon cubes, crushed
Cook for 1 hour at 15 pounds pressure. When the bean mixture is cooked, in 2 batches purée in a blender or food processor while still hot. Then add:
1/2 teaspoon herb salt
2 tablespoons fresh lime or lemon juice
1-1/2 tablespoons sherry
Heat to serving temperature and serve, garnished with:
Thin lemon or lime slices
Minced hard-cooked egg
Makes 10 servings

LENTIL SOUP

Cook in a pressure cooker for 15 minutes at 15 pounds pressure:
1/2 cup lentils
2 quarts water
2 cups tomato juice or stewed tomatoes
1 small carrot, finely chopped
2 cups minced onion
3 stalks celery, finely minced
1/2 green bell pepper, finely chopped
1/2 cup chopped parsley
1/2 cup finely chopped cabbage
3 bay leaves
1/4 teaspoon freshly ground black pepper
2 cloves garlic, minced
1 tablespoon Soup Herb Blend
10 vegetable bouillon cubes, crushed
Discard bay leaves and serve.
Makes 8 to 10 servings

Variation If you wish to make this soup a main dish, use 1 cup lentils. This will make a delicious, rich soup.

SOMETHING FROM RUSSIA

On a visit to New York, I stayed at the home of an old friend whose mother had come over from Russia, bringing many of the wonderful dishes of that country with her. While I was there she served chilled beet borsch, and of course I took her recipe for it and watched to see just how she made it. I usually omit the egg yolk from this recipe since I do not care for the flavor of uncooked egg yolk, but many people like it; it is a matter of individual taste. Some like chopped beets in this soup, others like to shred them to add texture. Still others like it clear, without any of the body of the beet. Also optional is whether or not the skins are left on the beets.

BEET BORSCH

Shred, using the coarse cone of a gricer, or grate over the coarse portion of a flat hand grater, but do not peel:
3-1/2 pounds beets
Cook in a pressure cooker for 15 minutes at 15 pounds pressure:
Shredded beets
6 cups water
1 large onion, finely chopped

1 tomato, chopped, or
1/2 cup tomato sauce
Juice of 1 large lemon, or to taste
1 teaspoon salt
1 teaspoon granulated white sugar
1 teaspoon Soup Herb Blend
3 fresh sorrel leaves (optional)

When cooked, put through a Foley mill or sieve. Using as much pulp as necessary to achieve desired thickness of soup, add while still hot:

1 egg yolk, lightly beaten with small amount of juice from straining (optional)

The mixture should be very piquant in taste. Cover and chill, preferably overnight.

Cook in a pressure cooker for 10 minutes at 15 pounds pressure, then reduce pressure immediately:

4 potatoes
1 cup water

When *just* cool enough to handle, peel and halve the potatoes. Divide beet mixture among 8 soup bowls. Add to each bowl:

1/2 potato
1 tablespoon finely chopped cucumber
1 heaping tablespoon sour cream

The potato must be very hot when dropped into the cold soup.
Makes 8 servings

BEET AND CABBAGE BORSCH

Shred, using the coarse cone of a gricer, or grate over the coarse portion of a flat hand grater, but do not peel:

1-1/2 pounds beets

Cook in a pressure cooker for 10 minutes at 15 pounds pressure:

Shredded beets
4 cups water

In a blender or food processor, purée in 2 or 3 batches:

Cooked beets
3 quarts water

Cook in a (large) pressure cooker for 10 minutes at 15 pounds pressure:

5 large stalks celery, finely chopped
1-3/4 pounds cabbage, finely chopped
1-1/2 green bell peppers, finely chopped
1 pound onions, finely chopped
3 carrots, finely chopped
3 cloves garlic, finely chopped
1-1/2 teaspoons Soup Herb Blend
1-1/2 teaspoons salt
10 vegetable bouillon cubes, crushed
2 tablespoons fresh lemon juice
4 cups water

In a soup kettle, combine the beet and vegetable mixtures and heat to serving temperature. Serve, garnished with:

Whipped sour cream
Chopped parsley

Makes 10 servings

salads

ABOUT SALADS

After experimenting with as many as ten varieties of lettuce in our Ranch House garden, we have settled on a few favorites, selected for characteristics of flavor, texture and color. The bronze types are wonderful for color, and what can equal the Boston butter and the bibb lettuce for taste and texture? The Kentucky bibb may be called limestone on a restaurant menu.

It is most important that the lettuce be fresh and very crisp and dry when used in salads. It can be washed and stored in plastic bags in the refrigerator at about 40°F, ready for use as needed.

If you seem to have trouble with your favorite tossed green salad, perhaps you have been using lettuce that is not dry. The dressing will mix with the water remaining on the lettuce and run off into the bottom of the bowl, diluting the dressing so much that most of the flavor will be lost. Remember, lettuce should be fresh, crisp and dry. These three things will make a difference and improve your salad immeasurably.

The dressing should be at room temperature. If too cold, it will cling to the lettuce, not dressing but smothering it. Have the bowl very cold and the lettuce chilled and this will chill the dressing.

Some interesting recipes for salads and salad dressings follow, but first here is the inevitable famous Caesar salad, so that if you are passionate about salads you can, after a considerable amount of practice, demonstrate your expertise before unbelieving friends.

CAESAR SALAD

When my sister, Dorothy Hooker Nye, was director at KGO-TV in San Francisco, she had a cooking show on which there appeared many famous chefs as guests. One of her guests was the maître d' at a renowned restaurant in San Francisco. I have enjoyed the excellent food there, and when Dorothy found out that I wanted the recipe for their Caesar salad, she asked and he gave it to her.

This is a very difficult salad to make, no matter how easy it looks when an expert does it at your table. The lettuce (and only romaine will do, no other will stand the number of tossings necessary in the making) must be very fresh, exceedingly cold and dry, dry, dry. Next, the manner of tossing the salad is most important. Follow the directions explicitly. You will have to experiment, and when you have found the proportions of everything, you will have something with which to astound your friends, confound your enemies and delight yourself every time you make the famous Caesar salad. And, most important, it must be made at the table, not ahead of time and brought on.

Into a bowl that is nested in crushed ice, put for each serving:
Romaine lettuce, cut crosswise in 1/2-inch-wide strips (about 1 cup)
Coddle (immerse in hot water) for 1 minute, no longer:
1 egg (sufficient for 4 servings)
Break the egg right into the lettuce and toss. Add and continue to toss:
Juice of 1/2 lemon
Add:
Dash paprika
Dash salt
3 turns of the pepper mill (coarse grind)
Generous dash Worcestershire sauce
1/3 teaspoon dry English mustard (sufficient for 4 servings)
Toss salad thoroughly again and add:
1-1/2 tablespoons garlic olive oil
1-1/2 tablespoons freshly grated Parmesan cheese
Toss thoroughly for the last time. Serve, then place on each serving:
1 tablespoon small croutons

The classic, nonvegetarian version also calls for 1 or 2 anchovies. Notice that the ingredients are added in a certain order and the salad is thoroughly tossed at certain points in the procedure. This is very important to the final result. It may look easy, but your first few failures will prove it isn't. So follow directions exactly and may the blessings of all salad gods that watch over hardworking chefs be with you.

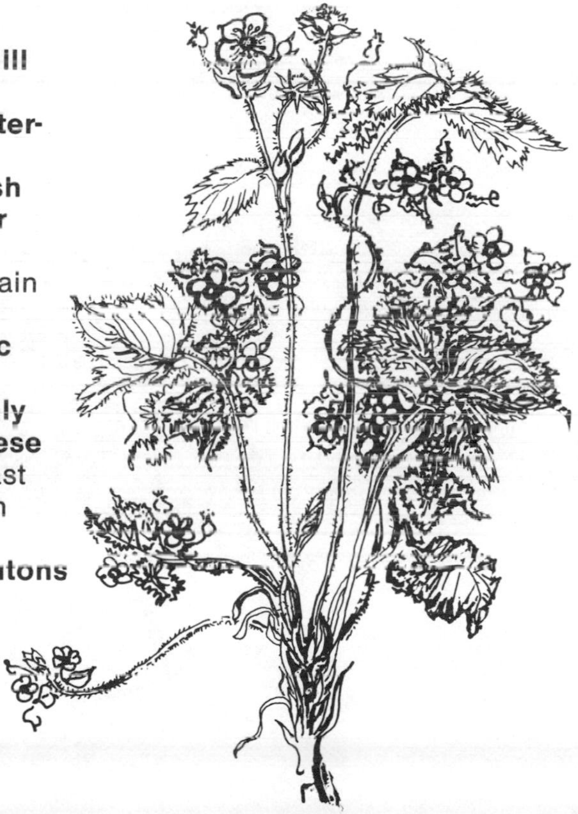

Note To prepare garlic olive oil, steep 1 garlic clove, halved, for at least 24 hours in 1/2 cup olive oil.

RAW SPINACH SALAD

For each person prepare:
1/2 cup trimmed spinach leaves
Mix together well and marinate spinach leaves in mixture for at least 30 minutes:
1 cup dry sherry
1/2 cup wine vinegar
3/4 cup olive oil
1-1/2 tablespoons herb salt
1/4 teaspoon freshly ground black pepper
Pinch curry powder
Use just enough of the marinade to thoroughly coat the leaves. Reserve any unused marinade in a jar with a tight-fitting lid in the refrigerator for your next spinach salad. Arrange spinach leaves on individual salad plates. Garnish with:
Canned pimiento strips
If desired, arrange along edges of spinach:
Hard-cooked egg slices
Sliced marinated mushrooms

RAW VEGETABLE SALAD SUPREME

In the spring when, if you have a garden, new carrots, beets, turnips and the ever-present radishes are available, a colorful and very interesting salad can be made. Wash all vegetables well, but do not peel them. Put them through the finest cone of a gricer to make long threads. If you do not have one, a grater will do if it can make the long threads. First the turnips, then radishes, then carrots and lastly the beets, so you won't have to wash the gricer between each use. On a plate which has been dressed with a bronze lettuce leaf, pile one mound each of carrots, turnips and beets in a triangle. In the center, place the radishes. They are a bit peppery and your taste will have to determine the amount. Pass a bowl of Sour Cream Dressing (page 51) that is slightly green from the addition of a few drops of food coloring. This salad will bring raves from your guests.

COOKED VEGETABLE SALAD

For those who for one reason or another will not or cannot eat raw foods, the following salad is excellent.

Peel, cut into 1-inch lengths and cook until tender in:
Water to cover
Very small carrots
(If only large carrots are available, peel and thinly slice them.) Drain the carrots (reserving the cooking water for preparing soup) and chill. Cook *separately* until just tender in:
Water to cover
Lima beans
Cauliflower or broccoli flowerets
Green beans
Corn kernels
Drain the vegetables (reserving the cooking water for preparing soup) and chill. Thin slightly with:
Sour cream
Mayonnaise
Season mayonnaise mixture with:
Garlic salt to taste
Mix the vegetables with the mayonnaise mixture until all are coated. Line a large plate or an unusually beautiful bowl with:
Lettuce leaves
Pile the dressed vegetables on top of the lettuce and garnish the entire top with alternate strips of:
Cooked shoestring beets
Long strips of cream cheese
(To make the cutting of the cheese easy, wrap the knife blade with a piece of the paper that is used to wrap cubes of butter, and the knife will not stick to the cheese.) Dot the areas in between the strips of cheese and beets with:
Sour Cream Dressing (page 51)

BUFFET SALAD

On one of my visits to England I helped to set up the vegetarian kitchen of Brockwood Park, a private school. Because there were young English girls as *femmes de cuisine,* it was important to give them something they could prepare every day without further instruction—something that would provide variety without the necessity of extra teaching.

Run through the fine cone of a gricer to form thin threads and place in separate large bowls:
Chilled lettuce
Chilled watercress
Peeled raw carrots
Peeled raw turnips
Peeled raw beets
In separate bowls, place:
Hard-cooked egg slices
Shredded cheddar cheese
Line platters with:
Bronze lettuce leaves
Pile on top of the lettuce:
Thinly sliced cucumbers zucchini, celery and mushrooms
Tomato wedges
Arrange the platters among the bowls of vegetables. On a tray, set several types of salad dressings and olive oil and vinegar decanters and let your guests prepare their own individual salads.

This salad was so popular at the school that we always served it, varying only the vegetables used. We sometimes prepared raw peas and cubed cooked carrot and celery mixed with mayonnaise, or cooked cauliflowerets and sliced carrots mixed with mayonnaise and topped with sliced cooked beets. In some areas of the country, jícama imported from Mexico is available, and this crisp vegetable, peeled and cut into slices or strips, makes a wonderful addition. This variety salad is excellent for serving a large family or a party.

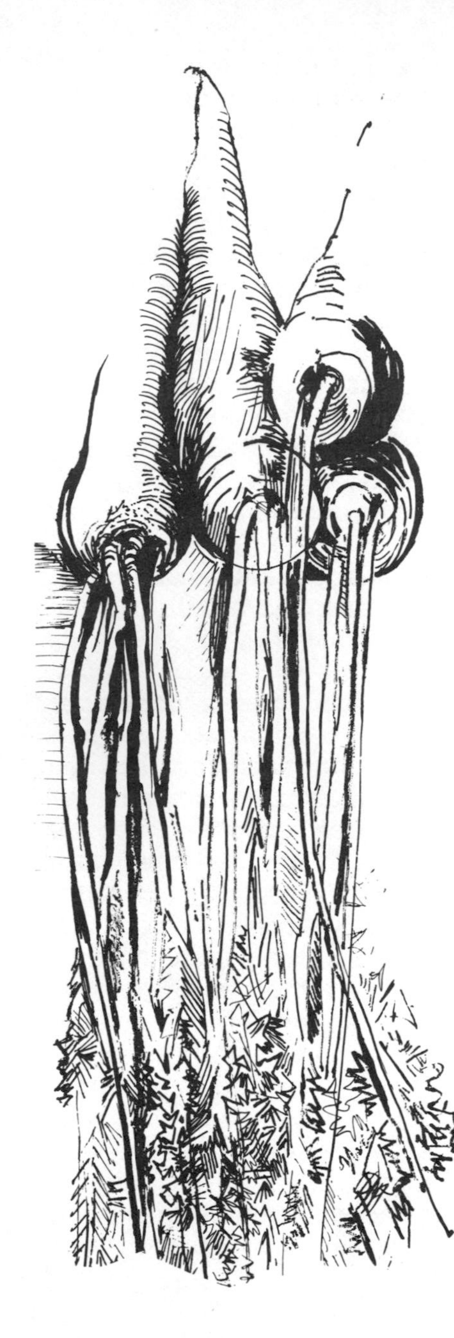

ZUCCHINI AND CARROT SALAD

This salad has had tremendous customer acceptance at the Ranch House.

Separately, very finely shred (with the fine cone of a gricer):
Zucchini
Carrots
Gently mix together zucchini and carrot and arrange in a ring on a plate lined with:
Lettuce leaves
In the center of the ring, place a large dollop of:
French Mustard Dressing (page 48)
Arrange around the ring, a border of:
Cherry tomato halves, rounded side up
Sprinkle the center of the ring with:
Grated Parmesan cheese
Paprika

ITALIAN SALAD

Many years ago, an Italian friend made a pizza for me and served it with the following salad.

Cook until tender but not mushy in:
Water to cover
Green beans
The beans may be left whole, sliced or French-cut, as you desire. Very thinly slice:
Large onions
Make a marinade by combining:
1 cup olive oil
1/2 cup fresh lemon juice
2 tablespoons red wine vinegar
Dash sugar
Pinch crumbled dried marjoram
Pinch crumbled dried thyme
Pinch crumbled dried basil
Pinch freshly ground black pepper
1/2 teaspoon salt
1/4 teaspoon garlic salt
Mix the marinade thoroughly with a wire whip. In separate containers, pour some of the marinade over the beans and onions and let stand for about 15 minutes so the marinade can thoroughly penetrate. (If there is not enough marinade to cover the vegetables thoroughly, increase the amount proportionately.) If this is done properly, the vegetables will absorb the flavor of the marinade, and it will not be usable again. For each serving, pile on:
1 bronze lettuce leaf
Small amount well-drained beans
6 or 8 rings well-drained onions

Lay across the top for garnish:
Canned pimiento strips or shoestring beets
This is an excellent salad to accompany any of the starches, such as spaghetti.

MANY BEAN SALAD

This is a very simple salad to make and very good if the entrée is not too rich and heavy. It consists of as many varieties of beans as desired, all marinated in the same marinade described in the preceding recipe, Italian Salad.

Use red beans, pinto beans, garbanzo beans, etc. Soak them overnight in water to cover, and then cook them all together the next day in a generous amount of water so they will not stick or become gummy. Drain well and marinate them in the Italian Salad marinade. Now cook some green beans, cut up or whole, until just done. They should not lose their color. Marinate them in the same marinade, drain and lay them as you would stack cord wood (pile them side by side) on each side of a lettuce-dressed plate. Drain the other beans and place them in the middle of the plate between the green beans. Top with some finely chopped green onion tops and a bit of pimiento for color. Be sure all the beans are well drained so that there is not a pool of marinade remaining on the plate when the salad is eaten.

QUICK MEXICAN SALAD

This salad is a change from the ordinary tossed green salad. If the ingredients are already on hand, it is very easy to prepare.

In a chilled salad bowl, toss together lightly:
2 heads Boston or iceberg lettuce, chilled and torn into pieces
1 (4-ounce) can pimientos, drained and cut into strips
1 (7-ounce) jar marinated artichoke hearts, drained and quartered
1 cup shredded mild cheddar cheese
1 large avocado, sliced
Add and toss again lightly:
1/2 cup French Olive Oil Dressing (page 48)
Serve with toasted tortilla chips or any type of crisp cracker.
makes 4 servings

GUACAMOLE

Combine:
1 large tomato, cut into small cubes
1 small onion, finely chopped, or
2 green onions and tops, finely chopped
2 fresh hot green chili peppers, seeded and finely chopped
2 tablespoons white vinegar
Grind in a mortar:
1 teaspoon salt
1/2 teaspoon garlic salt
8 fresh coriander leaves
Combine the mixture from the mortar with the tomato mixture and mix well. Add, no more than 30 minutes before serving:
2 large avocados, cut into 1/2-inch cubes
(If the avocados are added too far in advance, they will darken.)
Spoon the mixture onto a platter lined with:
Lettuce leaves
Garnish with:
Canned pimiento strips
Makes 4 servings

POTATO SALAD WITH COUNTRY BOILED DRESSING

When I was young and living in the Midwest, mayonnaise as a product on the grocer's shelf was unknown. When it first appeared, everyone said it was too oily, for we were accustomed to boiled salad dressings made without oil of any kind. Here is a boiled dressing that can be served hot over hot boiled, cubed and salted potatoes and chopped green onions—a delicious old-fashioned potato salad. (The amount of dressing sufficient for six medium potatoes.)

Mix together in a saucepan:
1 cup water
3 tablespoons granulated white sugar
1/4 cup white vinegar
3/8 teaspoon salt
3/4 teaspoon dry mustard
Beat into mixture:
1 egg
Bring to a boil and pour immediately over potatoes and onions.

WATERCRESS AND EGG SALAD

Here is another delicious, old-fashioned salad my English grandmother made, using the same boiled dressing as in the previous recipe, but this time served cold.

Wash and remove hard stems from:
Watercress
Mix in:
1 green onion, finely chopped, for each cup watercress
Hard cook:
2 eggs for each cup watercress
Slice the eggs into eighths lengthwise and lay them on the watercress in an old-fashioned bowl. Pour over:
Chilled boiled dressing
Garnish with:
Paprika
Chopped parsley

BEET AND EGG SALAD PIQUANT

Threaded through Ohio is a group of recipes making a fabric of food and cooking habits that originally came from the Pennsylvania Dutch. This setting did not include much fresh produce in the wintertime; they "made do" with what was available. One of their delightful salads is still a very good change from the usual tossed green salad we are accustomed to.

Remove tops and cook in a pressure cooker at 15 pounds pressure for 15 minutes in:
2 cups water
2 bunches small beets
Drain beets, reserving liquid, and when cool, remove skins. Add to beet liquid, stirring in well:
2 tablespoons granulated white sugar
1/2 cup white vinegar, or to taste

Return beets to liquid and add:

6 hard-cooked eggs (or more, if desired)

Refrigerate for at least 2 days so that the beet juice will penetrate the eggs. It will turn the whites a beautiful purple.

To serve, slice the beets and eggs separately with an egg slicer. Lay the slices in a neat pattern on a bed of:

Bronze lettuce leaves

Top each slice with a dab of:

Sour Cream Dressing (page 51)

Top each dab of dressing with:

Chopped canned pimiento

Chill well before serving.

Makes 6 servings

Variation Put a mound of cottage cheese on the lettuce, surround it with the egg and beet slices, and decorate with the dressing, being careful not to cover the golden color of the egg yolks. Scatter on chopped pimiento.

PERSIMMON AND AVOCADO SALAD

About Christmas time in most states Japanese persimmons begin to appear in the market. Select them when they are nearly ripe if you are not planning to use them immediately, but do not refrigerate. During the ripening process, the skin of the persimmon takes on a semitransparency and it becomes quite soft to the touch. If the skin is not of this texture, then the strong alumlike bitterness has not yet disappeared. Some people have said they do not like persimmons because they are "puckery." This is because they have not had perfectly ripe ones.

At about the same time, Fuerte avocados come in season. They are nutlike in flavor and the seed is not too large. These two delicacies are the foundation for this salad.

Gently grasp the ripe persimmon so as not to puncture it. If it is ripe enough, this is difficult. Gently twist the dried stem end out (if it is still in). Stand the persimmon on a cutting surface with the pointed end up, and, with a very sharp, thin knife, cut into 4 even quarters—in segments like an orange. Peel and cut the avocado into strips.

Put a small mound of cottage cheese in the center of a bronze lettuce leaf on a plate and lay 2 quarters of the persimmon on each side. Lay strips of avocado on top of the persimmon. Top with Grenadine Sour Cream Dressing (page 51).

Pomegranates are also in season and a few dark red seeds make a wonderful garnish on top of the pink dressing. Shredded fresh coconut is a nice added touch.

COMBINATION FRESH MELON SALAD

Peel and seed as many types as possible:

Melon

Slice the melon in lengthwise strips. Line an individual salad plate with:

Bronze lettuce leaf

Place on the leaf a mound of:

Cottage cheese

Arrange the melon strips around the cottage cheese. Top the cottage cheese with:

Sour Cream Grenadine Dressing (page 51)

Sprinkle on top of the dressing:

Freshly grated coconut

Serve chilled.

BROILED PEACH SALAD

Place under a broiler until very hot:
Cling peach halves
Lay the peach halves, pit side up, on individual salad plates lined with:
Lettuce leaves
Put in indentations:
Chopped walnuts
Dribble over each peach half:
Peanut Butter Dressing (page 51)

Variations

- To make a very fancy salad, soak the peach halves in cognac before broiling.
- Next to each hot peach half, put a small scoop of cold cottage cheese. The hot-and-cold combination is very interesting and delicious.
- Fill the pit side of each peach half with Pineapple-Guava Chutney (page 147) before broiling it, then top with Peanut Butter Dressing after broiling. This makes a very rich combination and should be served on the plate with the entrée rather than separately as a salad.
- Fill the pit side of each peach half with Green Ginger Sauce (page 175) before broiling. Serve without any dressing. Garnish with freshly grated coconut.

PEACH SALAD

Place on:
Lettuce leaf
Broiled peach half, pit side up
Fill center with:
1 teaspoon chopped candied ginger, including syrup
1 date, pitted and chopped
To make dressing, whip until fluffy:
8 ounces cream cheese
Add:
2 tablespoons sweetened pineapple juice
2 tablespoons sour cream
Whip for 1 minute. Place a large spoonful of dressing on each peach half, but do not cover it entirely. (This amount of dressing is sufficient for 6 to 8 peach halves.) Place on top of each peach half:
1/2 walnut meat
Chill well before serving.

ABOUT SALAD DRESSINGS

A friend said, speaking of restaurant dining: "That ubiquitous baked potato—how I abhor it!" I feel that way about the salads offered in most restaurants—the equally ubiquitous salad, with choice of dressing: "Will you have French, Thousand Island or Roquefort dressing?" So, at the Ranch House we have tried to avoid the usual—and how far out we have gone you will have to decide for yourself. We like them, but then, we make them, and that may be the reason. Our customers, however, also like these dressings and that is very important in a restaurant operation.

WINE VINEGAR

To start off, here is a suggestion about wine vinegar. It is so easy and so simple and you can vary it as you wish, adding other herbs or varieties of wine. Sometimes a blend of wine makes an interesting flavor variation.

First, get a large wine bottle, dark glass preferably. Measure the following into it:

1 tablespoon fresh tarragon leaves
or 1-1/2 teaspoons crumbled dried tarragon
4 cloves garlic, quartered
2 quarts rich red wine
2 quarts cider vinegar (5% acidity)

Put this away in the dark for at least a week (a month is better) to age it. When ready to use, decant and use as you would any wine vinegar.
Makes 4 quarts

ALL-PURPOSE DRESSING

This versatile dressing will keep in the refrigerator for weeks in a tightly covered jar. When you wish to use it, remove it from the refrigerator and put it in a pan of hot water to bring it to room temperature. Use just as much as you need, then return the remainder to the refrigerator. Once you make this dressing, you will never be without a bottle of it in your refrigerator. It is standard fare for all kinds of vegetable salads.

In a bottle or jar with a tight-fitting cap, put:
1 cup Wine Vinegar (page 47)
Add:
2 cups olive oil
(Other oils may be used, but the sweetness of olive oil will be lacking and the dressing will have too sharp a flavor.)
Grind together:
1 teaspoon herb salt
1 teaspoon Salad Herb Blend
Add to mortar mixture, mix well, then add to bottle:
1 teaspoon dry English mustard
Makes 3 cups

Variations Add 1 avocado, diced, 4 ounces blue cheese, crumbled, or 1 cup shredded cheddar cheese to the finished dressing.

FRENCH DRESSING

The simplest French dressing may after all be the very best. I have seen a waiter mix this one in the bottom of a well-chilled wooden bowl and then dump in sliced, ice-cold romaine or butter lettuce and just toss lightly. And what a salad it was, too!

Rub chilled wooden bowl with:
Cut garlic clove
Add and mix:
1 part vinegar
2 parts olive oil
Dash of salt
Freshly ground black pepper

FRENCH OLIVE OIL DRESSING

Mix together well:
1 cup tarragon wine vinegar
1 teaspoon dry mustard
1/2 teaspoon freshly ground black pepper
1/2 teaspoon salt
2 teaspoons herb salt
4 teaspoons paprika
1/2 teaspoon crumbled dried oregano
1/2 teaspoon crumbled dried basil
1/2 teaspoon crumbled dried thyme
1/2 teaspoon crumbled dried rosemary
(The amount of herbs may be adjusted to taste.) Add and mix in or shake in stoppered bottle:
2 cups olive oil, at room temperature
Makes approximately 3 cups

FRENCH DRESSING FOR FRUIT

In a blender or food processor, mix for 2 minutes:
1/2 cup water
1/2 cup cider vinegar (5% acidity)
1/4 cup fresh lemon juice
1 teaspoon salt
1 teaspoon capers
2 cloves garlic
1 tablespoon paprika
1 teaspoon Salad Herb Blend
1 fresh sage leaf
6 fresh lemon verbena leaves
1 cup peanut oil or other salad oil
Makes approximately 2-1/4 cups

Note For a blander dressing, add more water.

UNUSUAL FRENCH DRESSING

Put in mortar and grind together:
1 teaspoon salt
2 teaspoons paprika
1/2 teaspoon black peppercorns
Add and grind again:
1/2 teaspoon dill seeds
1 teaspoon dry mustard
1/4 teaspoon celery seeds
1 teaspoon onion salt
Add and grind again:
3 cloves garlic
Put in blender container and mix for 2 minutes:
3/4 cup cider vinegar (5% acidity)
1 cup peanut oil
2 tablespoons sugar
3/4 cup water
2 tablespoons achiote oil (page 140, optional)
Ground spice mixture
Makes approximately 2-3/4 cups

PARSLEY FRENCH DRESSING FOR VEGETABLES

In a blender or food processor, mix for at least 2 minutes:
1-1/2 cups parsley leaves
1/4 cup cider vinegar (5% acidity)
1/4 cup water
3/4 cup fresh lemon juice
2 tablespoons sherry
1/4 cup chopped chives, or 2 green onions and tops, chopped
1 teaspoon dry mustard
1/2 teaspoon salt
1 teaspoon Salad Herb Blend
1 teaspoon herb salt
1/2 teaspoon freshly ground black pepper
Add and blend for 1 minute:
2 tablespoons honey
1 cup peanut oil or other salad oil
Makes approximately 3 cups

FRENCH MUSTARD DRESSING

Whip together until creamy:
2 cups sour cream
6 ounces cream cheese
2 teaspoons herb salt
7 tablespoons moutarde de Dijon or Maille prepared Dijon mustard
2 teaspoons fresh lemon or lime juice

1 teaspoon liquid from bottled capers
Few drops yellow food coloring, or as desired
Makes approximately 3 cups

Note It is very important to use either of the imported mustards, for they contain excellent herb flavors.

FRENCH DRESSING WITH GERANIUM LEAVES

In a blender or food processor, mix for 2 minutes:
1-1/2 teaspoons herb salt
4 sprigs lemon thyme
1 sprig oregano
1 small sprig rosemary
1 fresh lemon geranium leaf
1 fresh lime geranium leaf
1 fresh nutmeg geranium leaf
1 fresh apple geranium leaf
1/2 fresh peppermint geranium leaf
2 teaspoons paprika
1 teaspoon dry mustard
1 tablespoon granulated white sugar
2/3 cup cider vinegar (5% acidity)
2 tablespoons water
Add and mix for 1 minute:
1 cup peanut oil or other salad oil
Makes approximately 1-3/4 cups

CUCUMBER DRESSING

For tossed green salads.

In a blender or food processor, mix for 2 minutes:

1/2 cucumber (unpeeled)
1-1/2 teaspoons herb salt
1/16 teaspoon freshly ground black pepper
1/4 cup cider vinegar (5% acidity)
1/2 cup sour cream
Dash granulated white sugar

Makes approximately 1-1/2 cups

AVOCADO AND BLUE CHEESE DRESSING

This dressing is excellent on sliced avocados and tomatoes, but is equally good on a tossed green salad.

In a blender or food processor, mix until thoroughly blended:

1 cup marinade for Italian Salad (page 42)
1 avocado
3 ounces blue cheese
3 tablespoons fresh lemon or lime juice
1/2 teaspoon herb salt
2 or 3 tablespoons water, or as needed to attain consistency desired

Makes approximately 2-3/4 cups

AVOCADO AND HORSERADISH DRESSING

Don't let the mention of horseradish put you off. The flavor is excellent.

In a blender, break:

1 egg, at room temperature

(It is important that the egg be at room temperature and not cold from the refrigerator.) In a very slow, steady stream, add with blender running at low speed:

1 cup salad oil, at room temperature

Add, while continuing to blend slowly:

4 teaspoons fresh lemon juice, or to taste

Now add and continue to beat slowly until thick:

1/4 cup salad oil, at room temperature

Grind in a mortar:

1 teaspoon herb salt
1 teaspoon Salad Herb Blend
1 teaspoon dry English mustard

Gently beat into thickened mixture:

Mortar mixture
1-1/2 tablespoons prepared horseradish
1 ripe avocado, cut up

Makes approximately 2 cups

ROQUEFORT DRESSING

Mix together thoroughly:

1 cup mayonnaise
2 to 4 ounces Roquefort cheese
1 cup half-and-half cream
1 teaspoon herb salt
1/2 teaspoon Salad Herb Blend

Makes approximately 2 cups

POPPY SEED DRESSING

For fruit salads.

In a blender or food processor, mix for 2 minutes:

1-1/2 cups cider vinegar (5% acidity)
2 tablespoons paprika
1/2 teaspoon freshly ground black pepper
1 tablespoon Salad Herb Blend
2 teaspoons poppy seeds
1-1/2 teaspoons salt

Add and mix for 1 minute:

2/3 cup honey
1-1/2 cups peanut oil
1 tablespoon herb salt
3 large fresh costmary leaves
4 fresh woodruff leaves
1/2 teaspoon freshly grated ginger root
4 pineapple sage leaves

Makes approximately 3-2/3 cups

SOUR CREAM DRESSING

Whip together until thoroughly blended:

2 cups (1 pint) sour cream or sour whipping cream
1 teaspoon onion salt
1/2 teaspoon garlic salt
1/2 teaspoon Salad Herb Blend
1/4 cup cream cheese

Makes approximately 2-3/4 cups

GRENADINE SOUR CREAM DRESSING

Once when I was whipping sour cream, I became occupied with something else in the preparation of the meal and allowed it to overwhip. It was only minutes before the guests were to arrive, and there was no time to get more sour cream. Out of desperation, I started grabbing and adding ingredients. When I tasted it I was delighted with the flavor of my concoction and used it on fresh fruit salad.

Whip together until thoroughly blended:

2 cups (1 pint) sour cream or sour whipping cream
2/3 cup powdered sugar
2 tablespoons grenadine
1/4 cup mayonnaise (optional)
1/4 cup cream cheese

Makes approximately 2-1/2 cups

BANANA SALAD DRESSING

For fruit salads.

Whip together for 3 minutes:

4 ounces cream cheese
2 ripe bananas
3 tablespoons honey
3 tablespoons sour cream
1/2 cup half-and-half cream
1 tablespoon fresh lemon juice
1/16 teaspoon ground cardamom

Makes approximately 2 cups

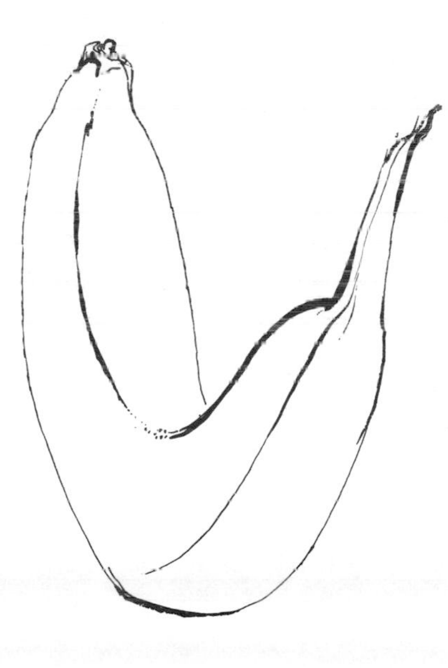

PINEAPPLE GUAVA AND CHEESE DRESSING

This is delicious on fruit salads.

Whip until very light and fluffy:

8 ounces cream cheese

Add and continue to whip until thoroughly blended:

1/4 cup chopped peeled California guavas
1 teaspoon Crème de Menthe Sauce (page 174)
Granulated white sugar to taste
Few drops green food coloring

Makes approximately 1-1/2 cups

Note If you are using Florida guavas, seed them as well.

PEANUT BUTTER DRESSING

Whip together until thoroughly blended:

1/4 cup cream-style peanut butter
1 cup mayonnaise
1/3 cup honey
3/4 cup half-and-half cream
1 tablespoon sauterne
1-1/2 tablespoons fresh lemon juice
4 ounces cream cheese
Pinch salt

Makes approximately 2-1/2 cups

Note If dressing is too thick, thin with additional cream.

vegetables

ORGANIC GARDENING

With all of the chemicals injected into animals to be slaughtered for food and all the insecticide sprays used in large-scale vegetable production, it is no wonder that more and more of us, in desperation, have decided to stop eating meat and to try raising our own vegetables, especially using the organic method.

If you're starting your own vegetable garden, bravo to you. The real hurdle is in beginning the project. Once it gets going, the rest is not too difficult and usually proves to be a happy experience. Your vegetables will not only be free of harmful chemicals, but will also be more nutritious and taste better.

People tend to speak rather loosely about nature as being organic and inorganic. Probably they have in mind things that are visibly growing, such as plant life (organic), and things that develop through a process, like the formation of crystals (inorganic).

In organic gardening, various types of soil bacteria act to make the nutrients in the soil available to the plants. Inorganic minerals provide no food for this bacterial growth so important in soil chemistry and soil rejuvenation. The breaking down of plant fibers releases their substances so that the bacterial action can take place. This process is easily accomplished by making a compost pile.

Set aside an area, about five feet by five feet, for your compost pile. Collect grass clippings, leaves, weeds, anything that will decompose, enough to cover the area to a depth of about a foot when leveled off.

Now add a three-inch-deep layer of weed-free manure. (Be sure it is weed free, not barnyard manure, or you will be pulling weeds all summer!) On top of the manure add a three-inch layer of soil. When you have enough material for another layer, repeat this process. Now wet it down with a hose, and keep it moist, not wet. Make at least four holes in the pile for ventilation. The pile is supposed to "burn" not rot. To do this it needs moisture and oxygen. I've seen five-foot-high piles with steam rising from the top of them.

When the pile is six weeks old, turn it completely over. Don't bother about keeping it in layered order. Keep it moist—do not flood it, just moisten it thoroughly. Again make four or five holes with a pole or iron bar. In another six weeks it should be turning black. Wonderful, light-textured soil is made this way, the kind that nature usually takes years to make.

When you begin to make your garden don't spread this wonderful compost soil all over it. Dig a trench for the row you are going to plant and put the enriched soil in it, then put the seeds directly on this soil. Cover them with the earth from the trench. After you have completed the planting, put

chicken manure *between* the rows, covering it completely to prevent odor or the breeding of flies. It is very strong and the leaching from it will feed the roots of your plants. You will be amazed at the results from this method of gardening.

Some gardeners find that keeping the soil around the plants moist discourages ants that put aphids at the tip of new growth. This avoids the necessity for spraying. If you plant early in the spring and the weather is cold, make—or buy from your nursery—small cone-shaped paper caps to put over each plant. This will speed the growth. *Don't let weeds get a start.* They are easy to deal with when small, and pulling out large weeds disturbs the roots of the vegetables.

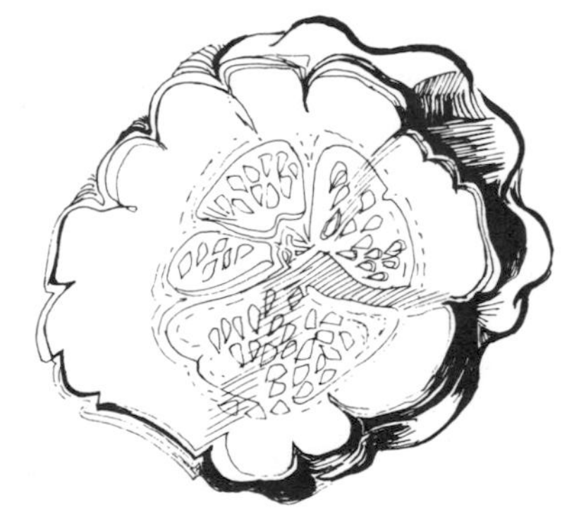

Eastern and Midwestern gardeners should find out about making cold frames for mid-winter and early spring gardening. This will extend the growing season and is worth the extra effort.

Select simple things that grow easily. In temperate climates Swiss chard, both red and green, grows wonderfully with little attention. Zucchini and yellow crookneck squash, eggplant and green peppers just grow like Topsy. Cabbage, red and green, is a fall crop. Radishes grow in six weeks, very easily.

Tomato plants are always great—watching those little blossoms turn into big red fruit is happiness. Don't plant them, however, unless you arrange some way to keep the vines up so that the fruit will not be lying on the ground where insects, chewing bugs and rot can attack it. The vines can be tied to poles. Four vines will produce more than enough fruit for the average family if properly tended, fertilized and watered. English peas, pole beans and scarlet runner beans take poles and tying up also. Cauliflower, broccoli and Brussels sprouts are all buds of the flower plant and have to be picked before they open and go to seed. Celery must be grown in a moist evnironment or it develops a bitter taste. Root crops—turnips, carrots, beets, rutabagas, parsnips and, if you have the space, potatoes—should be planted according to instructions on the seed packages. Edible pod peas, called Grey's sugar peas on some packages (the kind that are served in Chinese restaurants) grow very easily as a winter crop in moderate climates. With these vegetables and a small herb garden as suggested elsewhere in this book, you're all set for a wonderful year of taste enjoyment. There's nothing like being able to go out and pick things from your own garden.

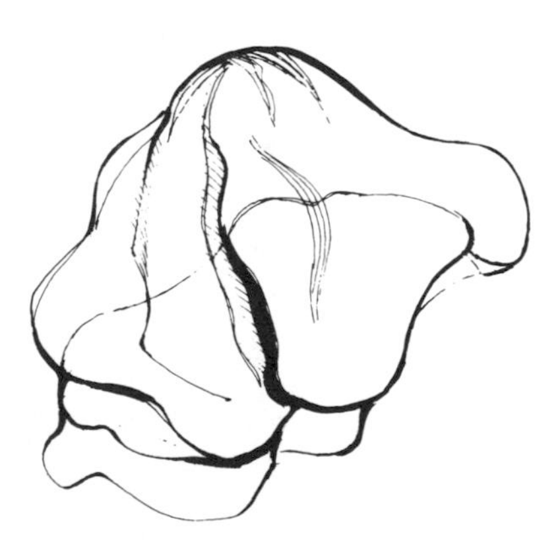

PREPARATION OF VEGETABLES

As soon as vegetables are picked, they start turning their sugar to starch for storage purposes, so it can be utilized by the germ in the seed for the necessary nourishment when sprouting for new growth. Yes, the vegetable likes to perpetuate itself just as humans do. So, the sooner you get the vegetable onto the table after it is picked, the more rich sugar flavor you will have. Remember the farmer's old saying about cooking sweet corn: "Put the water on the stove, and when it is about to boil, go out and pick the corn."

Authorities say vegetables more than twenty-four hours old, not refrigerated or preserved in some manner, have lost 90 percent of their nutritional value and much of their flavor. Here at the Ranch House people often remark about the wonderful flavor of the vegetables. There is no special magic in our methods, except that we make certain that the vegetables we use are fresh and we do not overcook them. If the cooking time is short, the natural sugar content is not all lost, does not bleed out into the water or get driven off in the steam along with the volatile oils. For this reason, we suggest pressure cooking. Also, nutritionists say the worst enemy of vitamins is heat in the presence of oxygen. The pressure cooker eliminates this for the air is dispersed by the steam before the cap is put on. Oxygen in the air "burns" all the vitamin A, and will turn freshly cut peaches brown. The quickness of the pressure cooking preserves the color of the vegetable, too. Then we serve them with a sauce that does not cover up the flavor, but only enhances it.

We often use the pressure cooker for vegetables without using the cap. Even without the cap there is more pressure than there would be in a kettle with the closest fitting lid. Some vegetables take only a half minute in the pressure cooker, so we use a timer to avoid overcooking. When the pressure cap is used, the kettle has to be cooled immediately to reduce the pressure and prevent overcooking. If you do not have a pressure cooker, however, use a saucepan that can be tightly covered.

Here are some of the terms used in explaining how to prepare vegetables for cooking. There are four degrees of thickness in chopping:

Minced Chopped very fine, almost to a mush.

Fine Sliced paper thin one way, and once across the other way.

Chopped Cut about 1/8 inch thick.

Coarse Cut about 1/2 inch thick.

These degrees are important for the sake of both texture and flavor. If a sauce is to be made in which only the flavor is needed, the vegetable is minced. If a slight texture is wanted, the vegetable is chopped fine. If texture is important but is still subsidiary to other ingredients, then "chopped" is used. In vegetarian cooking, when both flavor and texture are primary, the vegetable is coarsely cut.

ZUCCHINI

Zucchini should be picked when they are not more than 4 inches long. This way, the seedpods have not yet developed and the squash still retains its sweetness. Slice the zucchini exactly in half lengthwise. Season liberally with garlic salt (not the powder) and lay, cut side up, on a trivet in the pressure cooker with 1/4 cup of water. A second layer crosses the first, making squares between. Cook only 4 minutes without the pressure cap, and when through steaming, lift the lid. Remove the halves without breaking them and serve, cut side up, adding only a little soft butter.

ASPARAGUS

When cooking asparagus, select long, thick stalks. Wash well, being sure the little growing "flaps" on the sides of the stalks are clean. Hold the root end in one hand and, with the other hand, bend the stalk down; where it breaks is the line between the tough and the edible parts of the asparagus. Tie the stalks lightly in bunches, stand these bunches in 2 inches of water and boil until they can be pierced easily with a fork. The tenderer top part will be cooked by the steam and the tougher part by being immersed in the water. Remove the bunches, lay them down and cut the strings. Each stalk should be green and tender but not mushy. Salt lightly and add a sauce or just melted butter.

BEETS

The vegetable that suffers least from being canned is beets and they come a number of ways. They are, however, easily prepared whether canned or fresh. When cooking fresh beet roots, do not skin them. Scrub them clean and put them through a gricer (see page 176). Use very little water and cook them for 10 minutes at 15 pounds pressure. If they are young enough, only butter, pepper and salt need be added. There are, of course, fancier ways of serving beets. One treat not known to many people is to take the well-washed tops, if they are fresh and not wilted, put them whole into a pot with only a little water, cook them quickly, and then serve them with a sprinkling of herb salt and good sweet butter. Usually only those who have lived in the country have had this rare treat. Another rare treat is to take the new little beet tops and roots (only about the size of peas) that are taken out of the ground in the process of thinning the rows of growing beets, wash them thoroughly and cook them quickly, then serve buttered and salted.

LIMA BEANS

Frozen Fordhook limas are excellent with the addition of fresh or dried thyme and herb salt. Use the usual 1/4 cup of water, no trivet, and cook them only 30 seconds without the pressure cap. When the pot stops steaming, add plenty of butter and serve. Small cooked onions and limas make a wonderful combination.

GREEN BEANS

Green (string) beans have a very strong taste. If they are overcooked, this strong flavor increases until they become almost inedible. Green beans may be prepared in any one of three ways—left whole, French cut (that is, split down the center lengthwise) or cut across into 1-inch lengths. The French cut is quickest cooked, the 1-inch cut next, and the whole takes the longest. Here are the cooking times:
French Cut 1-1/2 minutes with cap, then cool quickly.
1-Inch 2 minutes with cap, then break pressure.
Whole 2-1/2 minutes with cap, then break pressure.
In European markets, a bouquet garni of a small bunch of summer savory and parsley is

always given with the purchase of green beans. Herb salt should be used generously; also, a liberal amount of butter when serving. Onions, sliced very thin, may be put on top of the beans when cooking.

CAULIFLOWER

Cauliflower can be such a good vegetable if it is not overcooked! It is also often served raw, the small buds added to vegetable salads. Since it is tasty without cooking, do not be afraid to leave it firm when you cook it.

Turn the cauliflower head upside down and make 4 to 6 cuts down through the stem, depending on the size of the head. Split the head apart and break off small pieces, leaving a piece of stem on each bud. Put the pieces in the pressure cooker on a trivet and use 1/4 cup of water. Cook for only 1-1/2 minutes, without the pressure cap. When done, remove lid immediately, and when it stops steaming, invert the lid. Lay on plate in small clusters and serve with topping of choice.

CARROTS

Carrots should be very tiny, long and thin, no bigger around than your finger. If larger ones are used, they should be thinly sliced on the diagonal. In cooking, use very little water and keep what is left. It makes a delicious addition to sauces and soups. Small carrots should not be peeled or skinned, for doing so lets out the flavor and natural sweetness. Cook them 3 minutes at 15 pounds pressure. At the end of this time, cool the pot immediately under running water. Lift and invert the lid. Serve whole, with a sauce spooned over them.

GREEN CABBAGE

Green cabbage is good cut into 1/2-inch squares and cooked quickly until just done but still crisp. Use *very little* water, so that when it is done there is practically none left. Add poppy seeds, herb salt, sliced green olives, butter, and half-and-half cream. Toss to incorporate all ingredients. Reheat, but do not boil. Each portion should be served in a small dish.

GREEN BUSH SQUASH

Green bush squash—the little flat round ones with slightly scalloped edges—should be cut into 6 or 8 pieces, like cutting a pie. Use a trivet in a saucepan, with a small amount of water. Season with dill seeds, a sprinkling of ground turmeric, butter and herb salt. Be watchful in the cooking, as one moment it will seem not to be done and seconds later it will be mushy.

SWISS CHARD

Swiss chard, red or green, is often served at the Ranch House. We use part of the white stem for texture. The long leaves with the stems attached are laid on the chopping board with the joint of the stems and leaves together. Thus all the stems can be cut off at once and kept separate. The leaves are coarsely shredded, about an inch wide, and cut crosswise; the stems are chopped about 1/4 inch wide. The chopped stems are put in the bottom of the pot, with just enough water to cover them. The leafy part is then laid on, and they are cooked 1-1/2 minutes without the cap. In serving, use equal parts of the stems and leaves. If only the leaves are cooked, they tend to settle down and become soggy.

CELERY

Celery, when used as a cooked vegetable, must be left firm and crisp. Cut the stalks into 1-inch pieces and season with herb salt to taste. Cook 2 minutes without the pressure cap. When finished steaming, invert the lid. For seasoning and color, plenty of butter, herb salt and chopped pimientos may be added. Celery is also good added to lima beans. Use 2 parts celery, 1 part limas, cooked separately and mixed together with butter and pimiento.

BROCCOLI

Broccoli is difficult to cook without losing the natural green color. It can be done, however. Split the larger stalks through the center into 2 or 4 pieces. Lay them in the pressure cooker on a trivet, cut side up. Use 1/4 cup water and cook only 30 seconds, with the cap, at 15 pounds pressure. When done, hold the cooker under a stream of cold water until the pressure is normal. Then lift and invert the lid. Serve, cut side down, with a sauce spooned over the top.

JERUSALEM ARTICHOKES

Long before Europeans landed on this continent, the natives were cultivating these tubers as one of their staple foods. How the name Jerusalem became attached to this member of the artichoke family is not clear—Webster suggests it may be a corruption of "girasole," the Italian word for sunflower. They are easy to raise—just plant the tubers in rows about 6 inches apart in well-drained soil. No need to cultivate them, and they will stand prolonged drought and neglect. A perfect plant for our leisure-loving gardener of today. Frost does not hurt them, and they are best left in the ground if they are not to be used immediately, for these thin-skinned tubers do not last very well after digging. They will keep for a few months refrigerated, however, if you have the storage space for them.

BUTTERED JERUSALEM ARTICHOKES

There are numerous ways to serve Jerusalem artichokes—au gratin, in a soufflé, raw in salads, mixed with other cooked vegetables, made into a cream soup, etc. One of the simplest ways, and one of the tastiest, is to butter-steam them.

In a pressure cooker without the cap or a saucepan that can be tightly covered, put:
1/4 cup water
4 tablespoons butter
2-1/2 teaspoons salt
Wash well (but do not peel as much of the flavor is just under the skin) and slice about 1/4 inch thick:
1 pound Jerusalem artichokes
Add the artichokes to the pan, cover and cook about 4 minutes. Shake the pan about as they cook instead of stirring them, so as not to break them up. When done, they should be tender but still crisp and no water should remain in the pan.
Makes 4 servings

JERUSALEM ARTICHOKE MELANGE

Cook in a pressure cooker without the cap for 2 minutes:
1/4 cup water
1 cup coarsely sliced carrots
1 cup coarsely sliced onions
1 cup coarsely sliced celery
1 cup coarsely sliced jícama (optional)
Combine with the vegetables:
1 cup hot steamed Jerusalem artichokes
Mix into the vegetable mixture:
Herb salt to taste
A generous amount of sweet butter
Some people find that Jerusalem artichokes served alone give them indigestion, but the addition of other vegetables relieves this problem.
Makes 6 servings

MUSHROOMS A LA VIENNOISE

I first had this dish at the Sacher Hotel in Vienna. Then my friend Wolfgang Puck, who was chef at Ma Maison for many years, gave me this recipe for it. He had learned how to prepare it in Vienna, where he had worked as a chef as a very young man.

Slice, with stems intact:
Large mushrooms
Dredge slices in:
All-purpose flour
Dip flour-coated slices in:
Beaten egg
Then dip slices in:
Fine dry bread crumbs
Deep-fry slices in:
Vegetable oil
Remove with slotted utensil and drain well on paper toweling.

Note These mushrooms are excellent served with béarnaise sauce with whipped cream folded in. Quick frying is the secret to the success of this recipe.

FRENCH-FRIED CAULIFLOWER

This is a simple recipe, but the result will surely delight you.

To make the batter, mix together well:
2 eggs
1/4 cup water
1/4 cup soy sauce
3/4 cup all-purpose flour
Break into flowerets:
Cauliflower
Coat the cauliflower with the batter and deep-fry until golden brown in:
Vegetable oil

Drain on paper toweling and keep warm until served.

Variations Substitute onion rings or carrot, green bell pepper or eggplant slices for the cauliflower.

FRENCH PEAS

Bring to a rolling boil in:
Water sufficient only to prevent sticking
2 cups shelled green peas
Grind in a mortar:
1/2 teaspoon onion salt
Pinch garlic salt
1/6 teaspoon ground marjoram, or 1/4 teaspoon fresh marjoram leaves
Pinch sugar (optional)
Add to the nearly cooked peas:
Mortar mixture
1/2 cup coarsely shredded (1/2 inch) iceberg lettuce
(Select the greenest part of the head lettuce for this dish.)
Continue cooking the peas until just done, but still firm. Remove from the heat and add:
2 tablespoons butter
Toss lightly and serve immediately.
Makes 4 servings

Note If using frozen peas for this dish, they need only be heated thoroughly.

BAKED ASPARAGUS AND PEAS

Boil until tender in:
Salted water to cover
1 pound asparagus, trimmed and cut into 1-inch pieces
Drain and set aside.
In a saucepan, melt:
2 tablespoons butter
Add and cook, stirring constantly, for 3 minutes:
2 tablespoons all-purpose flour
Add and cook, stirring, only until mixture begins to thicken:
2 cups milk or half-and-half cream
1/2 teaspoon herb salt
Remove the sauce from the heat and stir in:
Reserved asparagus
1 cup shelled green peas
Turn the mixture into a greased shallow glass baking dish.
Sprinkle over the top:
Dry bread crumbs
Grated mild cheddar cheese (not too much)
Dot with:
Butter
Place in a 325°F oven just until the sauce bubbles, about 15 minutes. Peas will cook in this amount of time and the top will be brown and crusty.
Makes 4 servings

GREEN BEANS CALIFORNIAN

Grind in a mortar and set aside:

1 teaspoon herb salt
6 sorrel leaves
2 costmary leaves
6 sprigs lemon thyme
1 sprig oregano
1 sprig summer savory
1 sprig marjoram

In a pressure cooker without lid, sauté in:

1 tablespoon butter
1 large onion, coarsely chopped

Place over onion:

4 cups French-cut green beans (about 1-1/3 pounds)

Add:

1/2 cup water
Mortar mixture

Cook for 1-1/2 minutes at 15 pounds pressure.
Makes 4 servings

GREEN BEANS HUNGARIAN

Try this recipe for a different vegetable dish with the taste of Eastern Europe.

Cook in a pressure cooker without cap about 3 minutes:

6 cups French-cut green beans (about 1-2/3 pounds)
1 onion, thinly sliced
1/2 teaspoon Savory Herb Blend
1 teaspoon herb salt
1/4 cup water

Drain, then add and stir in well without breaking up beans:

1/2 cup sour cream, whipped

Serve, topped with:

Dry bread crumbs, lightly browned in butter and seasoned with paprika

There won't be any leftover if you've followed this recipe!
Makes 6 servings

GREEN BEANS WITH SUNFLOWER SEEDS

The wonderful textures and flavors available in seed and nut meats should not be overlooked in cooking. This recipe is simple, but the results are quite extraordinary. The thin, pencil-type green beans will produce the best results for this recipe. If you have access to these, do not French cut them, but simply cut them in one-inch lengths.

Put in pressure cooker:
3 cups French-cut green beans (about 1 pound)
1/2 cup water
Scatter on top of beans:
1 large onion, thinly sliced
Grind in a mortar and sprinkle over onion:
1/2 teaspoon Savory Herb Blend
1 teaspoon herb salt
Scatter over the herbs:
1/4 cup hulled sunflower seeds
Cook without pressure cap until done to taste, about 4 minutes. Drain and add:
4 tablespoons butter, thinly sliced
Shake pot with rotary motion to mix butter into ingredients without breaking beans. Garnish just before serving with:
2 canned pimientos, chopped
This is the final touch to a delicious dish.
Makes 4 servings

GREEN BEANS AND CAULIFLOWER

Cook in a pressure cooker at 15 pounds pressure for 1-1/2 minutes:
4 cups French-cut green beans (about 1-1/3 pounds)
1/4 cup water
Reduce pressure, drain and set aside. Cook in a pressure cooker without cap about 2 minutes, or until just done but still firm:
1 head cauliflower, broken into flowerets
1/2 teaspoon poppy seeds
1/4 cup water
Drain and set aside. In a saucepan, melt:
4 tablespoons butter
Add and cook, stirring constantly, for 3 minutes:
2 tablespoons all-purpose flour
1-1/2 teaspoons herb salt
Add and cook until thickened, stirring constantly:
2-1/2 cups half-and-half cream
In the top pan of a double boiler, combine:
Cooked vegetables
White sauce
Stir gently over simmering water until heated through. Serve, topped with:
Toasted dry bread crumbs or fried sliced toasted almonds, lightly sprinkled with herb salt
Makes 6 servings

CHAYOTE SQUASH WITH SOUR CREAM SAUCE

Wash well and peel if skin is tough:
4 chayote squash
Slice about 3/4 inch thick and steam in a covered pan until just tender. Lay chayote slices on a warmed plate and keep warm. In a blender or food processor, whirl until finely ground:
3/4 teaspoon onion salt
1 teaspoon poppy seeds
1 teaspoon sesame seeds
1/2 teaspoon celery seeds
Pinch freshly ground black pepper
1/4 cup hulled sunflower seeds
Mix seed mixture with:
1/4 pound butter, melted
1-1/2 cups sour cream
Spoon sauce over chayote slices and serve.
Makes 4 servings

BEETS PIQUANT

Cut off tops, leaving about 1 inch of stems, then scrub but do not peel:

1-1/2 pounds beets (about 10)

Put beets through gricer fitted with coarse cone, making shoestring-size strips. Put the beet strips into a pressure cooker with:

1/2 cup water

Grate the rind, then halve and squeeze the juice from:

2 oranges

Add to the beets:

Juice from 2 oranges
Grated rind from 1 orange

Place on top of beets, open side down to form 4 little hats:

Orange skin halves left from juicing and grating

Spoon over orange "hats":

1/4 cup honey

Cover with lid and cook for 10 minutes at 15 pounds pressure. Remove orange skins and set aside. Add to beets:

1/2 teaspoon herb salt
2 tablespoons butter, melted
Juice of 1/2 lemon
1/2 teaspoon ground cardamom
1 tablespoon cornstarch, dissolved in a little water

Reheat beets, stirring gently, until sauce is thickened. Cut the reserved orange skins into pie-shaped pieces, about 12 to each half, and lay in pie pan, grated side up. Spoon over pieces:

1/4 cup honey

Sprinkle with:

Ground cinnamon

Heat until warmed through. Serve beets, with orange skins on separate dish as a relish.
Makes 6 servings

ORANGE BEETS

Drain, reserving the juice:

2 (16-ounce) cans beets

In a saucepan, combine:

1/4 cup orange juice
1/4 cup honey
2 tablespoons white vinegar
1 tablespoon freshly grated orange rind
2 tablespoons white corn syrup
1/6 teaspoon ground cardamom
Reserved beet juice

Place over medium heat and stir in:

2 tablespoons cornstarch, dissolved in 1 tablespoon water

Stirring constantly, heat until thickened. Then pour the thickened juice over the drained beets and add:

2 tablespoons butter

Place beet mixture in the top pan of a double boiler placed over simmering water until heated through. Remove from the heat and let stand to marinate for at least 4 hours, then reheat before serving.
Makes 8 servings

BROCCOLI IN CHEESE SAUCE

To make the sauce, scald:

2 cups milk

Stir into milk:

1/4 cup all-purpose flour, mixed with a little water

Mix together and add to sauce:

2 tablespoons butter, softened
1 tablespoon Bakon yeast
1/2 teaspoon herb salt

Cook over low heat, stirring constantly, until thickened.
Cook in:

Salted water to cover
1 pound broccoli, coarsely cut

Drain and add:

8 ounces sharp cheddar cheese, cut into 1/2-inch squares

Fold sauce into broccoli, turn into a casserole and bake in a 350°F oven for 30 minutes.
Makes 4 servings

BAKED ONIONS, CELERY AND CARROTS WITH CHEESE

Cook separately in water until just done, equal portions of:

Pearl onions

Celery, cut into 1-inch lengths

Drain vegetables and add them to:

Rich Cream Sauce (page 16)

(There should be just enough sauce to completely coat the vegetables.) Turn the mixture into a well-buttered casserole and stick down into mixture, the amount according to taste.

1/2-inch-long sharp cheddar cheese wedges

Adding the cheese in this manner keeps it from blending into the mixture. The taste of the cheese will retain its character and complement the vegetable mixture. Bake in a 350°F oven until the top begins to brown and the cheese melts, about 15 minutes.

BAKED ONIONS WITH CHEESE

Peel and cut in half, in quantity desired:

Good, firm onions

Place onions in baking pan, cut side up. Sprinkle with:

Crumbled dried basil

Herb salt

Dry bread crumbs

Grated Parmesan cheese

Cover and bake in a 350°F oven for 15 to 20 minutes, or until tender.

Serve garnished with:

Canned pimiento strips

FRIED OKRA, SOUTHERN STYLE

Wash, then cut off tops without breaking into pods:

Okra

In a skillet, heat:

Olive oil or peanut oil for frying

Dip okra, which should still be damp from washing, in:

Coarse cornmeal

Fry okra on both sides until lightly browned. Serve immediately.

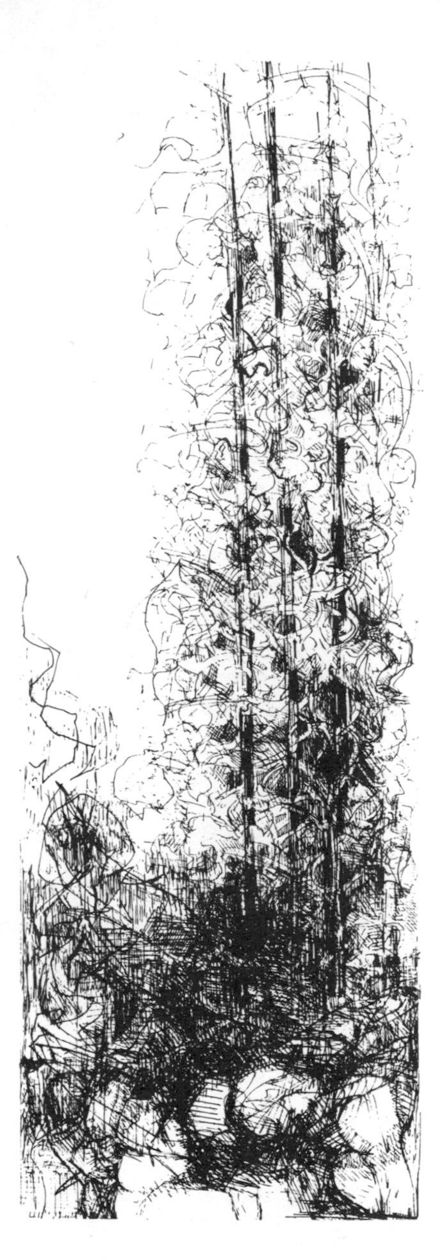

TOMATOES AND FRESH OKRA

In a saucepan, cook until clear in:
2 tablespoons olive oil
2 cloves garlic, minced
Wash and stem, without cutting into seedpods:
1 pound okra
Add okra to garlic in saucepan with:
2 tablespoons water
Cover and cook slowly until tender, about 15 minutes. Core, cut into quarters and add to okra:
1 pound tomatoes
Grind together and add:
1 teaspoon Tomato Blend
1 teaspoon herb salt
Cover tightly and bring just to a boil, being careful not to overcook the tomatoes. Then add:
2 tablespoons butter
Remove from the heat and let stand for 10 minutes to blend flavors before serving.
Makes 6 servings

EASY BROILED TOMATOES

Core, then cut in half crosswise:
6 very large, ripe tomatoes
Place tomatoes on a baking sheet, cut side up.
Mix together:
2 tablespoons crumbled dried basil
2 teaspoons herb salt
Approximately 3/4 cup grated Parmesan or Romano cheese
Sprinkle the cheese mixture over the tomato halves and broil the tomatoes until just soft. Serve immediately.
Makes 6 servings

TOMATOES PORTUGUESE

Brown in:
Butter
Rounds cut from bread slices
Brown in:
Butter
Thick tomato slices
Add to:
Rich Cream Sauce (page 16)
Grated Swiss cheese
Put tomato slices on bread rounds, pour sauce over and sprinkle with:
Grated Swiss cheese
Brown lightly under broiler and serve immediately.

CARROTS AND PINEAPPLE

In a saucepan, cook just until tender:

2 to 2-1/2 pounds large carrots, peeled and sliced 1/2 inch thick on the diagonal
1/2 teaspoon herb salt
1/2 cup water

Remove from the heat, drain and set aside.

In a saucepan, combine:

1 (14-ounce) can crushed pineapple and juice
1-1/2 cups unsweetened pineapple juice
1-1/2 teaspoons ground cardamom
1 teaspoon poppy seeds
1/2 teaspoon herb salt
1/2 cup firmly packed brown sugar
1 tablespoon cornstarch, dissolved in a little water

Cook over medium heat until slightly thickened, then add, stirring in well:

4 tablespoons butter

In the top pan of a double boiler, make alternate layers of the cooked carrots and pineapple sauce and heat over simmering water until warmed through.

Makes 6 to 8 servings

CARROTS WITH SHERRY

This recipe is much too simple to taste so good!

In an electric skillet, melt:

1/4 pound butter

Peel and thinly slice:

Approximately 2 pounds carrots

Put the carrots in the skillet (they should be about 1 inch deep), cover and set temperature at 250°F. (Do not add any water.) Cook the carrots until they are very soft and tender. The cooking time will depend upon the age of the carrots, so allow plenty of time if using mature ones. When the carrots are done to your taste add:

1/4 cup sweet sherry

Cover again and cook until the flavor of the sherry thoroughly permeates the carrots, about 10 minutes.

Makes 6 servings

LOUISIANA SWEET POTATOES

For a time I lived in the French Quarter in New Orleans, in the studio of my friend Audye Reynolds Tuttle, who now lives here in Ojai. Her cook had a marvelous way of concocting a dish of sweet potatoes. The recipe was Audye's own, and when she moved to Ojai she gave it to me. Jersey sweets, which are not the same as yams, are not suitable for this recipe. The yummiest yams you can find are the best to use.

Scrub and grate:

6 medium yams

The yams with the dark, purplish skins are best. Add to the yams and mix well:

1 cup milk
1 teaspoon ground nutmeg
1 teaspoon ground allspice
1/2 teaspoon ground cardamom
2 eggs, beaten
1 cup firmly packed brown sugar

Spread the yam mixture in a buttered glass flameproof baking dish. Pour over it evenly:

1/4 pound butter, melted

Bake in a 400°F oven for 30 minutes, or until tender when pierced with a knife. Before serving, dot with:

Miniature marshmallows (or large ones, cut up)

If desired, press into mixture:

Whole pecan meats

Place under the broiler to melt and lightly brown.

Makes 6 servings

YAMS WITH FRESH ORANGE SAUCE

Cook until tender in:
Water to cover
6 medium yams
Peel and slice yams and arrange in a buttered glass baking dish. Combine in a saucepan:
1 cup orange juice
1 tablespoon cornstarch, dissolved in a little water
3 tablespoons butter, melted
1/3 cup firmly packed brown sugar
1/3 cup granulated white sugar
Grated rind of 1/2 orange
2 tablespoons white corn syrup
Cook over medium heat, stirring, until thickened. Pour the sauce over the yam slices and bake in a 350°F oven for 45 minutes.
Makes 6 servings

SAUERKRAUT

In a skillet, melt together:
2 tablespoons butter or margarine
2 tablespoons Bakon yeast
Add:
1 (16-ounce) can sauerkraut, drained
1/2 onion, minced
Cover and cook over low heat 30 minutes.
Makes 4 servings

FLUFFY POTATO PANCAKES

Prepare:
1-1/2 cups grated raw potatoes
Beat together until stiff, glossy peaks form:
3 egg whites
3/4 teaspoon salt
Beat until lemon colored:
3 egg yolks
3/4 teaspoon salt
With a wire whisk, gently but thoroughly fold the yolks into the whites. Then combine and sift in:
3 tablespoons all-purpose flour
1/6 teaspoon freshly ground black pepper
Gently fold in the raw potatoes and add:
3 tablespoons finely minced onion
In a deep griddle or skillet, heat:
Peanut oil to a depth of 1/4 inch
With a large cooking spoon, drop batter into oil, forming pancakelike shapes. Baste the cakes with the oil as they fry so they will not break apart when turned. Turn with pancake turner aided with a spoon.
Makes 4 servings

CREAMED POTATOES HAROLDO

Cook until tender in:
Water to cover
4 large potatoes
Drain, peel and cut into 1/2-inch squares. Mix into the potatoes:
1/2 teaspoon herb salt
1 teaspoon plain salt
In a saucepan, melt:
4 tablespoons butter
Add and cook, stirring constantly, for 3 minutes:
4 tablespoons all-purpose flour
1/2 teaspoon herb salt
Add and bring just to a boil, stirring constantly:
1-1/2 cups milk
1-1/2 cups half-and-half cream
Add potatoes to milk mixture, heat through and turn into a serving bowl. Sauté lightly in:
Butter
4 green onions, cut into 1/4-inch lengths
3 tablespoons finely chopped parsley
Garnish potatoes with onions and parsley. If desired, sprinkle on top, then brown under broiler:
Grated cheese of choice
Makes 6 servings

BAKED SOYBEANS

Soak overnight in:
Water to cover
1/2 pound soybeans
(Let the beans stand over a pilot light if you have a gas stove.) Pour off soaking water and add to beans:
4 cups water
1 teaspoon salt
Cook in pressure cooker for 45 minutes at 15 pounds pressure. Do not overcook; the beans should be tender but still retain their shape. Sauté until golden in:
4 tablespoons butter
1 clove garlic, finely chopped
1 large onion, chopped (1-1/2 cups)
1/2 cup finely chopped celery
1/2 cup finely chopped parsley
1/2 teaspoon crumbled dried summer savory
Add the sautéed mixture to the beans and stir in well. Turn into a baking dish and bake in a 300°F oven until water is absorbed, but do not allow beans to dry out. Toward the end of the cooking period, cover so that the beans will not become dry on top.

This is a high-protein dish and should always be served with a green vegetable and a salad. Beans are a hearty dish and are difficult for some people to digest without the aid of roughage.
Makes 4 servings

ZUCCHINI TORRE

Cut into 1-inch-thick lengthwise slices:
1-1/2 pounds zucchini
In an electric skillet, heat to 450°F:
Peanut oil sufficient to fry the zucchini
(Peanut oil is essential because the zucchini must be cooked at high temperature.) Fry the zucchini on both sides in the hot peanut oil until tender and almost transparent. Grind in a mortar:
3 fresh coriander leaves
3 dried or fresh red chili peppers (deseeded, if desired)
1 sprig rosemary
4 cloves garlic
1 teaspoon salt
Combine in a saucepan:
Mortar mixture
1 (6-ounce) can tomato paste
1 (15-ounce) can tomatoes, broken up
Cook over medium heat for 5 minutes, stirring constantly. Remove from heat. Line the bottom of a 12-by-15-inch earthenware casserole with the cooked zucchini and spread the sauce over the top. Arrange on top of sauce a single layer of:
Thickly sliced sharp cheddar cheese
Cover with a lid or aluminum foil and bake in a 400°F oven for 45 minutes.
Makes 4 servings

bread

HOMEMADE MIRACLES OF BREAD

In a vegetarian diet, bread is basic. Wheat is almost a complete food in itself. In order to make good bread, something should be known about the ingredients that are to be used.

Bread flour is of two basic types: soft winter wheat flour and hard spring wheat flour. The softness or hardness can be detected by rubbing a pinch of flour between thumb and forefinger; soft flour feels silky soft and hard flour feels gritty.

Soft flour has less gluten and therefore the structure of its dough is weaker. This is the dough used for cake, cookie and pie crust baking where toughness is not desirable. Hard flour, the harder the better, is used for Vienna and French breads and it is largely their toughness that gives these their splendid character.

There are also two basic types of yeast: the cake type, which can be bought at a grocery or in one-pound bricks at a bakery, and the dry yeast, which comes in little packets. Cake yeast is ready for use. The dry type must be reconstituted, but this does not take too long, just long enough for it to start its growth, about fifteen minutes.

In discussing bread making with a woman recently, she said, "I'd love to make bread, but I am afraid to." I asked her what she was afraid of and she said, "the yeast." She knew nothing about yeast, its action, why it was used, etc., so we talked about it. I told her that yeast is a plant and during its period of growth it consumes food that is usually some form of sugar or honey. The byproducts are water and carbon dioxide gas, which make the dough rise. The best temperature for the growth of yeast is 85° to 90°F. Therefore, when setting the dough aside to rise, it must be kept at about this temperature. In addition, the dough should be covered while it is rising so that the top does not dry out and form a crust.

In the old days, bread makers scalded the milk before using it in making bread. This was done to kill off undesirable types of yeast that had collected in the milk from the air, which always carries what is called "wild yeast." This "wild yeast" produces all sorts of molding and souring in foods. Millions of dollars have been spent by processors of commercial yeast to isolate one particular strain of tough, durable and hardy yeast that will do the best work in raising the bread dough. If other types of yeast are present, the rising time of the dough will be unpredictable. Commercially, it is desirable to have a standardized yeast, the use of which will produce the same result over and over. Also, this type of yeast will stand more heat and cold before being killed and will grow faster than other varieties. If cake yeast is used, freshness is important. (If cake yeast is slightly brown when you take it out of the wrapping, it probably is still good.) Dry yeast, reconstituted with lukewarm water and sugar, is excellent and easier to find in most grocery stores. The gluten in the flour is what makes a paste that is tough enough to hold the bubbles of gas released by the growth of the yeast.

Some doughs are raised with baking powder or baking soda. Even pie dough rises a little, if handled correctly. This rising produces the flakes which are so desirable in good pie crust.

Unless the type of bread is unusual there should be two risings. After the dough has been mixed and set aside for the first rising to double its bulk—then it is punched down, the air knocked out of it so that it can be divided into loaves, kneaded, molded and put into the pans. Then it is again set in a warm place, covered with a cloth and allowed to rise to double its bulk. It will rise some in the oven but not enough to make a too light loaf.

Using very little liquid other than water will give the best texture to a loaf of bread, but such fine texture is gained at the expense of flavor. Butter, milk and sweetening (more than the yeast needs for its growth)

are used to get the delicious flavor we look for in homemade bread.

The difference in the cost of butter as compared to that of vegetable shortening or margarine is so slight that, unless one is on a low-cholesterol diet, it seems foolish to use any substitute for it. For whole milk there is an acceptable substitute in powdered milk, which can be reconstituted according to the directions on the package and used in place of fresh milk in any recipe.

A simple fact to keep in mind is that salt deters the action of yeast and tends to stabilize and control its growth and raising power in bread. If the bread rises too fast at room temperature (72° to 75°F), perhaps the recipe does not call for enough salt or the salt is not being mixed with the yeast and sweetening.

For the beginner, kneading the dough should not be a difficult task. All that is meant by the word is that the dough should be pushed down with both hands, then flattened so that it can be folded over and pushed down again—that is kneading. This develops the gluten content in the flour—the part that is rubbery and that makes it possible for the bubbles of gas to blow up and expand and raise the dough. Pushing and pulling the dough causes the gluten to absorb water (reconstitute itself). When properly kneaded the dough should be smooth and soft and rubbery.

An old lady who was an excellent baker said that bread should feel "as warm and soft as a baby's bare behind," and this is the best description I have found. The temperature of the ingredients and the room where the bread is being made will have a definite effect on the rising time of the dough, varying it from twenty-five minutes to an hour. In summer the dough has to be protected from excessive heat. In mixing, if the flour is cold, the liquid should be correspondingly warmer than usual. These are things experience will teach you to watch for as you mix and knead and bake your loaves.

WHOLE-WHEAT BREAD

The story of the development of our whole-wheat bread is interesting, I think, and typical of many of the methods and recipes still in use at the Ranch House, with improvements added through experience.

When we moved to Ojai it was with the intention of making everything we could, growing everything we could and in every way avoiding all types of processed and "tampered with" foods. The idea of having a cow and fresh milk from her soon went out the window, for the man who owned the cow on the ranch where we first lived told us that he had kept books on the milk production and could have bought the milk for the price he paid for the feed and cost of maintaining the cow, not counting the twice daily milking chore.

But we had our own garden, and our experiment with natural living began. I started making whole-wheat bread and it did taste very good. The owner of the health food store asked me to bring some loaves for him to sell and charged me no commission on his sales.

He also suggested that I use stone-ground meal instead of the graham flour I was using, and I began experimenting with the recipe. After many months I came to understand the properties of this meal and the resulting loaf was excellent. Everyone loved it and soon many were buying loaves to take home after they had dined with us.

Demand for the bread increased and it was becoming physically impossible to do the gardening, cooking, and pastry and bread making along with all the other things that are connected with running a restaurant. A friend in Santa Barbara brought me an old-fashioned bread mixer, the type that fastened to the table and had a handle at the top to turn. This was fine but I still had to turn the handle! I looked around for some mechanical assistance. We had an old washing machine from which I intended to remove and sell the motor. I began thinking about how I could attach that motor to the handle of the bread mixer; then an idea struck me—why not convert the washing machine itself into a bread mixer? I called a machinist who took the washing machine and stopped the drain with a stainless steel plug, removed the wringer and filled the bottom of the agitator with metal so that it would be easy to clean and we were in business!

When I started using the machine I did not know that this method would make an entirely different loaf of bread because it would undermix the dough. The walls of the bubbles in the dough would be thicker and so a flavor of undeveloped gluten would be baked into the loaf and a heavier loaf with a coarser texture and much more flavor would result. (I had always wondered why most commercial bread has so little flavor. Most bakeries are interested in producing a high, soft, light loaf of bread. The shopper, picking up such a soft loaf will feel it and think that it must be fresh. This may be so but the loaf is also without much flavor.) As Lill Kraus once said when she was given a fresh, hot slice, "It is actually old-time peasant bread!" A lighter loaf, though it may be twice the size, will have only half the flavor. In all our breads flavor comes first, texture and lightness second.

Whole wheat, and the reference here is to stone-ground wheat flour, contains the entire wheat berry with nothing taken away or added to it. It is crushed between stone burrs and ground slowly so that the wheat germ oil is pressed into the flour, not lost on the machinery or vaporized by heat generated by the speed of steel rollers.

Because of the amount of bran and other coarse outside parts of the wheat berry in this flour, it takes a high amount of gluten of good, tough quality to hold the dough firm so that in the rising process the little bubbles caused by the action of the yeast will not burst; if these little bubbles burst they make holes in the bread. If too much of this bubble bursting takes place, the inside of the loaf is too porous and heavy. The flour must make a dough that will hold together and not break easily when stretched. This is important for texture as well as flavor.

White or brown sugar are adequate sweeteners, but honey gives more flavor and tends to keep the bread from drying out. Molasses is sometimes used for sweetening and it is excellent for those who like it, though it does tend to mask the true flavor of the wheat. There are recipes that call for about four times the amount of honey we use in our recipe. This also masks the true wheat flavor. These variations are a matter of individual taste, giving you a chance to develop your own special recipe.

Wheat is grown in various parts of the country and in different soils. Some is harder and some softer because of these conditions. If the dough seems inclined to be too sticky, maybe it needs a slight increase in the amount of flour over that previously used, even though the flour is the same brand and purchased from the same supplier. Add or hold back only a small amount, a few tablespoons as an experiment, if the dough does not handle properly.

As a variation, wheat germ can be added to the recipe without changing the texture. This is done by substituting one ounce of wheat germ for one ounce in each pound of flour used. Soy flour is sometimes added only in small quantities without seriously changing the texture of the loaf. If you wish to experiment, substitute about 10 percent to begin with and add more in small amounts until you get the desired loaf.

Nutritionists say that the whole wheat berry contains a wonderful array of vitamins and minerals. The importance of this is for the individual to decide.

Now for the recipe. It may not be the best in the world but it has found favor with those who have bought and eaten it in Southern California for thirty years.

RANCH HOUSE STONE-GROUND WHOLE-WHEAT BREAD

Using a metal pan that can be warmed, mix together and heat to 85°F.
1/2 cup water
2-1/4 cups milk
1 tablespoon butter
1/3 cup honey
2 teaspoons salt
Add and stir in well:
2 packages active dry yeast
Let stand until yeast dissolves and little bubbles begin to appear. Then add and mix in well, first with a spoon, then by hand to get in all the flour:
5-3/4 cups stone-ground whole-wheat flour
(Accurate measurement is important.) Knead until thoroughly mixed. It should be moist and slightly sticky. Cover with a cloth and set in a warm place. Let rise to double its bulk, about 15 to 20 minutes. Turn out onto a floured board and knead again for at least 10 minutes, pressing it down flat, folding it over and turning it around until all the large air bubbles are squeezed out. This is to make a good texture. Dough should be springy to the touch, good and tough.

Mold into loaves in this way: Cut dough into 2 equal pieces; flatten each piece out and fold over, doing this again and again until, when rolled up, it will make a "log" the size of the bread pan. Have loaf pans, 7-1/2 by 3-1/2 inches, well greased with shortening—butter burns off and lets the bread stick. When the dough is put in the pan be sure that the upper surface is smooth and unbroken, for this is to be the top of the loaf and should not have a break that would let the dough break out in a bubble. Let rise until dough is about 1 inch higher than the pan. Bake for 45 minutes at

375°F. Remove loaves from pans and place on rack to cool.

A few comments. If the dough is allowed to rise too long the first time it will be sticky and impossible to handle without drenching the board with flour. This additional flour will dry out the dough and make a dry loaf. If the dough is too "young," as the expression goes in the baking business, it will not be springy enough and will take too long to rise the second time. When making the "log," seal the 2 edges together and lay the log seam side down in the pan.

Fruit and/or nuts can be added to this dough as it is being mixed. Walnuts, pecans, sunflower seeds, shredded fresh coconut, cashews, or a cup or so of raisins, currants or pitted dates—all of these give wonderful flavor and texture. Also, if it is available to you, fresh coconut milk is a wonderful substitute for cow's milk. What a flavor, with the addition of the freshly grated coconut! What fun you can have experimenting with these various combinations!
Makes 2 loaves

WHOLE RYE BREAD

Because it is very difficult to find a commercial bread that does not contain wheat, a doctor friend asked me to create one so that she could recommend it to her patients who are allergic to that grain. I experimented with rye flour, and here is the result.

Using a metal pan that can be warmed, mix together and heat to 85°F:
1-1/4 cups milk
3/4 cup water
2 tablespoons butter
2 tablespoons molasses
2 tablespoons honey
2 teaspoons salt
Stir in well:
2 packages active dry yeast
1-1/2 tablespoons caraway seeds (optional, but excellent)
Let stand until yeast dissolves and little bubbles begin to appear, about 15 minutes. Then add and mix in well with a spoon:
2-1/2 cups medium rye flour
Again add and mix in well:
2-1/2 cups medium rye flour
Unless you have a mixer with a dough hook for bread making, you will have to get in with your hands to mix this dough thoroughly. Yes, it is very sticky and messy, but pay no attention to that. The end result will be worth it. There is very little gluten in rye flour and it must all be developed by mixing.

When mixed so it forms a firm mass, put in a bowl, cover with a cloth and let stand in a warm place to rise to double in bulk, about 1 hour. Turn out onto a floured board and knead for at least 5 minutes. Divide into 2 loaves. Prepare as directed in Stone-Ground Whole-Wheat Bread recipe (preceding). Put into 2 well-greased 7-1/2-by-3-1/2-inch loaf pans, cover and let rise again, but not as high as the whole-wheat dough or the loaves will fall in the oven. There is not enough gluten in the dough to hold it up that high. Bake in a 360°F oven for 40 minutes. Remove from the oven and brush tops of loaves with:
Melted butter
Remove loaves from pans and place on rack to cool.
Makes 2 loaves

SESAME-SOY BREAD

The baker who has been with the Ranch House for sixteen years recently told me that years of experimentation have taught him never to heat the milk and water to more than 85°F for this bread. If you do, the bread will not rise properly.

Using a metal pan that can be warmed, mix together and heat to 85°F:
1 cup milk
3/4 cup water
1 tablespoon butter
1/4 cup wheat germ
1/2 cup soy flour
2 teaspoons salt
1/4 cup honey
Stir in well:
2 packages active dry yeast
Let stand until yeast dissolves and little bubbles begin to appear, about 15 minutes. Then add and mix in well with a spoon:
2-1/2 cups sifted unbleached white flour
Again add and mix in well:
2-1/2 cups sifted unbleached white flour
When mixed to form a firm mass, put in a bowl, cover with a cloth and let stand in a warm place to rise to double in bulk, about 1-1/2 to 2 hours. Turn out onto a floured board and knead for at least 10 minutes. Divide into 2 loaves. Prepare as directed in Stone-Ground Whole-Wheat Bread (page 74). Put into 2 well-greased 7-1/2-by-3-1/2-inch loaf pans. Brush tops of loaves with a mixture of:
Egg white and a little water
Sprinkle over the tops:
Sesame seeds
Cover and let rise to about 1 inch above the rim of the pans. Bake in a 360°F oven for 40 minutes, or until nicely browned. Remove loaves from pans and place on rack to cool.
Makes 2 loaves

RAISIN BREAD

This bread is easy to make. Simply add 2 cups raisins to the Sesame-Soy Bread dough (preceding). Do not top the loaves with sesame seeds. When the bread comes out of the oven, glaze it with a mixture of powdered sugar and a little water. The less water, the thicker the coating.

OATMEAL BREAD

In a double boiler, cook for 30 minutes:
1 cup old-fashioned rolled oats
1 cup water
Remove to mixing bowl and add, mixing in well:
2 tablespoons butter
1-1/2 teaspoons salt
5 tablespoons honey
Mix together and let stand until little bubbles appear, about 15 minutes:
1/2 cup warm milk (90°F)
2 packages active dry yeast
When oatmeal has cooled sufficiently, add yeast mixture and mix well. Then add and mix in well:
3 tablespoons hulled sunflower seeds
3 tablespoons chopped walnuts
1 cup white bread flour
Mix in:
2-1/4 cups white bread flour
When a firm mass is formed, put into a bowl, cover with a cloth and let stand in a warm place to rise to double in bulk. Divide into 2 loaves. Prepare as directed in Stone-Ground Whole-Wheat Bread (page 74). Put into 2 well-greased 7-1/2-by-3-1/2-inch loaf pans, cover and let rise again, but not too high, as they will sink in the

oven because the dough does not have enough gluten in it. Brush the tops of the loaves with a mixture of:

Egg white and a little water

Sprinkle over the tops:

Uncooked old-fashioned rolled oats

Bake in a 375°F oven for 45 to 50 minutes. Remove loaves from pans and place on rack to cool.

Makes 2 loaves

DATE-NUT BREAD

In a small pan or bowl, combine:

5 ounces chopped pitted dates
2-1/2 tablespoons butter
1/2 teaspoon salt

Pour over dates and let stand 10 minutes:

1-1/4 cups water, boiling

Mix together well:

1 egg
1-1/4 cups granulated white sugar

Sift together:

1-7/8 cups white bread flour
1/2 teaspoon double-acting baking powder
1-1/2 teaspoons baking soda

Stir together the date mixture and the egg mixture, add these to the flour mixture and beat in well, using an electric mixer. Add and mix in well:

1-1/2 cups chopped walnuts
1 teaspoon vanilla extract

Divide batter between 2 loaf pans (7-1/2 by 3-1/2 inches) lined with brown paper that has been brushed with vegetable shortening. Bake in a 375°F oven for 45 to 50 minutes, or until the tops rise up and crack a little. Unless these cracks appear, the insides of the loaves are not completely baked. Remove loaves from pans and place on rack to cool.

Makes 2 loaves

NANCY'S ONION AND CHEESE BREAD

Mix together and let stand until small bubbles appear, about 15 minutes:

1/4 cup warm water (90°F)
1 package active dry yeast

Add yeast mixture to:

4 tablespoons butter, melted
1/4 cup granulated white sugar

Mix together:

1 cup milk
1 egg, beaten

Add to milk mixture:

1/2 cup hot mashed potato
1/2 cup grated sharp cheddar cheese
1/4 cup grated Parmesan cheese
1/3 cup grated onion and juice from grating
5 cups white bread flour

Combine milk mixture and yeast mixture and mix well to form a firm mass. Put into a bowl, cover with a cloth and let rise in a warm place until double in bulk, about 1 hour. Turn out onto a floured board and knead for 5 to 10 minutes, until smooth and elastic. Form into 3 long (French bread type) loaves and place on a baking sheet, seam sides down. Brush loaves with:

Melted butter

Cover and let rise again to double in bulk. Bake in a 300°F oven for about 1 hour. Remove from the oven and cool on a wire rack. This makes excellent toast.

Makes 3 loaves

GERMAN FRUIT BREAD

Using a metal pan that can be warmed, mix together and heat to 90°F:

1-1/2 cups milk
1 tablespoon butter
2 tablespoons soy flour
1/2 cup honey
3/4 teaspoon salt

Stir in well:

2 packages active dry yeast

Let stand until yeast dissolves and little bubbles begin to appear, about 15 minutes. Then beat lightly and mix in well:

1 egg

Add and mix in well with a spoon:

2 cups sifted white bread flour

Again add and mix in well:

2-3/4 cups sifted white bread flour

Dredge:

1/2 pound mixed candied fruit, in
1/2 cup white bread flour

Add to fruit, but do not dredge:

1-1/2 cups coarsely chopped walnuts

Mix nuts and fruit into dough. When a firm mass is formed, put dough in a bowl, cover with a cloth and let stand in a warm place to rise to double in bulk, about 2 to 3 hours. Turn out onto a floured board and knead for at least 10 minutes. Divide into 2 loaves. Prepare as directed in Stone-Ground Whole-Wheat Bread recipe (page 74). Put into 2 well-greased 7-1/2-by-3-1/2-inch loaf pans, cover and let rise again until nearly double in bulk. Bake in a 350°F oven for 40 minutes. Remove from the oven and brush tops of loaves with a mixture of:

Powdered sugar and a little water

The less water, the thicker the glaze. Remove loaves from pans and place on rack to cool. Makes 2 loaves

CALIFORNIA SPICE BREAD

Using a metal pan that can be warmed, mix together and heat to 90°F:

1 cup milk
3/4 cup water
1 tablespoon butter
1/4 cup wheat germ
2 teaspoons salt
1/4 cup honey
3/4 cup sifted soy flour

Stir in well:

1 package active dry yeast
2 teaspoons ground cardamom
2 teaspoons ground coriander
1 teaspoon ground nutmeg
1 teaspoon ground allspice

Let stand until yeast dissolves and little bubbles begin to appear, about 15 minutes. Then add and mix in well with a spoon:

2 cups sifted all-purpose flour

Again add and mix in well:

2 cups sifted all-purpose flour

Mix well to form a firm mass. Put into a bowl, cover with a cloth and let rise in a warm place until double in bulk, about 1 hour. Turn out onto floured board and knead for 5 to 10 minutes. (For better texture, let bread rise again 10 minutes and knead again for 10 minutes.) Divide into 2 loaves.

Prepare as directed in Stone-Ground Whole-Wheat Bread recipe (page 74). Put into 2 well-greased 7-1/2-by-3-1/2-inch pans, cover and let rise to about 1/2 inch above rims of pans. Bake in a 360°F oven for 35 minutes, or until top is nicely browned. Remove from the oven and brush the tops with:
Melted butter
Remove loaves from pans and place on rack to cool. This bread is excellent toasted for breakfast.
Makes 2 loaves

JUDY'S PUMPKIN BREAD

This bread will stay fresh in the refrigerator for a week, if you can keep people away from it.

Mix together well:
4 eggs, beaten
3-1/2 cups granulated white sugar
1 cup safflower oil
Add and mix in well:
3 cups all-purpose flour
1-1/2 teaspoons salt
1 teaspoon vanilla extract
1 teaspoon ground cinnamon
1 teaspoon ground nutmeg
2 teaspoons double-acting baking powder
2 cups pumpkin purée
2/3 cup water
1 cup raisins (preferably sultanas)
1 cup chopped walnuts
Divide the mixture between 2 standard loaf pans that have been well greased. Bake in a 350°F oven for 1 hour and 10 minutes, or until a wooden pick inserted in the center comes out clean.
Makes 2 loaves

LUXURY CORN BREAD

Mix together well:
1-1/2 cups yellow cornmeal
1/2 cup all-purpose flour
1/4 cup granulated white sugar
1/2 teaspoon baking soda
1 teaspoon salt
1/2 cup raisins (optional, but delicious)
Beat together and add, mixing well but lightly:
1 egg
1-1/4 cups sour cream, or 1 cup milk and 4 tablespoons butter, melted
Pour into a well-greased shallow 9-inch baking pan and bake in a 425°F oven for 20 to 25 minutes. Cool on a wire rack. This bread can be split when cold, then toasted and drenched with melted butter to make it extra rich.
Makes one 9-inch square

SCOTCH SCONES

Mix together with a pastry blender or 2 knives, then by hand until as fine as cornmeal:
4 cups all-purpose flour
2 teaspoons cream of tartar
1-1/2 teaspoons baking soda
1 teaspoon salt
6 tablespoons butter
Add and mix in well:
6 tablespoons granulated white sugar
Mix together, then add to the flour mixture, combining until just mixed in (too much mixing will toughen the dough):
1-1/2 cups buttermilk
2 eggs, beaten
Drop by spoonfuls onto a greased baking sheet, or pour into 2 well-greased 9-inch cake tins. Bake in a 400°F oven for 8 to 10 minutes, or until nicely browned on top. Remove to a wire rack to cool. The scones tend to burn on the bottom if they are left in the oven too long because of the sugar in the batter. They can be slit open when cold and toasted and buttered.
Makes approximately 36 scones

ATOMIC MUFFINS

I am periodically besieged by one or another of the multitude of food faddists. I seem especially to attract every crackpot with a real food neurosis.

One day, after a particularly deadly onslaught complete with reasons why I should eat in what they call the "health way," I set out, with great glee, to make a concoction that I knew was going to be so horrible that even the most dedicated faddist could not stomach it. I put together everything I had ever heard of that would bring dynamic, vibrant, radiant, bubbling, creative, irritating good health, and then put this potential dynamite into a muffin tin and baked it.

I have to report that those muffins turned out to have a marvelous flavor and gave a quite noticeable jolt of energy. But nobody is going to influence me, and I can resist their ideas by refusing to make these abundantly delicious bits of good health. However, there is no reason why you should not try them, so go to the health food store and buy the ingredients.

Place in a mixing bowl and mix well:
1/2 cup soy oil or safflower oil
3/4 cup firmly packed brown sugar
2 tablespoons blackstrap molasses
2 eggs
Add and mix again:
1 teaspoon salt
3/4 cup wheat germ
1/4 cup soy flour
1/2 cup dry milk powder
1/2 cup sesame meal
1/2 cup brewer's yeast
1 cup stone-ground whole-wheat flour
1/2 cup hulled sunflower seeds
1-1/2 cups milk
2-1/2 teaspoons double-acting baking powder
Add and mix again:
1 cup raisins
1 cup chopped nuts of choice
2 tablespoons old-fashioned rolled oats
Divide among 24 muffin-tin wells and bake in a 375°F oven for 18 minutes. Cool on a wire rack.
Makes 24 muffins

POTATO MUFFINS

Mix together and let stand until little bubbles appear, about 15 minutes:
1/3 package (1 teaspoon) active dry yeast
1 cup warm milk (90°F)
Combine, mix with yeast mixture and let stand for 5 hours:
3 small potatoes, boiled, peeled and put through a gricer
1 teaspoon salt
1 teaspoon vegetable shortening
1 tablespoon butter
1 tablespoon granulated white sugar
2 eggs, well beaten
4 cups all-purpose flour, or as needed to make a stiff dough
Punch down, knead briefly and, with a rolling pin, roll out 3/4 inch thick on a lightly floured board. Cut with a biscuit cutter in size desired, transfer to a

shallow pan, spacing far enough apart to prevent their touching when they rise, cover and let rise in a warm place for 2 hours. Bake in a 425°F oven for about 10 minutes. Remove to a wire rack to cool.
Makes approximately
36 muffins

PARKER HOUSE ROLLS

At home, birthdays, holidays and other special days were always celebrated by making these wonderful, fragrant, delicious rolls named for the famous inn of long ago—the Parker House in Boston. It is well worth the little bit of extra work it takes to make them. Try some—you will be as delighted as we always were.

Mix together:
1 cup warm milk (90°F)
1/2 package active dry yeast
1/4 cup granulated white sugar
Let stand until small bubbles appear, 15 minutes, then add and mix well:
1-1/2 teaspoons salt
4 tablespoons butter, melted
2 cups all-purpose flour
Add and mix in:
1 egg, lightly beaten
Add and continue to mix:
2 cups all-purpose flour
Transfer dough to a lightly greased bowl, cover with a cloth and let dough rise to double in bulk, about 1 to 2 hours. Turn out on floured board, knead until smooth and smooth dough to about 1/2-inch thickness. Cut with small biscuit cutter into rounds. Crease each round with the dull edge of a knife blade, putting the crease just a little off center. Brush the smaller side with:
Melted butter
Fold the smaller side over the larger side. Place the rolls in a shallow pan far enough apart to prevent their touching one another when they rise. Cover and let rise until double in bulk, then bake in a 400°F oven for 15 to 20 minutes, or until nicely browned on top. Remove to a wire rack to cool.
Makes approximately twenty-two 2-1/2-inch rolls

WAFFLES

Place in mixing bowl:
2 cups sifted cake flour
2 tablespoons granulated white sugar
Add and mix in lightly:
1 cup milk
1/4 cup water
Beat together, then add to flour mixture:
3 egg yolks
1/2 teaspoon salt
Add and mix in well:
6 tablespoons butter, melted
Add and mix again:
1 tablespoon double-acting baking powder
Beat until stiff, glossy peaks form:
3 egg whites
1/2 teaspoon salt
(Whipping the eggs with the salt stiffens them without making them dry.) Fold the egg whites gently but thoroughly into the batter. (The steps in this recipe are very important and should be followed just as they are given. This procedure makes a light batter that will hold up until the last waffle is cooked.) Do not grease the griddle and proceed according to manufacturer's directions for your griddle. Serve with:
Melted butter and hot maple syrup, or
Maple Butter (page 178)
Makes 4 medium waffles

rice & grains

A CHEF'S WAY WITH RICE AND GRAINS

The northern peoples of the world are, as a rule, wheat eaters; the southern folks are rice eaters. Because of climatic conditions, this is surely a most natural thing: Wheat is the grain of the cool north, rice the grain of the warm south. More than two-thirds of the world's people use rice as a major part of their diet.

In serving this wonderfully nourishing starch keep in mind that it is mostly just that—rich starch. A few other hints may be of value to you as you experiment with rice cooking. Wheat and rice are dried seeds and the cooking process reconstitutes them for human consumption. They must be made to re-absorb the moisture that went out of them as they ripened for harvesting.

Authorities say there are more than fifty varieties of rice. For our rice dishes we will suggest only the three familiar categories—white, brown and wild rice. Actually, the last named one is not a rice, but rather a cereal gathered by the North American Indians. They harvest it by knocking it into their canoes as they paddle along the shores of American and Canadian lakes where it grows. A limit has been set on the amount of wild rice that can be gathered, and the Indians have the sole right to harvest it. It is an important part of their diet and this explains why there is such a small amount that reaches the market and why its price is so high.

White rice is natural brown rice with the outside covering removed by a process called polishing. Nutritionists say the outside covering is rich in the vitamin B complex and do not recommend the use of polished rice. Many people, however, prefer white rice, depending on other foods and vitamin pills for their supply of the vital B complex vitamins.

COOKING RICE

There are two main methods of cooking rice. One way is to slowly introduce the rice into a pot of rapidly boiling salted water, so that the water does not stop boiling as the rice is added. The rice is covered, cooked until tender over low heat, usually about 20 minutes, and then poured into a large strainer to drain any remaining water. Hot water is run over the rice to wash away the starch that comes out in the cooking. The rice is then put in a pan in the oven to reheat before serving. This method, which keeps the rice from being sticky, makes a nice pot of rice.

The other method of cooking rice is to put oil or butter in a pan that can be tightly covered and when it has melted, stir in unwashed rice and salt. The pan is then put over a very hot flame until the grains begin to look a little white. Immediately boiling water is poured over the rice and it is stirred and covered, then put over low heat to simmer. The proper method is to get the rice as hot as possible without browning it at all, so that when the water is added it will continue to boil up vigorously until the cover is put on. The heat is then turned to simmer, so as not to evaporate the water. If this method is followed correctly, all the water will have been absorbed by the rice when it is done. It will be fluffy, with little holes like tiny volcanos scattered through it. Never under any circumstances should the rice be stirred after the water is added. Stirring will break up the structure of the cooking rice grains that seem to form themselves together and to lift up the entire mass. Rice cooked this way can be kept in the pan over a warm burner with a couple of asbestos pads under it for at least an hour without losing too much of its goodness and texture.

Either of these methods may be used in cooking wild rice. Some people may not like the strong flavor of wild rice. To get rid of this, using the washed rice method, cook it about twenty minutes, then drain it. Wild rice needs something

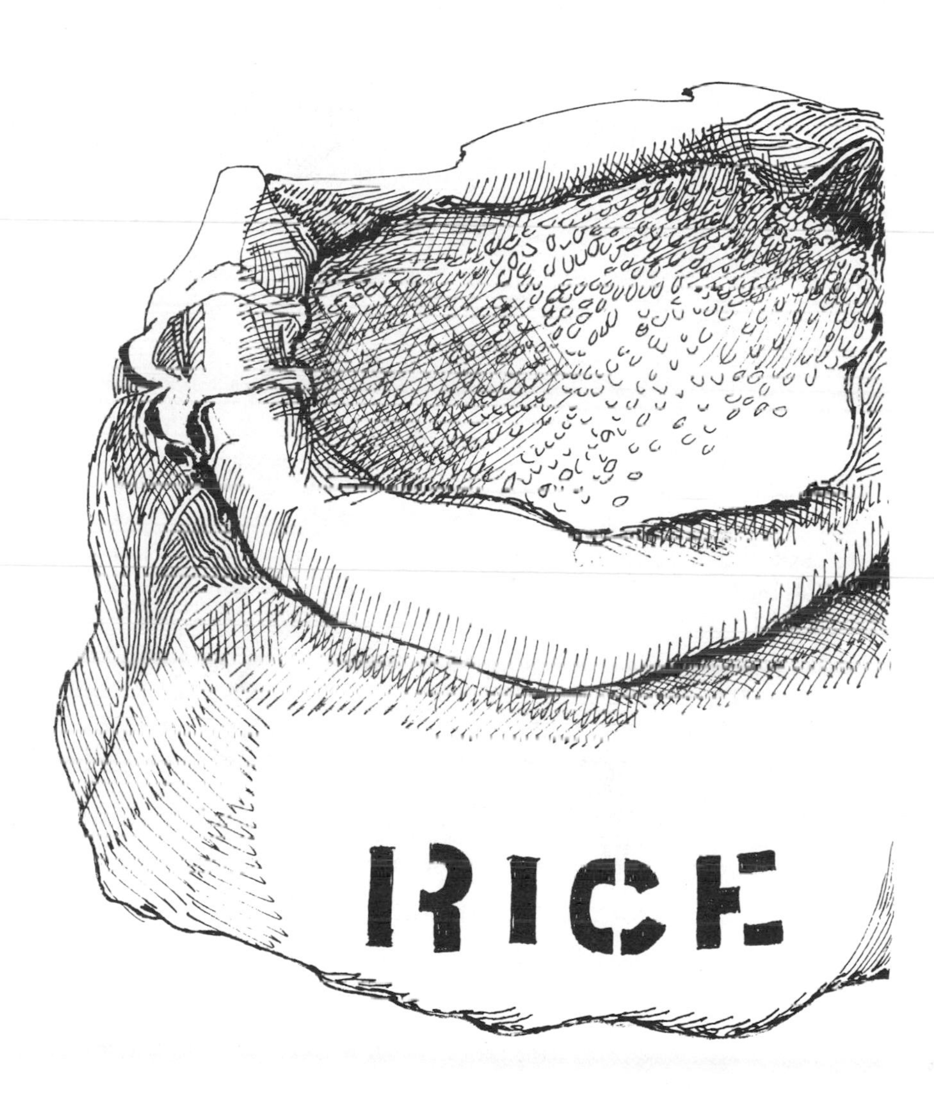

strong to complement its dominant flavor.

There are so-called quick-cooking brands of rice on the market. Personally, I do not like these "prefabricated" time savers—they do not have the right flavor. To me, they taste like a poor variety of popcorn.

Rice is included in this chapter on the cereal grains, for even if there is controversy about it being a grain, it is cooked the same way and often served the same way.

SPROUTING GRAINS

You might be interested in experimenting with something the so-called health-minded people use. (What an expression! As if only certain people were interested in health!) Select a small pyrex or other glass dish that can be covered. Lay four thicknesses of paper toweling on the bottom. Soak a half cup of any grain or seeds, such as whole wheat, alfalfa, soybeans, mustard, cress, in a cup of lukewarm water for a half hour. Drain off enough water so that when you pour the seeds into the bowl they will not float.

Every day add a cup more water and drain off the excess. In about five days, you will have sprouts ready to eat. These sprouts are delicious used in fresh salads—filled with "vital electricity" they say. Maybe they are! Anyhow, I love the fresh crunchy taste of them.

Use your own sprouting arrangement if you can find a better way than the one I have described. In Switzerland they have a very elegant gadget called a Bio Snacky. It is made by Samen Mauser in Zurich. It has four levels with a hole in each of the top three so the water can run down. With it, three different types of grain can be sprouting at the same time.

COOKING GRAINS

Grains provide a good source of protein, so important in the vegetarian diet. They are easily prepared and delicious served plain or with vegetables and herbs for flavor.

The simplest method of cooking grains seems to be the one that provides the most flavor—practically the same method used in cooking rice: Boiling water is added to the grain after it has been heated in a pan or kettle that has a tight-fitting lid, with or without the addition of salt and oil or butter. A little of the boiling water should be added at first so it will not boil over, then add the remainder and do not let it stop boiling; this is important. Cover immediately, turn to low heat and let it simmer. Don't let it stop bubbling slightly, but it should not boil hard, as that will evaporate the water before the grain is reconstituted and it will be hard and inedible.

The package usually tells how long to cook the grain but a good rule is to let it cook for at least half an hour before looking at it. By no means remove the cover before then and let out the steam! Also, *don't stir the grain during the cooking process.* As the grain cooks, the expanding kernels push each other up to form a network. If this structure is broken before the grain is completely cooked, it becomes a soggy mess that is unpalatable.

After the grain is cooked, it can be stirred, other things can be added—it doesn't matter. It can be stored in the refrigerator and reheated the next day in a covered pan with the addition of a little water. But all of this is possible only after it has been thoroughly cooked.

Here are suggestions for cooking and serving the various grains.

MILLET

Follow the cooking method suggested for grains, using:
1 cup millet
4 cups water, boiling
1/3 teaspoon salt
Cook for at least 30 minutes before removing the lid, then try for doneness; tastes differ about this. Serve, topped with:
Sweet Pepper Butter (page 21)
Makes approximately 3 cups

BULGUR WHEAT

The simplest way to cook this grain is to put into a saucepan:
2 cups water
Bring to a boil and add:
1 cup bulgur
1 teaspoon salt
Lower the heat to simmer and cook, covered, for about 20 minutes, or until it is done to your taste. Serve, topped with:
Garlic Butter (page 21)
Makes approximately 3 cups

STEEL-CUT OATS

Cook this grain in the same way as the bulgur, page 85, but add a little more water after about 20 minutes. When done properly, the oats will have a delicious crust on the bottom. Also, after it has cooked for a while, it must be gently stirred, for it does not form a structure in the same way that other grains do. By nature, it is too sticky to do this.
Makes approximately 3 cups

BROWN RICE

In a saucepan with a tight-fitting cover, melt:
2 tablespoons butter
Add:
1 cup unwashed brown rice
Stir rice with a wooden spoon over low heat while adding:
1 teaspoon salt
Do not brown rice in butter; heat only until very hot. Add:
2 cups water, boiling
Stir, cover, reduce heat to low and cook until tender (Texas and Louisiana brown rice, 30 minutes; California brown rice, about 1 hour). Serve, topped with:
Green Onion Butter (page 21)
Makes 3 to 4 cups

SOUTHERN RICE

In a skillet or heavy saucepan with a tight-fitting lid, melt:
1 tablespoon butter, margarine or vegetable oil
Add:
1 cup unwashed rice of choice
Stir rice with a wooden spoon over low heat while adding:
1 teaspoon salt
Do not brown rice; heat only until very hot. Add:
2 cups water, boiling
Stir, cover, reduce the heat to low and cook until tender (white rice, 20 minutes; Texas and Louisiana brown rice, 30 minutes; California brown rice, 1 hour).
Makes 4 servings

Note Adding 1 teaspoon ground turmeric with the salt is an excellent way of adding color and flavor to this dish. We do this at the Ranch House all the time.

RED RICE

In a skillet or kettle with a tight-fitting cover, melt:
1 tablespoon butter or margarine
Add:
1 cup unwashed rice of choice
Stir rice with a wooden spoon over low heat while adding:
1 teaspoon salt
Do not brown rice in butter; heat only until very hot. Add:
2 cups water, boiling
1 teaspoon paprika
2 canned pimientos, diced
Stir, cover, reduce the heat to low and cook until tender (white rice, 20 minutes; Texas and Lousiana brown rice, 30 minutes; California brown rice, 1 hour).
Makes 6 servings

GREEN PEPPER RICE

In a skillet or kettle with a tight fitting cover, heat:
2 tablespoons vegetable oil
Add:
1 cup unwashed rice of choice
Stir rice with a wooden spoon over low heat while adding:
1 teaspoon salt
Mix together and add, keeping rice very hot:
1 teaspoon chopped celery leaves
1/2 green bell pepper, cubed
1/4 cup minced parsley
1/4 cup chopped green onion tops
Mix together and add:
2 cups water, boiling
2 drops green food coloring
Stir, cover, reduce the heat to low and cook until tender (white rice, 20 minutes; Texas and Louisiana brown rice, 30 minutes; California brown rice, 1 hour).
Makes 6 servings

OLIVE CHOW YUK

In a saucepan, melt:
2 tablespoons butter
Add:
1 cup unwashed rice of choice
Stir rice with a wooden spoon over low heat while adding:
1/2 teaspoon salt
Do not brown rice in butter; heat only until very hot. Add:
2 cups water, boiling
Stir, cover, reduce the heat to low and cook until tender (white rice, 20 minutes; Texas and Louisiana brown rice, 30 minutes; California brown rice, 1 hour).
Prepare:
2 cups diagonally sliced (3/4 inch thick) celery
2 medium onions, quartered and layers separated
1 cup green bell pepper strips
Combine these vegetables and cook for 10 minutes in:
2 tablespoons olive oil or other vegetable oil
Dissolve in:
1 cup hot water
1/4 teaspoon granulated white sugar
1 vegetable bouillon cube
Add water mixture to vegetables, cover and cook 10 minutes.
Mix together:
1 tablespoon soy sauce
1 tablespoon cornstarch
Drain off liquid from vegetables and mix liquid with cornstarch-soy mixture. Add this to the vegetables, along with:
3/4 cup chopped black olives
Stir in well and cook a moment or so to thoroughly combine ingredients and thicken juices slightly. Serve on the prepared hot rice.
Makes 4 servings

Note: You may substitute any vegetable desired in this recipe. Let your inspiration guide you.

GREEN RICE

This dish is preferably prepared in a large stainless steel skillet.

In a large skillet, cook slowly until clear in:
2 tablespoons vegetable oil
1 onion, finely chopped
1 clove garlic, finely chopped
Add and bring to a good rolling boil:
1 (4-ounce) can long green chili peppers, seeded, if desired, and cut into 1/4-inch dice
1/2 cup finely chopped celery leaves
1/2 cup finely chopped parsley
1/2 cup finely chopped French sorrel
1/2 cup finely chopped broccoli flowerets
1/2 cup finely chopped Swiss chard tops
2 teaspoons salt
3 cups water, boiling
Few drops green food coloring (enough to make a nice green color)
In a separate skillet, melt:
2 tablespoons butter
Add:
2 cups unwashed white rice

Stir the rice with a wooden spoon over low heat until very hot. Add the rice to the boiling vegetable mixture, stir, cover, reduce the heat and cook until tender, about 20 minutes.
Makes 6 servings

INDIA RICE SPECIALE

Steep for at least 30 minutes in:
1/2 cup hot water
1 teaspoon saffron threads, or 1/8 teaspoon powdered saffron
In a saucepan with a tight-fitting cover, melt:
2 tablespoons butter
Add:
2 cups unwashed white rice
Stir rice with a wooden spoon over low heat while adding:
1 teaspoon salt
Do not brown rice in butter; heat only until very hot. Add to saffron water:
3-1/2 cups water, boiling
Add this to the rice, stir, cover, reduce heat to low and cook until tender, about 20 minutes.
Serve, garnished with:
Chopped or slivered blanched almonds, lightly toasted if desired
White raisins
Makes 6 servings

JAVANESE RICE

An unusually fine cook who was born in Java of Dutch parents and lived many of her young years there taught me to prepare this dish. She would cook her rice, then rinse off the extra starch, drain the rice and dump it into a large saucepan. To each three cups of cooked rice, she would add the following ingredients.

Cook until just tender in:
Boiling water to cover
1 cup inch-long green bean pieces
(My friend was able to get what are called 3-foot beans. They are a very thin pencil-like green bean, a little crisper than a regular green bean.)
Sauté just until tender in:
Butter
1 large onion, thinly sliced
Lightly toss together the beans, onions and rice and then gently reheat at serving time if making ahead. For an extra touch, my friend would sometimes sprinkle on top:
Raisins
Makes 4 servings

CASSEROLE OF THE EAST

In a saucepan, bring to a boil:
2 cups water
Add:
1 cup washed brown rice
Cover, reduce the heat and cook until tender, 30 minutes to 1 hour, depending on type of rice used. Rinse off starch as directed in general instructions for cooking rice.
Mix together:
1/2 cup Ranch House Béchamel Sauce (page 15)
1/8 teaspoon curry powder
(Measure the curry powder carefully. The curry flavor should not be too strong.) Combine the cooked rice and curried sauce and mound up in a flameproof casserole.
Cut in half:
Several fresh figs
Lay the figs, cut side down, on the mounded rice in a circular fashion, but do not cover it completely. Sprinkle over the mound:
A generous amount of pine nuts
Place under a broiler until pine nuts are lightly browned. This will heat the figs and rice to just the right temperature. Serve immediately.
Makes 4 servings

Note This recipe is one of many delicious dishes served at Gleich's, a fine vegetarian restaurant in Zurich, Switzerland. Manfred Gleich gave it to me especially for this book.

BROWN RICE PILAU WITH HERBS

Grind in a mortar:
1 teaspoon salt
2 teaspoons onion salt
1/2 teaspoon dried summer savory
1/2 teaspoon dill seeds
Add to the herbs and spices and grind well:
1 clove garlic
In a skillet with a tight-fitting cover, melt:
2 tablespoons butter
Add:
1 cup unwashed brown rice
Stir rice over low heat until very hot; do not brown. Add:
2 cups water, boiling
2 bay leaves
Mortar mixture
Stir, cover, reduce the heat to low and cook until tender (Texas and Louisiana brown rice, 30 minutes; California brown rice, 1 hour).
Makes 4 servings

INDONESIAN RICE

In a skillet or saucepan with a tight-fitting cover, melt:
4 tablespoons butter
Add:
2 cups unwashed white rice
Stir rice with a wooden spoon over low heat while adding:
1 teaspoon salt
Do not brown rice in butter; heat only until very hot. Add:
4 cups water, boiling
Stir, cover, reduce heat to low and cook until tender, about 20 minutes. In a pressure cooker without cap and using very little water, layer vegetables in order given:
1/2 cup thinly sliced carrot strips (2 inch)
1/2 cup thinly sliced celery (2 inch)
1/2 cup French-cut green beans (2 inch)
1/2 teaspoon Savory Herb Blend
Cook about 2 minutes, then drain and add:
Enough butter to thoroughly coat vegetables
Add vegetables to rice, toss until mixed and sprinkle on generously:
Sliced roasted almonds
(Hot but not browned pine nuts may also be added to vegetables or sprinkled on as garnish. Cashew nuts may be used as well, but not combined with other nuts. They make an excellent variation.)

This combination of rice and vegetables is the central dish on one type of *rijsttafel,* an elaborate meal served in Indonesia. By spreading the rice on a large platter and arranging all manner of vegetables around it, then garnishing the rice with nuts, one can make this the main dish of a buffet luncheon or a dinner.
Makes 6 servings

RICE ORIENTAL

In a large skillet, heat:
2 tablespoons peanut oil
Add:
2 cups unwashed brown rice
Stir rice with a wooden spoon over low heat while adding:
2 teaspoons salt
1/2 teaspoon ground turmeric
1/2 teaspoon ground cardamom (optional)
Do not brown rice; heat only until very hot. Add:
4 cups water, boiling
1 (4-ounce) can diced pimientos
1/2 cup chopped parsley
1 tablespoon chopped fresh coriander (optional)
Stir, cover, reduce the heat to low and cook until tender. (Texas and Louisiana brown rice, 30 minutes; California brown rice, 1 hour).
Makes 6 servings

WILD RICE AND MUSHROOMS

When we first opened our dining room to the public, I had to invent meatless dishes that would be acceptable to the meat eaters who often came to dine. I hit on the idea of making the broth for wild rice with vegetable bouillon cubes, and it worked very well. The cubes, plus the herbs that I add along with the broth, give the wild rice a fine flavor.

Wash thoroughly in at least 3 changes of water, watching for small stones:
1 cup (6 ounces) wild rice
In a large skillet with a tight-fitting lid, melt:
2 tablespoons butter
Spread the washed rice in the skillet and stir with a wooden spoon. Do not brown the rice; heat only until very hot. Add:
3 vegetables bouillon cubes, dissolved in
3 cups boiling water
1/2 teaspoon herb salt
Stir, cover, reduce the heat to

low and cook for about 1 hour, or until the rice is tender and has swelled to the proper size.

Wash and drain well in a colander:
1 pound mushrooms
Remove the stems with a sharp knife and slice the stems into 1/4-inch-thick slices. Cut the caps into 1/6-inch-thick slices. Set the mushrooms aside.
Grind in a mortar:
1 teaspoon onion salt
2 pinches garlic salt
2 pinches dried basil
2 pinches dried thyme
2 pinches dried rosemary
2 pinches dried marjoram
2 pinches freshly ground black pepper
2 pinches celery seeds
(Do not omit any of these herbs and spices, for they are balanced in this proportion.)
Add the herbs and spices to:
4 cups half-and-half cream
Combine the cream and mushrooms in a saucepan and heat, but do not boil. Stir into the saucepan:
6 tablespoons cornstarch, dissolved in a little water
Heat gently, stirring, until thickened, then add:
1/4 cup cream sherry
Serve the creamed mushrooms with the wild rice.
Makes 6 servings

WILD RICE IN CASSEROLE

Wash thoroughly in at least 3 changes of water, watching for small stones:
1 cup (6 ounces) wild rice
Boil for 20 minutes in:
3 cups water
Washed wild rice
Drain the rice and set it aside.
In a skillet, melt:
2 tablespoons butter
Add and cook for 5 minutes:
1/2 pound mushrooms, chopped
1 green bell pepper, seeded and chopped
2 onions, chopped
Add and cook for 10 minutes over medium heat:
2 cups tomato juice
Then add, mix in well and remove from the heat:
1/2 cup chopped parsley
1/4 teaspoon paprika
1/4 teaspoon crumbled dried thyme
1 teaspoon salt
Prepare:
3/4 cup grated mild cheddar cheese
In a casserole, layer half of the wild rice, mushroom mixture and grated cheese. Repeat the layers with the remaining ingredients. Bake in a 350°F oven for 45 minutes.
Makes 6 servings

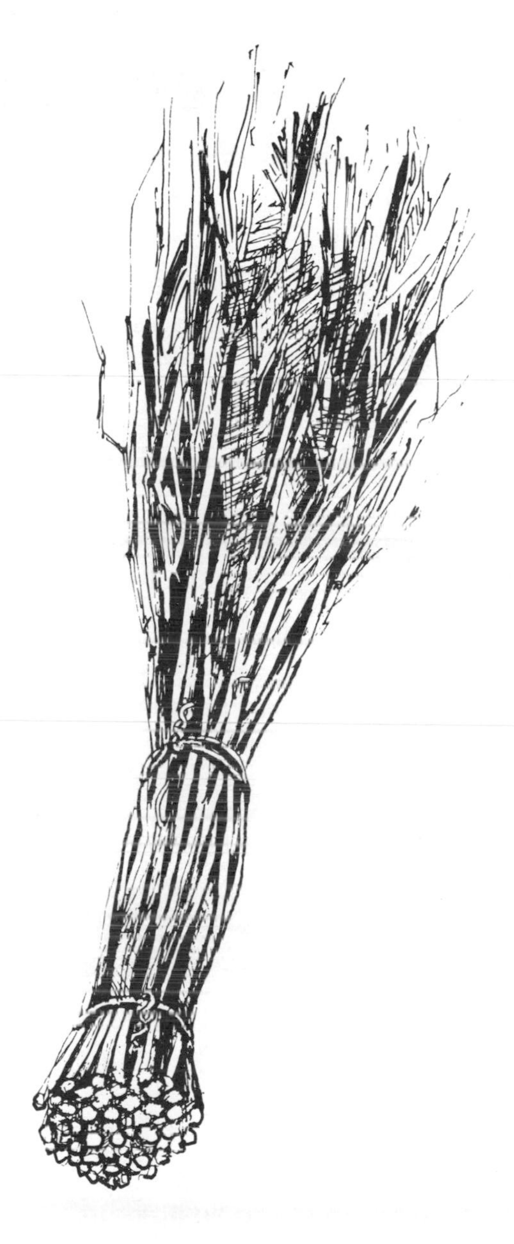

eggs, cheese & noodles

EGGS

Here are a few things about eggs you may not have discovered—especially if you are a younger, less experienced cook.

The whites of eggs have very little flavor. Their mission in cookery is to bind things together or lightly hold other ingredients. Their main value, then, is their viscosity, their "stick-togetherness." This capacity is enhanced when they are being beaten, by the addition of small amounts of salt or sugar. (Never use flour or anything of that dry nature that has to be reconstituted.)

Even a tiny drop of any oil, or a bit of the yolk with its high oil content, may prevent eggs being whipped satisfactorily.

When a recipe calls for whipping both the yolks and whites, I add the salt of the recipe equally to each and whip the yolks first. Yolks have a much heavier body and so hold up longer, and it takes longer to whip them. They should be beaten until they are lemon colored.

The whites whip in less time and will not hold up very long, so they should be whipped just before they are to be folded in. A folding motion should always be used, to incorporate even more air in them and thus counteract the loss of air during the mixing process.

The yolks, though having less lightness, have most of the flavor that is in the egg, and add richness to everything containing them.

SOUFFLE SECRET

I believe I have discovered a way of easily making soufflés so that they do not collapse immediately as they are removed from the oven. I had thought that the thickness of the white sauce was what held the soufflé up, but now I think the way the yolks are handled is the secret of controlling the structure. The yolks should never be heated before they go into the oven. They should not be added to the white sauce until it is cool. Then about one-third of the beaten whites are stirred into the egg yolk-cheese sauce mixture. Adding some of the beaten whites in this way thins the mixture without making it so liquid that it goes to the bottom when it is poured over the rest of the beaten whites and gently folded in.

As the soufflé bakes, the thickening of the yolks establishes the structure and lightness, and produces the wonderful brown hat that appears. The tendency to collapse seems to be practically eliminated.

You can, if you wish, brush the bottom and sides of the soufflé dish with butter (or spray with a nonstick coating), then sprinkle them with grated Parmesan cheese. This also helps hold the soufflé up.

CHEESE SOUFFLE

In a saucepan, melt:

3 tablespoons butter

Add and cook 3 minutes, stirring constantly:

3 tablespoons white bread flour

Add and cook until thick, stirring constantly:

1 cup milk

Remove from the heat and stir in:

8 ounces sharp cheddar or aged Swiss cheese, grated

Let cool, then beat in:

6 egg yolks
1/2 teaspoon Worcestershire sauce
Dash cayenne pepper

Beat until stiff, glossy peaks form:

6 egg whites
1/2 teaspoon salt

Fold one-third of the whites into the cheese mixture to lighten it. Turn this mixture into the rest of the whites and fold in gently. Put in an ungreased 2-quart baking dish and bake in a 350°F oven for about 45 minutes, or until a knife inserted in the center comes out clean.
Makes 4 servings

For the cheese soufflé recipe given here, use a two-quart pyrex casserole with slightly flared sides rather than straight ones like the traditional soufflé dishes. The soufflé rises about half of the depth of the bowl. The usual test for doneness is to insert a knife, and, if it comes out clean, the soufflé is done.

SPINACH SOUFFLE

In a saucepan, melt:
3 tablespoons butter
Add and cook 3 minutes, stirring constantly:
3 tablespoons all-purpose flour
Add and cook for 3 minutes, stirring constantly:
1 cup milk
1/2 cup chopped cooked well-drained spinach
1 canned pimiento, chopped (optional)
1/2 teaspoon herb salt
Remove from the heat and let cool. Mix in well:
6 egg yolks, beaten
Beat until stiff, glossy peaks form:
6 egg whites
1/2 teaspoon salt
Fold one-third of the whites into the spinach mixture to lighten it. Turn this mixture into the rest of the whites and fold in gently. Put in an ungreased 2-quart baking dish and bake in a 350°F oven for 45 minutes, or until a knife inserted in the center comes out clean. Serve with:
Light cheese sauce
Makes 4 servings

LAZY SUSAN SOUFFLE

Spread lightly with:
Butter
5 slices white bread
Spread over the butter a light coating of:
Prepared mustard
Cut the bread into cubes and put into an ungreased casserole. Mix together and pour over the bread cubes:
4 eggs
3 cups milk
1 pound sharp cheddar cheese, grated
1/8 teaspoon herb salt
1/8 teaspoon Worcestershire sauce
Dash cayenne pepper
Bake in a 375°F oven for 1 hour, or until a knife inserted in the center comes out clean. Serve with:
Light cheese sauce or Light Tomato Sauce (page 19)
Makes 4 servings

MUSHROOM SOUFFLE

Sauté until tender in:
2 tablespoons butter
1/2 cup minced celery
Drain, reserve juice and set celery aside. Sauté until tender in:
1 tablespoon butter
1 pound mushrooms, chopped
Drain, reserve juice and set mushrooms aside.
In a saucepan, melt:
4 tablespoons butter
Add and cook for 3 minutes, stirring constantly:
6 tablespoons all-purpose flour
Add and cook until thick:
Reserved celery and mushroom juice, plus enough milk to make 2 cups liquid
Then add and bring to gentle boil:
1/2 cup grated cheddar cheese
1/4 teaspoon paprika
When sauce boils, stir in:
Reserved celery and mushrooms
Remove from the heat and let cool. Mix in well:
6 egg yolks, beaten
Beat until stiff, glossy peaks form:
6 egg whites
1/2 teaspoon salt
Fold one-third of the whites into the mushroom mixture to lighten it. Turn this mixture into the rest of the whites and fold in gently. Put in an ungreased 3-quart casserole and bake in a 350°F oven for 45 minutes, or until a knife inserted in the center comes out clean.
Makes 8 servings

ARTICHOKE SOUFFLE

Cook until clear in:
4 tablespoons butter
1/2 onion, minced
Add and cook, stirring constantly, for 3 minutes:
3 tablespoons all-purpose flour
Add and cook for 2 minutes, stirring constantly:
1 cup milk
1/2 teaspoon herb salt
Add and mix in well:
6 cooked artichoke hearts, chopped
3/4 teaspoon double-acting baking powder
Remove from the heat and let cool. Mix in well:
6 egg yolks, beaten
Beat until stiff, glossy peaks form:
6 egg whites
1/2 teaspoon salt
Fold one-third of the whites into the artichoke mixture to lighten it. Turn this mixture into the rest of the whites and fold in gently. Put in an ungreased 2-quart casserole and bake in a 350°F oven for about 45 minutes, or until a knife inserted in the center comes out clean.
If desired, serve with:
Light cheese sauce
Makes 4 servings

SPOON BREAD

Spoon bread is actually a cornmeal soufflé, and when properly made is almost as light (taking into consideration the coarse texture of cornmeal) as any other soufflé.

I have found that yellow cornmeal is too heavy in texture for spoon bread. The white cornmeal is by far a better choice. Prepare this exactly as you do any other soufflé, adding the egg yolks when the cornmeal mixture is cool.

Scald:
4 cups milk
Add and cook until thick:
1 cup white cornmeal
2 tablespoons butter
Cool only until lukewarm, then add:
4 egg yolks, beaten
1 teaspoon salt
Beat until stiff, glossy peaks form:
4 egg whites
3/4 teaspoon salt
Fold one-third of the whites into the cornmeal mixture to lighten it. Turn this mixture into the rest of the whites and fold in gently. Put in a deep, greased 2-quart baking dish and bake in a 400°F oven for 45 minutes or until firm to the touch.
Makes 8 servings

Variation If fresh corn is available, reduce white cornmeal measure to 1/2 cup and add 2 cups fresh corn kernels.

EGGS FLORENTINE

Cook in very little water for about 5 minutes, or until wilted:

4 bunches fresh spinach, trimmed

2 teaspoons herb salt

Drain well and spread on the bottom of a baking dish to make a layer about 1 inch deep.

Make 8 depressions, evenly spaced, in the spinach and break into each:

1 egg

The eggs must be carefully broken into the depressions so the yolks are not broken. In a saucepan, melt:

4 tablespoons butter

Add and cook 3 minutes, stirring constantly:

4 tablespoons all-purpose flour

Add and cook until thick, stirring constantly:

2 cups milk

1/2 teaspoon salt

Spoon the sauce over the spinach and eggs and sprinkle over the top:

Grated cheddar cheese

Bake in a 350°F oven for 30 minutes, or until eggs are set. If you prefer hard yolks, bake a little longer.

Makes 8 servings

OMELET WITH TWO FILLINGS

For each person, prepare an omelet by beating together:
2 eggs
2 tablespoons heavy cream
Dash herb salt
In an omelet pan or skillet, melt:
1 teaspoon butter
Pour in eggs, tilt pan to evenly distribute them, turn flame down and cook quickly, lifting edges of eggs to let uncooked portion run underneath. When almost done, spoon one of the following fillings on one side, lift the other half over it, and cook a bit more until brown.

For mushroom filling, sauté in:
1 tablespoon butter
1 cup chopped mushrooms
1/4 teaspoon herb salt
Add and cook until thickened, stirring frequently:
2 tablespoons Gravy Quick
2 tablespoons cornstarch, dissolved in 2/3 cup water

For Spanish filling, cook together for 4 minutes:
1/4 cup water
1 large onion, coarsely chopped
4 stalks celery, coarsely chopped
1/4 cup finely chopped parsley
Add and heat to serving temperature:
3 canned pimientos, coarsely cut
1 teaspoon salt
1/2 teaspoon crumbled dried basil
1/2 teaspoon crumbled dried marjoram
1 cup tomato paste
2 tablespoons sugar

Note Depending on the number of omelets you are serving, you may find that you have some of the filling left over. Either filling can be kept in the refrigerator for at least 3 days. The mushroom filling is delicious added to scrambled eggs or butter-steamed onions and served over toast.

EGGS LILI KRAUS

One day when we were having lunch in the kitchen of the old Ranch House, in walked a beautiful woman with long black braids hanging down her back. It was Lili Kraus. She was giving a series of concerts at Happy Valley School, and the school had sent her to us. How many times I have cooked for her! She used to practice at the school and then come over famished, wanting something "quick and good." She especially liked the flavor of green peppers with eggs, and so between us we concocted the dish given here, which I named for her because it would never have existed without her.

Sauté in:
Butter
1 green bell pepper, seeded and finely minced
1 green onion and top, finely minced
2 mushrooms, finely minced
Dash Omelet Herb Blend
Beat together:
2 eggs
2 tablespoons heavy cream
Dash herb salt
Dash Omelet Herb Blend
In an omelet pan or skillet, melt:
1 teaspoon butter
Pour in eggs, tilt pan to evenly distribute them, turn flame down and cook quickly, lifting edges of eggs to let uncooked portion run underneath. When almost done, spoon the mushroom mixture over the surface and sprinkle with:
Grated cheddar cheese
Place under broiler until top puffs and begins to brown. Slide it gently onto a plate and serve immediately.
Makes 1 serving

ENGLISH EGGS

Allowing 1 or 2 for each serving, prepare:

Hard-cooked eggs

In a bowl, mix enough of the following ingredients together to form a medium-thick cold sauce to cover the eggs:

Mayonnaise

Heavy cream or evaporated milk

Few drops white vinegar or fresh lemon juice

Prepared mustard (optional)

Peel the eggs and drop them into the sauce. Garnish with:

Finely minced celery, green onions or parsley or finely shredded carrots

To serve, spoon plenty of the sauce over the eggs. Serve accompanied with a salad or as part of a luncheon buffet.

CURRIED MUSHROOMS AND EGGS

Sauté in:

4 tablespoons butter

1 clove garlic, minced

2 onions, minced

2 tablespoons minced parsley

Add and cook, stirring constantly, for 1 minute:

2 cups sliced mushrooms

1-1/2 tablespoons curry powder

1/4 cup all-purpose flour

Add and cook, stirring constantly, until thickened:

2 cups milk

Then add and mix in:

3 tablespoons orange marmalade or jam

2 tablespoons fresh lemon juice

1/2 cup shelled green peas

Slice into eighths:

4 hard-cooked eggs

Lay the eggs on a plate and spoon the curry mixture over them. Garnish with:

Paprika

Chopped cashews or whole pine nuts

Makes 4 servings

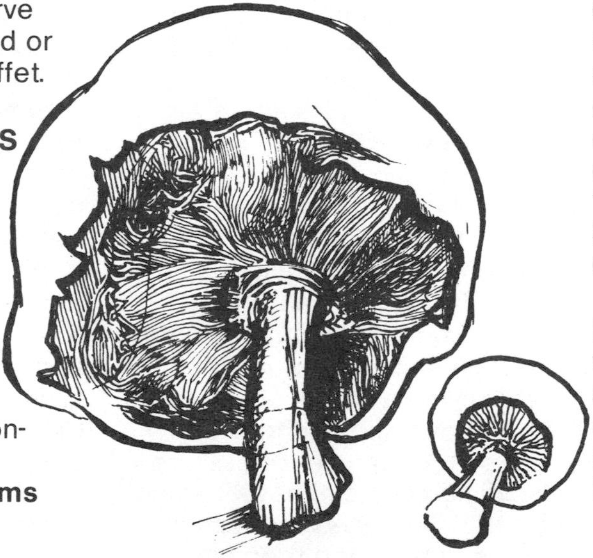

EGGS TETRAZZINI

Cook just until tender in:

Boiling salted water

4 ounces medium-cut Fresh Noodles (page 105)

Drain and set aside. Cook until tender but not mushy in:

2 tablespoons butter

2 large onions, coarsely sliced

1 green bell pepper, seeded and thinly sliced

1 bunch parsley, minced

1/4 teaspoon Omelet Herb Blend

1/2 teaspoon herb salt

Mix together:

Cooked vegetables

1/2 pound mushrooms, thickly sliced

Cooked noodles

Spread the noodles mixture in a shallow rectangular baking dish and make 8 evenly spaced depressions in the top. Into each depression, break:

1 egg

Sprinkle the top liberally with:

Grated Parmesan or sharp cheddar cheese

Bake in a 325°F oven until the whites of the eggs are just set and casserole is heated through. Garnish each egg with:

Minced parsley

Makes 8 servings

ZUCCHINI FRITTATA

This is not the traditional frittata of Italy, but rather a version served in a small Italian restaurant in La Jolla. Patrons line up for it there at lunch time.

Separate:
4 eggs
Add to both the yolks and whites:
1/4 teaspoon salt
Grind in a mortar:
1/2 teaspoon dried basil
1/2 teaspoon dried marjoram
Add to the mortar mixture:
1/4 cup all-purpose flour
Beat the egg yolks until light yellow and thick. Beat the egg whites until stiff, glossy peaks form. Fold the yolks into the whites, then gently fold in:
Herb-flour mixture
Then gently fold in:
2 cups thinly sliced, lightly salted, cooked zucchini
In a large skillet, heat:
Peanut oil
Spoon large spoonfuls of the zucchini mixture into the hot oil, pushing the batter off the spoon and pressing it down to make them as flat as possible. Cook on both sides until nicely browned. Serve very hot, with the following sauce poured over.

To make the sauce, cook until clear in:
6 tablespoons olive oil
2 large onions, thinly sliced
Stir in:
2 large tomatoes, peeled, deseeded and chopped
4 sprigs oregano
4 sprigs basil
2 vegetable bouillon cubes, crushed
2 cups water
Bring to a boil and add, stirring constantly until thickened:
3 tablespoons cornstarch, dissolved in a little water
Makes 4 to 6 servings

Variations Thinly sliced cooked Jerusalem artichokes or artichoke hearts may be substituted for the zucchini.

INVERTED ITALIAN FRITTATA

Put through the medium cone of a gricer or medium blade of a food processor:
2 stalks celery
2 green bell peppers
3 zucchini
Add to the vegetables:
1 bunch green onions and tops, minced
Beat together and set aside:
4 eggs
1/4 cup half-and-half cream
1/4 teaspoon herb salt
Dash freshly ground black pepper
In a large flameproof skillet placed over an asbestos pad to prevent burning, heat:
3 tablespoons peanut oil
3 tablespoons butter
When hot, add:
Vegetables
1/2 teaspoon herb salt
1/2 teaspoon Vegetable Herb Blend
Cook vegetables until they are just crisp, then spread over them:
1 cup grated sharp cheddar cheese
Pour the reserved egg mixture over the vegetables, cover and continue to cook until eggs are set and very light in texture, about 4 to 5 minutes. Place skillet under the broiler to brown frittata slightly. It must not brown too much or it will dry out. Serve immediately, cut into wedges. This is an excellent luncheon dish, accompanied with a tossed salad.
Makes 6 servings

EGG FOO YUNG

Combine in a large bowl:
1 cup chopped parsley
1/2 cup finely chopped green onions and tops
1 large green bell pepper, seeded and cut in julienne
1 bunch watercress tops (optional)
1/2 cup chopped celery leaves
1 cup water chestnuts, sliced 1/4 inch thick
1/2 cup thinly sliced bamboo shoots
1/2 pound bean sprouts
Beat together:
8 egg yolks
1/2 teaspoon salt
Beat until stiff, glossy peaks form:
8 egg whites
1/2 teaspoon salt
Gently fold beaten yolks into whites. Sift into egg mixture:
1/2 cup all-purpose flour
Fold flour in gently, with only enough strokes to incorporate completely. Then fold egg mixture into vegetables.
In a large skillet or deep griddle, heat:
Peanut oil
The oil should be hot enough to make the batter sizzle around the edges when it is dropped into the oil. Drop a large tablespoonful of batter into the oil for each cake. Spoon some of the hot oil over the cakes to seal them. When browned on the underside, turn with a large spatula aided by a spoon, and brown on the second side. If this is done correctly, there will be no splashing of the batter at the edges of the cakes. Don't worry about the vegetables getting done; they will cook just enough if the oil is the right temperature.

To prepare the sauce, combine in a saucepan:
4 cups water
1 teaspoon Savita, or 1 vegetable bouillon cube, crushed
1/4 cup soy sauce
Place over medium heat until a gentle boil is reached, then add:
6 tablespoons cornstarch, dissolved in a little water
Cook, stirring constantly, until thickened

Put 3 cakes on each plate, lapping one over the other, and spoon the hot sauce over them. Serve with:
Steamed white rice
Makes 8 servings

CHEESE

"Milk's leap toward immortality." —Clifton Fadiman

If you are going to melt cheese into a sauce or fondue, keep in mind that new, green cheese will not melt but turns into a sort of gum. In fact, it is well to remember that all protein, unless somehow modified, will curdle, thicken or become rubbery when heated. Eggs, cheese and wheat gluten get leathery; milk will curdle at the least error.

In cheese, the process of aging somehow affects the cheese so that it will melt; therefore, cheese for dishes such as Welsh rarebit should always be aged. A simple way to tell whether or not cheese is aged is to break it. Aged cheese will crumble easily; green cheese will not. It takes at least a year to age good cheese properly. I think none of the so-called "processed" cheeses will satisfy those who appreciate natural cheese, nor will processing ever take the place of natural aging in cheese.

WELSH RAREBIT

Don't be put off if it's called Welsh Rabbit—it is all the same dish! The important thing is to use a well-aged cheese. Cheddar is used most often, but other varieties, such as Swiss and Gruyère, are also used.

I shall always remember having Welsh rarebit late at night in the basement dining room of the old Deshler-Wallick Hotel in Columbus, Ohio. I think it was the best rarebit I ever had, and always when I make it this remembered taste is what I try to recreate; imitate, even, if you wish, for I don't feel guilty about trying to imitate a dish I have especially enjoyed. It is a lot of fun, if you are interested in cooking, to try duplicating what you have liked.

Here is a recipe especially liked by many people—very rich and heavy when not diluted with cream or any other sauce. You can dilute if you wish, but I will take it straight, served on toast and very hot. It must be heated slowly to keep it smooth and free from roughness in texture.

Put into the top pan of a double boiler:

8 ounces cheddar cheese, grated
2 tablespoons butter (preferably unsalted butter)
1/4 cup stale beer (preferably English ale)
1/4 cup heavy cream or Ranch House Béchamel Sauce (page 15, optional)

Melt to a smooth consistency over gently simmering water. Then beat in:

1 egg

Season with:

1/4 teaspoon Worcestershire sauce
1/4 teaspoon paprika
Dash cayenne pepper
1/4 teaspoon dry mustard (optional)

Serve over:

Toast

This dish can also be served in individual flameproof casseroles, which should be put under the broiler for a moment to make sure the servings are piping hot. Alternately, serve it fondue style in a chafing dish or kept warm on an electric tray, and accompany with long strips of toast, to be used for dipping.
Makes 4 servings

GREEN ONION AND CHEESE CASSEROLE

Cook until tender in:

4 tablespoons butter

1 bunch green onions and tops, chopped

1/4 cup hulled sunflower seeds

Remove from the heat. Beat together, then mix with the cooked onions:

4 eggs

1-1/2 cups milk

8 ounces cream cheese, crumbled

1/4 teaspoon herb salt

1 tablespoon minced parsley

Spread on:

2 slices white bread

Butter

Cube the bread and lay the cubes in a buttered casserole. Pour the onion-egg mixture over the bread cubes and bake in a 375°F oven for about 25 minutes, or until a knife blade inserted in the center comes out clean. Serve immediately.

Makes 4 servings

Note This is a subtly flavored dish. People who like strongly flavored food may find it too bland.

CHEESE FONDUE, AMERICAN STYLE

Scald, then remove from the heat:

2 cups milk

Add and mix together well:

8 ounces sharp cheddar cheese, grated

4 cups fine soft bread crumbs

1 tablespoon butter

When mixture is cool, add and fold in well:

9 egg yolks, well beaten until yellow in color

1/2 teaspoon salt

Beat until stiff, glossy peaks form:

9 egg whites

1/2 teaspoon salt

Fold whites into cheese mixture, one-half at a time, and turn into a baking dish. Bake in a 350°F oven for about 30 minutes. Spoon over servings:

Light cheese sauce or white sauce with plenty of chopped parsley added

Makes 6 servings

SWISS FONDUE

Use a pyrex or other glass vessel that will withstand direct heat. Rub the inside with:

Cut garlic clove

Pour into baking dish:

1-1/2 cups dry white wine

Add and mix well:

1 pound well-aged Swiss cheese, grated

(Be sure the cheese is well-aged, or it will toughen into a rubbery mass.) Stir constantly over low heat until cheese is melted. This may look hopeless at first, but persist. It will come out partly thin and partly thick. Add and stir until thickened:

3 tablespoons potato flour, dissolved in 3 tablespoons water

Then add and stir in well:

2 tablespoons kirsch

Dash ground nutmeg

Serve the fondue in a heated casserole or chafing dish and accompany with pieces of:

Sourdough French bread

Very good for a party, especially if accompanied with good beer.

Makes 6 servings

SWISS CHEESE PIE

Cook until tender in:
4 tablespoons butter
1 large bunch green onions and tops, chopped
Mix together to form consistency suitable for lining a pie plate:
33 soda crackers, crushed into crumbs
6 tablespoons butter, melted
Line a deep 9-inch pie plate with the cracker mixture, pressing it on firmly. Spread the cooked onions over the crust, then mix together well and pour over the onions:
2 eggs
3/4 cup sour cream
2-1/2 cups grated Swiss cheese
1/2 teaspoon salt
Dash white pepper or cayenne pepper
Bake in a 350°F oven for 40 minutes, or until a knife inserted in the center comes out clean.
Makes 6 servings

CHEESE BLINTZES

The former mayor of Ojai, James Loebl, requested this dish for his holiday party at the Ranch House this past year. He asked for it because on his first visit to the restaurant thirty-one years ago he had enjoyed a supper of cheese blintzes.

To make the pancake batter, place in an electric mixer and mix well:
1 egg
5 tablespoons milk
5 tablespoons water
Pinch salt
(The milk should be directly from the refrigerator and the water should be cold from the tap. These temperatures are important, as a warm mix tends to fry too quickly and stick to the pan.) Sift into the mixer bowl, then beat at high speed for at least 5 minutes:
1/3 cup all-purpose flour
Refrigerate for at least 1 hour so froth will settle.

With a pastry brush, grease a 7-inch skillet that is shiny clean. Place over medium heat and allow the pan to get very hot. The grease should be smoking slightly. Lift the pan from the heat and spoon into it a large cooking spoonful of batter, tilting the pan quickly so as to cover the bottom with batter. Return the pan to the heat for 45 seconds. Remove from the heat and invert the pan onto a greased board to release the pancake from it. Repeat with the remaining batter, being sure to stir the batter well before each spoonful is taken out.

To make the filling for the blintzes, beat together thoroughly:
1 cup crumbled hoop cheese (soft baker's cheese)
1 egg
Add and beat well again:
2 teaspoons fresh lemon juice
2 teaspoons pineapple juice
1 tablespoon sugar
Pinch salt
Dash ground cardamom
Dash ground cinnamon
Put a large cooking spoonful of the cheese mixture on the browned side of each pancake and roll into a cylinder, turning the edges in. Lightly brush one side of each blintz with:
Melted butter
Cook, buttered side down, on a grill or in a skillet until browned. Lightly brush top side of each blintz with:
Melted butter
Turn the blintzes and cook second side until browned.
Makes 4 servings
(3 blintzes per person)

CHEDDAR CHEESE QUICHE

Cook until clear in:
2 tablespoons butter
2-1/2 cups thinly sliced onion
Mix together to form consistency suitable for lining a pie plate:
33 soda crackers, crushed into crumbs
6 tablespoons butter
Line a deep 9-inch pie plate with the cracker mixture, pressing it on firmly. Spread the cooked onions over the crust. Scald, then remove from the heat:
1-1/2 cups milk
Add:
8 ounces sharp cheddar cheese, grated
Stir until the cheese has melted and the mixture has cooled slightly, then add:
3 eggs, beaten
1 teaspoon salt
1/4 teaspoon freshly ground black pepper
1 teaspoon Worcestershire sauce
Stir well, then pour over the onions in the pie plate. Bake in a 350°F oven for 40 minutes, or until a knife inserted in the center comes out clean.
Makes 6 servings

Variations Lightly toast 1/2 cup roasted almonds, then sprinkle with herb salt and toss with melted butter. Place the almonds on the crust before adding the onions. You may also add 1 teaspoon Bakon yeast to the almonds with the herb salt, or substitute chopped cashews or pecans or whole pine nuts for the almonds—lightly toasted of course.

Sauté 1 cup thinly sliced mushrooms in butter until tender, lightly salting them. Spread them on the crust before adding the onions. Or substitute sliced zucchini or chopped eggplant or green bell pepper, or a combination of vegetables for the mushrooms.

Eggs are the integral part of the liquid, but half-and-half cream may be used in place of the milk, or you may use vegetable juices, such as tomato, celery or carrot juice.

The simplest crust to make is the one given in the recipe, but one made with white or whole-wheat flour is delicious. This quiche can also be made in small tart pans to serve as appetizers. Be sure the crust is browned on the edges and crisp.

NOODLE DISHES

Whenever possible, prepare fresh noodles for your pasta dishes. Their flavor and texture is superior to the dried ones.

FRESH NOODLES

Mix together:
1-1/2 cups white pastry flour
1 teaspoon salt
Make a well in the center of the flour and add:
2 whole eggs
5 egg yolks
With a long fork, stir the eggs into the flour, being careful not to get the eggs on the sides of the bowl. Be sure the mixture is completely combined, then, take it out of the bowl and knead on a floured board until it feels smooth.

An alternate method of mixing, which I find is easier, is to use a KitchenAid mixing machine. Put the flour in the mixing bowl, making a well in the center. Then add the eggs to the well, and by hand with the flat beater—not the wire whip—gently mix together the flour and eggs. When it is rather well incorporated, put the beater in the machine and finish the job. This gets all the eggs into the flour without losing any on the sides of the bowl.

Cut the dough into 4 equal portions. Working with one portion at a time and keeping the others covered, pat it out into a rectangular form on a floured board and then begin rolling it out with a lightly floured rolling pin. It should be as thin as paper, about 4 inches wide and very long. With a sharp knife, cut the dough lengthwise into the width you want the noodles. Let the noodles dry in a covered wicker basket (the basket permits air to circulate around them). Repeat with remaining dough.

To cook, put the noodles into:
A generous amount of boiling salted water
Cook until just tender—al dente—about 7 minutes.
Drain well.
Makes 12 ounces

FETTUCCINE ALFREDO

Many years ago in Rome I had the great pleasure of dining at Alfredo's fine restaurant in the Piazza Augusto. (This is the authentic Alfredo's; there are now several imitators in different places in Rome.) Alfredo showed me all through the kitchen. I met his charming sisters, each one at a cash register checking the food as it left the kitchen, and watched his chef prepare their famous fettuccine.

Stacked in one corner of the kitchen were wicker baskets containing the noodles, with a cloth over each one. The noodles are made in Alfredo's own factory, he told me, where six women work at making them. The chef took a three-quart saucepan, filled it about two-thirds full of water and added a little salt. When it was boiling, he put in a big handful of noodles—and his hands were unusually large, with huge thick fingers. The noodles were boiled a few minutes, then taken to a sink nearby and drained. Out of a wooden tub the chef scooped a handful of sweet butter and put it on a warm platter. The drained noodles were mounded on the platter and on top of them he put a tremendous handful of grated pecorino cheese. Pecorino is a little stronger than Parmesan, but not at all bitter. When Alfredo tosses the noodles in the dining room, the result is not stringy but very buttery and cheesy.

Alfredo makes a real production out of serving this, his most famous dish. It is brought in on the long white platter and Alfredo comes with a large spoon and fork to toss the noodles very deftly so that the butter and cheese are thoroughly mixed with them. The noodles are then divided among the guests and the large platter on which the fettuccine was served is always given to the most glamorous lady in the party. Long ago Mary Pickford and Douglas Fairbanks dined at Alfredo's, had the fettuccine, and later sent him a gold fork and spoon. Now, when VIP guests come they may use this gold fork and spoon. I was delighted to be thus honored. (By this time they probably have many duplicates for the tourist trade.)

With an ordinary wooden fork and spoon and some practice, you can serve American-style fettuccine with the same flourish that Alfredo serves his fettuccine. Follow Alfredo's method, using:
Fresh fettuccine noodles, cooked al dente
Sweet butter (plenty of it), at room temperature
Freshly grated Parmesan or pecorino cheese (be generous)

MANICOTTI

Here is a dish that is quite simple to make once you have prepared the Fresh Noodles (page 105). I first had it in one of the food stalls at the famous Farmers Market in Hollywood.

Prepare and cook wide Fresh Noodles (about 4 inches wide). Each noodle will be filled and rolled into a "little muff," as the name implies.

For the filling, mix together well:
1 pound ricotta cheese
1/4 teaspoon crumbled dried basil
1/4 teaspoon crumbled dried marjoram
When the noodles are cool enough to handle, spoon some of the filling on one end and roll the noodle up. Place the filled noodles in a baking dish, fold sides down. Make a light sauce by pressing the juice from:
Canned tomatoes
Add a sprinkling of:
Crumbled dried oregano
Crumbled dried basil
Pour the sauce over the noodles and place in a 325°F oven until just heated through. Do not heat too much, or the noodles will disintegrate. Serve immediately with a green vegetable.
Makes 4 servings

SPINACH MANICOTTI

Prepare:
Fresh noodle dough (page 105)
Roll out dough very thinly and cut into 4-by-6-inch rectangles. Dust them with flour and cook until just tender in:
Boiling salted water
Drain well and set aside. Blanch just until wilted:
1 pound spinach, trimmed
Drain well and set aside. In a saucepan, combine:
1/2 cup water
2 carrots, minced
1 stalk celery, minced
1 small onion, minced
1 cup white wine
Drain well, discard vegetables, reserve liquid and boil liquid until reduced to 1/4 cup. Combine:
Cooked spinach
Reduced cooking liquid
2 cups Ranch House Béchamel Sauce (page 15)

Lay noodles flat on a board and spread some of the filling down the center of each. Roll up and place seam side down in a baking dish. Heat in a 350°F oven just until hot. Serve 2 to each person, sprinkling before serving with:
Grated Romano cheese
Alternately, serve with:
Italian Sauce (page 18) or Light Tomato Sauce (pag 19)
Makes 6 to 8 servings

NOODLES AND SPINACH

Cook until al dente in:
Boiling salted water
1 pound medium-cut Fresh Noodles (page 105)
Drain and put into a long, shallow baking dish.
Cook until wilted in:
A small amount of water
1-1/2 pounds spinach, trimmed
Drain off any excess water and add to spinach:
4 vegetable bouillon cubes, crushed
Grind in a mortar:
1 teaspoon onion salt
1/2 teaspoon garlic salt
1/2 teaspoon Savory Herb Blend
1/2 teaspoon celery seeds
Add to spinach:
Mortar mixture
1-1/2 cups half-and-half cream
Stir well and spread over noodles in baking dish, then cover with:
1-1/2 cups grated cheddar cheese
Press cheese down into mixture. (If the cheese is not pressed into noodle mixture it will brown too much and not form the desired light crust.) Bake in a 350°F oven until cheese is melted and forms a nice, light crust. To serve, cut with a large metal spatula.

This is a famous recipe served at the coffee shop of the Sherman Hotel in Chicago. Serve with shoestring beets, buttered carrots or other vegetable of bright color.
Makes 8 servings

NOODLES MEXICALI

Cook until al dente in:
Boiling salted water
8 ounces medium-cut Fresh Noodles (page 105)
Drain and set aside. In a pressure cooker without cap, cook for 3 minutes:
2 tablespoons butter
1 teaspoon salt
2-1/2 cups coarsely chopped celery
2-1/2 cups coarsely chopped onion
3 cups coarsely chopped green bell pepper
Grind in a mortar, then add to vegetables:
1 teaspoon herb salt
1/4 teaspoon dried basil
1/8 teaspoon dried marjoram
In a saucepan, melt:
2 tablespoons butter
Add and cook, stirring constantly, for 3 minutes:
2 tablespoons all-purpose flour
Add and cook, stirring constantly, until thickened:
2 cups milk
Put in a large baking dish:
Half of the cooked noodles
Cover the noodles with:
Half of the vegetables
Sprinkle over the vegetables:
Salt
Lay over vegetables:
Strips of cheddar cheese
Top with:
1/3 cup cut-up deseeded chili peppers
Pour over the chili peppers:
Half of the white sauce
Repeat these layers and bake in a 350°F oven for about 30 minutes, or until the mixture bubbles.
Makes 6 servings

GNOCCHI

A friend of mine went to live in Italy and learned the language well enough, she said, to joke with her servants and get from them the following recipe.
It is *important* in this and the following gnocchi recipe that the Parmesan be *freshly grated.*

In a saucepan, combine and bring to a boil:
2 cups milk
2 cups water
Add and cook, stirring constantly, until mixture clings to a spoon:
2 cups semolina
Have a greased baking dish prepared. Spread the semolina mixture in it about 1/2 inch thick. When cool, cut into serving pieces of desired size.
Spread over the top:
Melted butter
Grated Parmesan cheese
Bake in a 350°F oven until golden brown, about 15 minutes.

If desired, a sauce may be added to the finished dish. Simmer until soft, then put through a sieve:
Chopped tomatoes
Heat to serving temperature and season with:
Crumbled dried or minced fresh basil and salt to taste
Makes 4 to 6 servings

GNOCCHI ALLA ROMANA

This recipe comes from the Ritz Hotel in London.

In a saucepan, bring to a boil:
4 cups milk
Add and cook, stirring constantly, for about 10 minutes until mixture thickens:
1/2 pound farina
Remove from the heat and add, stirring in thoroughly:
3 tablespoons grated Parmesan cheese
3 tablespoons butter, melted
2 egg yolks, beaten with a pinch of salt
Pour farina mixture on a buttered platter and smooth out to about 1/2-inch thickness. Let stand for several hours, then cut into diamond-shaped or round sections. Put a layer of the sections in a buttered baking dish and sprinkle with:
Grated Parmesan cheese
Make another layer of sections and sprinkle again with:
Grated Parmesan cheese
Drizzle over the top:
Melted butter
Dust again with:
Grated Parmesan cheese
Bake in a 400°F oven until lightly browned, about 15 minutes.
Makes 4 to 6 servings

HUNGARIAN-STYLE HERB NOODLES

Mix together well:
3 cups cake flour
1 sprig each basil, thyme, marjoram, costmary and chive, very finely minced
3 large sprigs parsley, finely chopped
1-1/2 teaspoons double-acting baking powder
3/4 teaspoon salt
Add and mix to consistency of cornmeal with a pastry blender or 2 knives:
2 tablespoons butter
Make a well in the flour mixture and add:
6 eggs, beaten
Mix well, then knead on a floured board to form a smooth dough. Divide the dough in 3 equal portions. Working with 1 portion at a time and keeping the others covered, roll out with a lightly floured rolling pin on a floured board into a very thin, large circle. Roll up the

sheet into a cylinder and cut into crosswise slices about 2/3 inch thick. Repeat with remaining dough. Unroll the slices and drop them, several at a time, into:
Boiling salted water
(If they are all put in at once, the water will stop boiling and the noodles will not cook properly.) Cook about 5 minutes, then lift from the water with a slotted utensil, draining well. Repeat with the remaining noodles.

If the noodles are to be kept awhile before serving, in a saucepan melt:
Plenty of butter
Add the noodles and shake them around until they are coated with the butter. This will prevent their sticking together and they can be kept for as long as an hour before serving.
Makes 6 servings

YOLANDA'S CASSEROLE

This recipe is named for a warm-hearted friend, who is also a marvelous cook.

Prepare:
Cooked Hungarian-Style Herb Noodles (page 105)

In a saucepan, put:
4 cups French-cut green beans
1/2 cup water
(Long, thin beans are best for this dish.)
Spread over beans:
1 large onion, thinly sliced
1/2 teaspoon Savory Herb Blend
1 teaspoon herb salt
Cook over medium heat until just tender, then drain. Generously butter a medium-sized casserole. On the bottom put a layer of:
Cooked noodles
Top with a layer of:
Cooked beans and onion
Top this with a layer of:
Small spoonfuls of cottage cheese
Small spoonfuls of sour cream
Thin slices of cream cheese
Repeat these layers until the baking dish is filled. Top with:
Sour cream
Sprinkle over the sour cream:
A generous amount of paprika
Bake in a 350°F oven until the mixture bubbles, about 15 minutes, then serve immediately. The heartiness of this dish depends on the amount of cottage cheese used, so govern yourself accordingly.
Makes 6 servings

entrées

If you are one of the many people now beginning a meatless diet, you may feel that one of your biggest problems is what to prepare for an entrée. Other parts of the meal are simple, but "All I know how to fix is macaroni and cheese!"

The change to a vegetarian diet will be easier and more fun if you start with a wholly new approach to eating, free of worry about substituting one thing for another. So many of the suggested "vegi" substitutes for meat are very dull, and eating things that don't start the digestive juices flowing will not create the proper digestive climate. I have tried to invent things that will inspire the appetite and please the palate.

Again I say, don't look for substitutes. There aren't any, really, although there are some so-called meat substitutes that are tasty and nutritionally valuable. Old habits may linger for a while, perhaps some cravings will plague you, but you have a new world of food to think about and if you ignore the old ways they will quickly fade. In deciding to change your eating habits you are probably beginning to listen to your own body wisdom. Just eat things that for you combine happily for texture and flavor—and enjoy your meal!

Of course there are dietary considerations, but no great complications. Common sense will safely guide you. Protein is necessary in the diet but perhaps not as much as we have assumed. It is said that too much protein produces an oversupply of uric acid, thus working the kidneys too hard. I have tried to put most of these entrées together so that dietary requirements will not be neglected. Some of the dishes are higher in protein and in minerals and vitamins than meat. Many types of nuts, seeds, cheese, grains and milk products are used. Soy protein is said to be superior even to meat. The easiest way to get this protein is in soy flour which can be added to many things. Avoid overuse of the many processed foods such as sugars, starches and fats. If you drink coffee or tea, be sure to get plenty of the vitamin B complex in your diet, this seems to be helpful in preventing the nervousness caffeine can cause. These stimulants are said to burn up the blood sugar and in the process use up the B vitamins.

Many books on nutrition and dieting say you must eat meat; just as many books say eating meat is a terrible dietary error. I say why not experiment and enjoy the experience of something different. Try one diet that appeals to you for a while, then try another; then go with the one that provides you with the most energy and harmony of spirit.

Here are some suggestions that may be useful. Try starting your meal with fresh raw fruit—an apple or an orange, a peach or pear, grapes or a melon, or with raw vegetables, perhaps

in a salad. Hard to chew vegetables like carrots, celery, cabbage and beets can be put through the gricer. Use an easily prepared dressing of oil and vinegar, or a simple French dressing. Eat small amounts, chewing everything well. The most wonderful flavors will be your rich reward.

Don't bother to think in terms of an entrée—prepare what you feel you would like to eat. Let your natural food wants, those the body will project, come to the surface. Perhaps to your surprise, this approach will result in a delicious and satisfying meal.

If you will pay attention to its messages your body will guide you. Become aware—listen carefully with great confidence! Experiment! Experiment! Experiment! If you choose wrongly now and then, what does it matter? You have found out something. Either you didn't like the taste of that dish or it was not suitable for you at the time you ate it. There are no mistakes; you are learning a completely different way of nourishing yourself. Don't depend on an outside authority. It's your body, unlike any other body. It is your problem to nourish it and enjoy the process. Your meat-eating friends will have things to say, such as: "Do you think you are getting enough protein?" or "Will all that raw stuff agree with you?" And, most tiresomely, you'll get "recommended" diets. Don't waste time giving logical explanations. Just tell them you're having fun trying something new.

Sometimes people get sick, and eventually we all die—what of it! For the time being we are alive—so be it!

STUFFED ARTICHOKES

With scissors, clip the tops from:
4 large artichokes
Cut off the stems and, with a melon ball maker, scoop out the "chokes." Only cut down to the bottom of the artichoke; do not cut into it. Cook artichokes and stems in a pressure cooker at 15 pounds pressure for 10 minutes with:
1/4 cup water
When cool enough to handle, spread apart the leaves slightly so the stuffing can be easily put in the center hole. To make stuffing, cook until clear in:
2 tablespoons butter
2 green onions and tops, finely chopped
Add and cook for 2 more minutes:
1/4 pound fresh mushrooms, finely chopped
Add and mix in well:
1 cup shredded mild cheddar cheese
1/2 cup dry bread crumbs
1/2 teaspoon salt
1/8 teaspoon crumbled dried chervil
Good dash freshly ground black pepper
Mix together and add:
2 eggs, well beaten
1/2 cup sour cream

Stuff the artichokes with this mixture. Remove skin from stems if it is tough. Chop stems and put on top of stuffing. Top with:
Grated mild cheddar cheese
Bake in a 400°F oven for 30 minutes. Serve with small dish of:
Drawn butter
Dip leaves into butter before eating.
Makes 4 servings

FRIENDS IN NEED

When we were in the process of building the new Ranch House and getting ready to serve the public, we needed help and enlisted the aid of two very good friends, Fred and Torre Taggart.

When we finally opened the restaurant and started serving, Fred made the whole-wheat and date-nut bread, struggling with an old broken-down oven that we bought for little money, and that never did work properly. Torre cooked and served with my help. In my opinion she is one of the best and most creative cooks I know. She left us a group of wonderful dishes, one of which is given here.

EGGPLANT ROMA

Slice in pieces 1/2 inch thick:
2 eggplants (unpeeled)
Broil the slices quickly as possible on both sides, and layer one-half or one-third of them at once in a crockery or glass baking dish. Sprinkle lightly with:
Salt
On each slice of eggplant, place a slice of:
Provolone cheese, about half the size of the eggplant slices
Sprinkle over them lightly:
Bakon yeast (optional)
Spoon over slices, without disturbing the yeast:
Italian Sauce (page 18)
Do not use too much cheese and tomato sauce. There should be 2, or perhaps 3, layers, depending on the size of the baking dish. Bake in a 350°F oven for about 30 minutes, or until the sauce begins to bubble gently around the edges. Overbaking will toughen the cheese and overcook the sauce and eggplant.
Makes 8 servings

RATATOUILLE

This dish can be found all through the Middle East. There's a legend that the first time it was prepared for a shah he became ill from its richness. We would probably say that the illness came from too much olive oil—the Turkish version calls for twice as much as is given in this recipe. The vegetables are generally cooked until they are quite mushy, but you may cook them the way that suits you best.

In a covered pan, cook until soft in:
1/3 cup olive oil
6 cloves garlic, minced
2 onions, coarsely cut
2 small zucchini, coarsely cut
1 pound mushrooms, sliced
1 eggplant, cubed
1 (28-ounce) can tomatoes, drained and minced
1/4 teaspoon crumbled dried basil
1/4 teaspoon crumbled dried marjoram
1 teaspoon salt
1/8 teaspoon freshly ground black pepper
Serve with:
Steamed millet (page 85), rice or plain lentils
Makes 4 servings

EGGPLANT A L'ALGERIENNE

Mix together:

3/4 teaspoon herb salt
1/2 teaspoon Savory Herb Blend
Pinch curry flour
1 tablespoon all-purpose flour

Sauté lightly in:

Butter
8 large mushrooms, sliced
1 shallot, chopped, or 1 tablespoon chopped onion

Add, stir in well and cook 2 minutes:

Flour mixture

Then add, blending in well:

1/2 cup half-and-half cream

Simmer a few minutes to reduce liquid slightly. (Any good mushroom sauce can be substituted for the preceding.)

Prepare:

Eight 1/2-inch-thick unpeeled eggplant slices

Either place under a broiler until tender and browned or dip slices first into:

Half-and-half cream

Then dip them into:

All-purpose flour

Fry the eggplant slices until golden brown in:

Vegetable oil

Prepare:

Eight 3/4-inch-thick unpeeled tomato slices

Dip the tomato slices in:

All-purpose flour

Fry the tomato slices until lightly browned in:

Vegetable oil

Spread over the bottom of a shallow rectangular baking dish:

1 cup Brown Rice Pilau with Herbs (page 89)

Arrange on top, alternating slices and overlapping edges:

Eggplant and tomato slices

Pour over the top:

Prepared mushroom sauce

Bake in a 350°F oven until the mixture begins to bubble, about 10 to 15 minutes. Do not overcook or the eggplant and tomato slices will become mushy.

Makes 8 servings

STUFFED EGGPLANT

Cut off 1 inch from tops of:

4 large eggplants

Reserve the tops and hollow out the insides of the eggplants, leaving a 1/2-inch-thick wall. Place the eggplants in a large kettle and steam for 9 minutes. Remove and allow to cool. To make the stuffing, mix together:

1 cup cooked rice of choice
1/4 cup minced onion
1/2 cup sautéed chopped mushrooms
3/4 cup shredded cheddar cheese
2 eggs
1/4 cup dry bread crumbs
1 teaspoon minced fresh basil, or 1/2 teaspoon crumbled dried basil
1/2 teaspoon herb salt
2 tablespoons chopped green bell pepper
2 tablespoons olive oil

Divide this mixture evenly among the 4 eggplants and stuff it into the cavities. Put on the reserved tops and bake in a 400°F oven for about 1-1/2 to 2 hours. Remove from the oven and slice the eggplants in half horizontally. Lift off the top halves with a spatula and invert them onto serving plates. Remove the remaining halves to serving plates. Top the eggplant halves with:

Light cheese sauce

Makes 8 servings

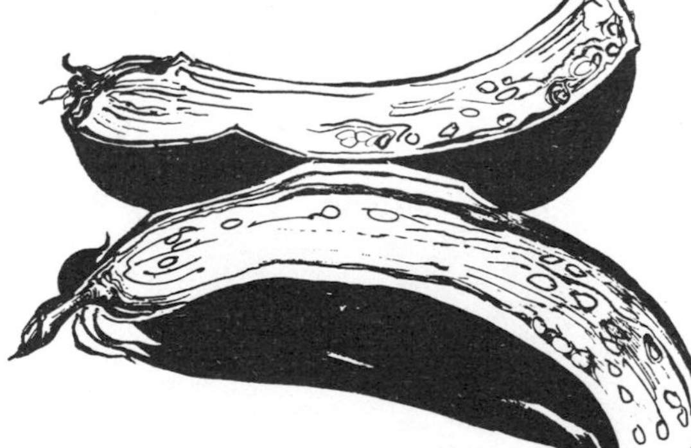

BROILED MUSHROOMS

I had an amusing experience on my first visit to the famous Antoine's in New Orleans, and the thing I remember most vividly is a dish of mushrooms. We asked the waiter about the various vegetarian dishes available and discussed each one—the sauces used, and so forth. Finally, we ordered a fairly simple meal. The waiter misunderstood, either deliberately or because he did not know English very well. Lo and behold! Two waiters began bringing in trays piled with dishes, enough to fill our large table and the one next to it!

After the first shock, I was delighted at this opportunity to sample such a variety of foods! Of all this largess, the dish that remains most clearly in my memory is a particular type of broiled mushrooms, as much as three inches in diameter, thick as a steak and dark in color. When you cut them, they were solid without being tough. I think they must have been broiled in butter, then turned upside down and the cap filled with a mixture of onion, garlic, Worcestershire and a bit of thyme. This flavor had permeated the mushrooms, making them absolutely divine. Here is the way we serve them at the Ranch House.

Use quantities of mushrooms and toast sufficient for the number of servings you need. Prepare:

Hot toast generously covered with lightly flavored garlic butter

Have ready:

Large, russet-type mushrooms

Select the largest, russet (brown) mushrooms available. The russet mushrooms have the most flavor and do not shrink in the cooking as much as other mushrooms do. The "skirt" should be tightly attached to the stem, for then they are freshly picked and not dry. Wash them well under cold, running water and scrub off any bits of dirt imbedded in the top or at the end of the stem. Do not peel them. Cut the stem off even with the bottom part of the mushroom; do not break it off for then a hole is left in the underside of the mushroom. In a skillet, melt:

A generous amount of sweet butter

Lay the mushrooms in the pan, cut side down. Cover and cook slowly until they feel as soft as the side of the forearm. Covering the pan is essential to keep the mushrooms from drying out. When done on the first side, turn them with tongs. Put onto each stem end:

2 or 3 drops Worcestershire sauce
Good dash herb salt

Cover and continue cooking until the second side is gently browned. Have ready a hot platter with the hot toast on it. Lift out the mushrooms without spilling any of the delicious juice in the caps. Turn them over on the toast so the liquor will soak into it. Any liquor left in the pan should be spooned over each serving.

These mushrooms make a delicious accompaniment to scrambled eggs, or are good served with cooked green vegetables or a salad. Surprisingly, they are enough, with any of these suggestions, to be a satisfying meal.

MUSHROOMS FLORENTINE

Wash thoroughly, then trim two-thirds of length of stem from:
3 bunches spinach
Steam the spinach until wilted, then drain well and set aside.
Cook until clear in:
2 tablespoons butter
2 cloves garlic, minced
1/2 small onion, minced
Add and bring just to a simmer, being careful not to boil:
4 ounces cream cheese, crumbled
1 cup sour cream
1-1/2 cups shredded sharp cheddar cheese
Mix into the reserved spinach:
1-1/2 teaspoons herb salt
1 teaspoon Savory Herb Blend
Cut the spinach coarsely and combine it with the cream cheese mixture. Keep it warm on the stove over an asbestos pad until needed.

Cover the bottom of a casserole with a single layer of:
Buttered white bread toast
Cut off stems even with bottoms of:
3/4 pound large mushrooms
In a skillet, melt:
Butter
Add the mushrooms, stem sides down, cover and cook until they give to the touch. Turn the mushrooms over and to the stem end of each add:
Few drops Worcestershire sauce
Dash herb salt
Spoon the reserved spinach mixture onto the toast in the casserole, then lay the mushrooms on top, cut side down, being careful not to splatter the juice from the stem. Warm the casserole in a 325°F oven until well heated through.
Makes 6 servings

EGG AND MUSHROOM CUTLETS

Sauté in:
4 tablespoons butter
1/2 teaspoon herb salt
2 cups sliced mushrooms
1 green onion, minced
In a separate skillet, melt:
3 tablespoons butter
Add and cook, stirring constantly, for 3 minutes:
3 tablespoons all-purpose flour
Add and cook, stirring constantly until thickened:
1 cup milk
1/2 teaspoon salt
2 teaspoons minced parsley
Hard cook:
6 eggs
When eggs are cool enough to handle, separate yolks from whites and rub each through a sieve. Set a little of the sieved whites aside for garnish.
Mix together:
Mushroom mixture
White sauce
Sieved yolks and whites
Enough dry bread crumbs to make a firm mixture
Spread the mixture on a platter, and when cool, form into 6 patties. Dip each patty into:
Beaten egg
Then dip each patty into:
Dry bread crumbs
In a skillet, fry patties on both sides until nicely browned in:
Butter
Garnish with:
Reserved sieved whites
Makes 6 servings

KAPUSTA PIROG

Mix together to form a coarse crumb mixture, as for pie dough:
1-1/2 cups all-purpose flour
1/4 pound butter, at room temperature
1 teaspoon salt
Make a well in the flour mixture and pour in:
1/3 cup buttermilk
Mix in the buttermilk just until the dough holds together. Divide the dough almost in half and roll out the larger portion on a lightly floured board to fit an 8-by-8-by-1/2-inch glass

baking dish. Line the dish with the dough and set aside with the remaining portion of dough.

To make the filling, melt:
2 tablespoons butter
Add and cook until soft, but not too mushy:
1 large onion, coarsely sliced
3 cups thickly sliced mushrooms
3 cups coarsely cut cabbage (1/2-inch-wide pieces)
1/2 teaspoon Omelet Herb Blend, ground in a mortar with 3/4 teaspoon herb salt
Add and stir in gently:
4 hard-cooked eggs, cut into eighths
3/4 cup Rich Cream Sauce (page 10)
Spread mixture in dough-lined baking dish and dot with:
A generous amount of sweet butter
Roll out remaining dough portion on a lightly floured board to form a top crust and cover baking dish, pressing down the edges to seal. Make a few slits in the top so that steam will escape. Bake in a 450°F oven for about 25 minutes, or until the crust is nicely browned. Cut into squares and serve immediately.
Makes 6 servings

FRESH MUSHROOM CUTLETS

These are easy to make but must be prepared at the very last minute or they will break up when fried.

Prepare:
1 cup finely chopped mushrooms and stems
1 green onion and top, finely chopped
Beat together, then mix with above:
2 eggs
1/2 teaspoon herb salt
Add and stir in well, but not until mushy:
1/2 cup dry bread crumbs
3/4 cup grated mild cheddar cheese
Divide mixture into 8 portions and form each portion into a patty 1/2 inch thick. Press each patty between 2 sheets of waxed paper.
In a skillet, melt:
Butter
Fry the patties on both sides until crisp on the outside and moist on the inside. Serve with:
Mornay Sauce (page 16)
Makes 4 servings

FRESH MUSHROOM AND SPINACH FRITTERS

Cook in water clinging to leaves until wilted, then drain well:
2 bunches spinach, trimmed
Set spinach aside. In a skillet, cook until tender and dry in:
1 tablespoon butter
1/2 pound mushrooms, sliced
Combine the spinach and mushrooms. Sift together:
1 cup all-purpose flour
2 teaspoons salt
1/4 teaspoon black pepper
1/4 teaspoon ground nutmeg
2 teaspoons baking powder
Combine the sifted mixture with the spinach-mushroom mixture, then mix in well:
2 cups soft bread crumbs
1 cup hulled sunflower seeds
2 tablespoons butter, melted
3 eggs, beaten
Set aside.
To make the sauce, prepare:
1 recipe Rich Cream Sauce (page 16)
Add to the sauce and keep hot until ready to serve:
2 tablespoons sherry
1/2 cup chopped parsley
1/4 cup chopped chives
1/2 cup grated sharp cheddar cheese
To cook the fritters, heat in a skillet:
Equal portions butter and peanut oil
Spoon in batter, making fritters in size desired. Fry until nicely browned, turning twice. Spoon sauce over the fritters and serve.
Makes 6 servings

PENNSYLVANIAN GREEN BEAN STEW

This is an excellent dish that, on first reading, may seem a bit too complicated. Actually, it isn't difficult. The vegetables are all cooked separately, then the gravy is made from the bean juice and all the ingredients are added and reheated—that is the simple way of it.

Cook in:
Boiling salted water
6 medium potatoes
Drain and, when cool enough to handle, peel the potatoes and cut them into eighths; set aside. Cook 5 minutes in a pressure cooker without a cap:
2 tablespoons butter
1 large onion, finely chopped
3 stalks celery, cut in 1-inch pieces
Grind in a mortar:
1 tablespoon herb salt
1/4 teaspoon dried summer savory

1/4 teaspoon dried thyme
Add to the mortar:
2 tablespoons Bakon yeast, mixed with 1 teaspoon salt
Put in a pressure cooker and cook for 1-1/2 minutes at 15 pounds pressure:
1-1/2 pound green beans, cut into 1-inch lengths
1/2 cup water
Mortar mixture
Drain liquid from beans into a saucepan and add:
Water to make 1-1/2 cups
Place over medium heat and add, stirring constantly until thickened:
1/4 cup all-purpose flour, blended with 4 tablespoons butter
When thickened, add:
Reserved potatoes
Reserved green beans
1 (7-ounce) can diced pimientos, drained
1 bay leaf
16 ounces fresh bean curd (tofu), cut into 1-inch cubes and browned in butter or vegetable oil
Heat to serving temperature and let stand for at least 30 minutes over an asbestos pad before serving. Remove the bay leaf and serve.
Makes 6 servings

STUFFED YELLOW SQUASH

Trim and cut in half:
18 medium yellow crookneck squash
Scoop out centers of squash with a melon baller or small spoon, being careful not to pierce the skins. Reserve the pulp. Cook until clear in:
2 tablespoons butter
4 cups minced onion
1 clove garlic, chopped
Add and cook just until tender, but not too soft:
Chopped squash pulp
2 large sprigs winter savory, chopped
2 large sprigs basil, chopped
1/4 cup chopped parsley
2 vegetable bouillon cubes, crushed
Add:
1 cup chopped English walnuts
1/2 cup dry bread crumbs
1/2 cup wheat germ
2 eggs
2 tablespoons grated cheese of choice
In a large kettle, steam squash halves until just tender, but not too soft, then place in a flat baking dish. Divide filling equally among them. Bake in a 375°F oven for 30 minutes.
Makes 6 servings

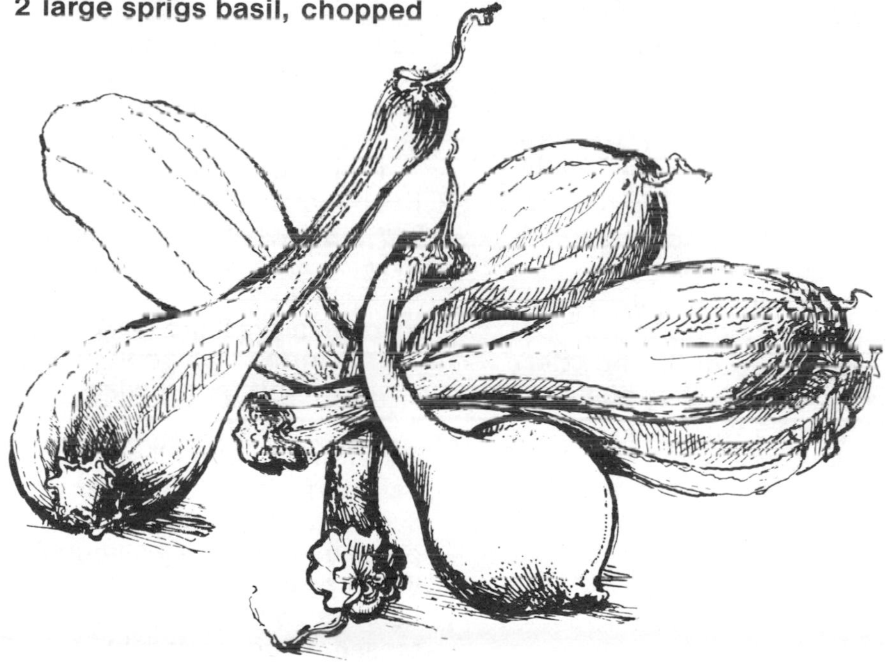

VEGETARIAN GUMBO

In a large saucepan, cook until just tender, about 15 minutes:
4 vegetable bouillon cubes, dissolved in 1 cup hot water
1-1/2 cups coarsely cut celery
1 cup coarsely cut onion
1/4 cup chopped parsley
1/2 teaspoon salt
1/4 teaspoon paprika
1 tablespoon sugar
4 bay leaves
1/4 teaspoon freshly ground black pepper
2 tablespoons butter
Add and boil for 5 minutes:
Half of a (28-ounce) can tomatoes, mashed
Stir in:
2-1/2 tablespoons cornstarch, dissolved in a little water
Stir over medium heat until thickened. Add and heat just to boiling, but do not boil:
2 cups cooked okra
Sprinkle in the saucepan and stir in immediately:
1 tablespoon filé powder
Heat again just to boiling point and serve with rice.
Makes 8 servings

LOW-CALORIE BROCCOLI WITH SAUCE

In a small saucepan, heat together:
2 cups buttermilk
1 cup plain yogurt
1/4 cup cornstarch, dissolved in a little of the buttermilk
Grind in a mortar:
1/2 teaspoon onion salt
1/4 teaspoon garlic salt
Dash dried winter savory
Add to mortar and grind together well:
1 teaspoon capers
1 teaspoon ground turmeric
Add the mortar mixture to the buttermilk mixture, then heat gently, stirring, until it thickens. Add to mixture, stirring until smooth:
1/4 cup sour cream
Keep the sauce warm in the top of a double boiler or placed over an asbestos pad until ready to serve.
Place in a pressure cooker:
2-1/2 pounds broccoli, stalks cut in half lengthwise
1/2 cup water
Cover and heat until steam has been escaping for 30 seconds. Put on cap and set pressure gauge at 15 pounds. When pressure is reached, cook 30 seconds, then cool pressure cooker immediately by placing under cold, running water. Remove lid immediately and allow steam to escape. To serve, place cooked broccoli, cut sides down, on a serving platter and top with sauce.
Makes 6 servings

ZUCCHINI CASSEROLE WITH RICE

Cut in half lengthwise, then steam until just tender:
12 medium zucchini
Set the zucchini aside. Cover the bottom of a casserole large enough to hold the zucchini in a single layer with:
3 cups cooked brown rice
Spread over the rice:
8 ounces sharp cheddar cheese, grated
Sprinkle over the cheese:
Savory Herb Blend to taste
Arrange the steamed zucchini, cut side up, on the rice. They should be close together so that the rice is completely covered. Heat together to blend thoroughly, but do not boil:
6 tablespoons tomato paste
1/2 teaspoon herb salt
3/4 cup sour cream
1/4 cup minced coriander leaves
Spread the tomato mixture over zucchini. Bake in a 375°F oven for 30 minutes.
Makes 6 servings

FRESH CORN CASSEROLE

In a large kettle, place over low heat to warm:

4 cups milk
1-1/2 pounds frozen corn kernels
2 teaspoons granulated white sugar
1-1/2 tablespoons butter

Grind in a mortar and add:

1 teaspoon salt
1/4 teaspoon dried thyme
1/4 teaspoon dried marjoram
1/4 teaspoon dried basil
1/8 teaspoon freshly ground black pepper

Then add:

5 eggs, lightly beaten
1/2 green bell pepper, finely chopped
2 canned pimientos, finely chopped
1/4 cup finely chopped parsley
1 green onion, finely chopped

Put into a buttered casserole and place the casserole in a pan with water to a depth of 1/2 inch. Bake in a 325°F oven for 1-1/4 hours.
Makes 8 servings

OHIO CORN PUDDING

Stand on end, cut only top of kernels off, then scrape down with knife to remove all milk from:

12 ears sweet corn

Combine corn with:

1 tablespoon granulated white sugar
1 tablespoon all-purpose flour
1 teaspoon salt
Dash freshly ground pepper
3 eggs, well beaten
1/2 cup half-and-half cream
1 cup shredded sharp cheddar cheese

Turn into a buttered casserole and bake in a 350°F oven for 45 minutes, or until set.
Makes 6 servings

DOROTHY'S HIGH-PROTEIN CASSEROLE

Keep these three cans on your shelf and you are always ready for unexpected guests.

Mix together well:

1 (15-ounce) can cream-style corn
1 (15-ounce) can soybeans
1 (15-ounce) can tomatoes, well drained and juice pressed out well
2 cups dry bread crumbs
1 egg, beaten
6 ounces sharp cheddar cheese, grated

Turn mixture into a casserole and bake in a 375°F oven for at least 30 minutes.
Makes 6 servings

TOMATO AND CELERY CASSEROLE

Prepare, reserving celery leaves:
3 cups 1-inch-long celery pieces
Add to the celery:
1/2 teaspoon herb salt
Steam the chopped celery in a very little water until just soft. Drain the celery and place it in a casserole. Cut into 1-inch cubes and spread over celery:
8 slices lightly buttered white or whole-wheat bread
Spread over celery and bread cubes:
2 cups grated sharp cheddar cheese
Drain and press seeds from:
1 (28-ounce) can Italian-style tomatoes
(Reserve the juice for soup stock.) Lay these flattened tomatoes over the cheese. There should be enough to cover it, but if not, another small can of tomatoes should also be used.
Mix together:
6 tablespoons half-and-half cream
6 tablespoons all-purpose flour
Add:
6 eggs, well beaten
1/2 teaspoon herb salt
1/2 teaspoon crumbled dried oregano
1/2 teaspoon crumbled dried basil
Add cream mixture to casserole, pressing down a little so it will penetrate into the layers. Finely chop and spread over the casserole mixture:
Reserved celery leaves
Bake in a 400°F oven for 45 minutes, or until egg custard is set but not dry. Cut in squares and serve, garnished with:
Chopped parsley
Makes 6 servings

NEXT-DAY CASSEROLE

Using slicing cone of gricer or a food processor, slice:
2 unpeeled potatoes
2 large onions
2 zucchini
2 green bell peppers
Grease a large baking dish and make a layer of half the sliced vegetables on the bottom, interspersing them with:
6 ounces sharp cheddar cheese, thinly sliced
Sprinkle on top of layer:
1/2 teaspoon herb salt, ground in a mortar with 1-1/2 teaspoons Vegetable Herb Blend
Repeat layer with remaining vegetables and an equal amount of cheese, and top with an equal amount of the herb salt and Vegetable Herb Blend.
Arrange on top:
Thinly sliced sharp cheddar cheese
Drizzle over the top:
1/4 cup water
Cover tightly and bake in a 350°F oven for at least 1-1/2 hours, or until potatoes are tender. Serve with a tossed green salad with avocado.
This casserole can be stored in the refrigerator for at least a week. Reheat in a moderate oven.
Makes 6 servings

STUFFED CABBAGE

Sauté in:
2 tablespoons butter
1 onion, chopped
1-1/2 cups sliced mushrooms
1 canned pimiento, finely chopped
1 teaspoon minced garlic
1 teaspoon Savory Herb Blend
Remove from the heat and mix in:
1 cup cooked white or brown rice
1 cup grated cheddar or Swiss cheese
Parboil for 8 minutes:
10 large cabbage leaves
Divide the rice mixture evenly among the cabbage leaves, roll up the leaves to form secure bundles and keep the rolls tightly closed with toothpicks. Place the cabbage rolls in a casserole or baking pan, cover and bake in a 350°F oven for about 25 minutes. To serve, remove the toothpicks and top each cabbage roll with:
Dollop whipped sour cream
Sprinkle on top:
Paprika
Makes 8 to 10 servings

STUFFED YORKSHIRE PUDDING

To prepare the stuffing, steam until tender, then drain well:
2 small zucchini, cut into 1/2-inch pieces
1/2 large onion, coarsely cut
1/2 cup coarsely cut celery
1/2 green bell pepper, coarsely cut
1/2 cup cubed (1/2 inch) jicama
6 green beans, coarsely cut
Add to the steamed vegetables:
1/2 cup fresh or thawed green peas
Set the vegetables aside and keep warm.
In a saucepan, heat:
1-1/2 cups Mornay Sauce (page 16)
Mix the vegetables into the sauce and keep hot until used.

To make the Yorkshire pudding, put into a blender or food processor and mix for 30 seconds, or until smooth:
2 cups milk
4 eggs
2 cups all-purpose flour
1-1/2 teaspoons salt
Put into each of 10 baking cups and preheat at least 5 minutes in a 400°F oven:
1 tablespoon peanut oil
(The baking cups should be pyrex and must be "cured" before using to prevent sticking. To cure them, brush each with peanut oil and place in a 400°F oven for 10 minutes. Cool completely before using.) Fill each preheated cup with about 1/3 cup of the batter and bake in a 400°F oven for 15 to 20 minutes, or until nicely browned. Remove the puddings from the oven, slide from the cups onto dinner plates and spoon into each an equal portion of the vegetable-sauce mixture. Serve immediately.
Makes 10 servings

Variation Buttered white toast may be substituted for the Yorkshire pudding.

ZUCCHINI ITALIANO

In harvesting zucchini from your garden, sometimes you will miss one of those long, green, fat ones until, when it is discovered, it seems too large to pick and cook in the usual way. But all is not lost—in fact you have a treat coming. Just let it grow until it gets to about a foot and a half long, then pick it and wash it well. Now your only problem is finding a vessel large enough in which to cook it. A canning kettle is usually adequate. Cut the zucchini in half lengthwise and remove the seeds and membrane. Put it in the kettle with about an inch of water and steam it until it is just a bit soft. Don't overcook, as you are going to bake it. Set aside to cool.

Prepare:
Cooked spaghetti, cut into 2-inch lengths
Combine spaghetti with:
Italian Sauce (page 18), enough to coat the noodles well
Place in a long baking dish, cut side up:
Zucchini halves
Stuff the halves with the spaghetti and sprinkle lavishly with:
Grated Parmesan cheese
Bake in a 325°F oven until the edges of the spaghetti bubble nicely.

If you want a richer dish, mix some of the cheese into the spaghetti before stuffing the zucchini. In any case, be sure there is plenty of good, sharp cheese, for the oil of the cheese should permeate the meat of the zucchini to give the desired flavor.

Place the long green boats on a serving platter and garnish with:

Well-buttered noodles, tossed with chopped pimientos and sprinkled with herb salt

Cut across in large slices and serve with some of the noodles. Makes 8 servings

WORKING PERSONS CURRY

This recipe is for people who work (and nowadays who doesn't?) and must come home and prepare food for themselves or their family. This dish can be prepared and stored for at least a week without spoiling. Remember the Hindus used spices to prevent spoilage.

Soak for at least 1 hour in:

Water to cover
2 cups lentils

Add to lentils:

3 cups water

Cook in a pressure cooker for 10 minutes at 15 pressure. Remove from the pressure cooker and set aside. Combine in a pressure cooker and cook for 2 minutes at 15 pounds pressure:

1/4 cup water
3 carrots, cut into 1/2-inch pieces
3 stalks celery, cut into 1/2-inch pieces
1 very large onion, cut into sixths
1 green bell pepper, cut into large pieces
3 zucchini, cut into 1/2-inch pieces

Stirring constantly, cook until clear in:

1 tablespoon butter
6 cloves garlic, minced
1 onion, minced
4 to 6 tablespoons curry powder, depending on hotness desired

Mix together, then add to curry mixture:

6 tablespoons apricot jam or jam of choice
3 tablespoons fresh lemon juice

Combine lentils and cooking liquid, vegetable mixture and curry mixture and heat just to boiling point. Do not cook or mixture will become mushy. Prepare:

Southern Rice (page 86) with turmeric
Pineapple Guava Chutney (page 147)

Serve curry with rice and chutney

Any leftover curry and rice can be stored in separate containers in the refrigerator. When you wish to reheat these leftovers, put a small amount of water into 2 separate kettles and spoon out the proper amount of rice and curry into each. Reheat slowly to prevent burning. If properly prepared, the rice will be as fluffy as it was the first time. This is a marvelous recipe for people who have guests drop in unexpectedly at mealtime. Additional condiments may be served, such as cashews, raisins, yogurt, pine nuts, grated coconut, etc. Makes 8 to 10 servings

QUICK CURRY

Cook until clear in:
2 tablespoons butter
2 cloves garlic, minced
1 large onion, minced
Add and cook for 5 minutes, stirring frequently, until a thick paste is formed:
2 tablespoons curry powder
Add and simmer for 30 minutes:
4 vegetable bouillon cubes, dissolved in 1 cup hot water
1 cup cooked lima beans
1 cup cooked cut-up zucchini
1 cup cooked cut-up green beans
1 cup cooked coarsely cut onion
1 cup cooked coarsely cut celery
1/2 cup cooked chopped mushrooms
Stir in:
1/2 cup sour cream
6 tablespons orange jam or marmalade
1/4 cup fresh lemon juice
Adjust seasonings with:
Salt
Serve with rice.
Makes 8 servings

CHOP SUEY AND SAUCE

Mix together:
8 stalks celery, thinly sliced on the diagonal
2 onions, thinly sliced
1/2 green bell pepper, thinly sliced
4 water chestnuts, thinly sliced
1/2 cup thinly sliced bamboo shoots
1/4 cup blanched whole almonds
2 cups bean sprouts
Put into a kettle with a tightly fitting lid and heat until very hot:
1/4 cup peanut oil
Add to the kettle:
Prepared vegetables
1/2 cup hot water
Cover and cook over medium low heat until just done but still crisp. Combine in a saucepan:
16 ounces fresh bean curd (tofu), pressed to remove excess liquid, cut into 1-inch cubes and browned in peanut oil
3 tablespoons soy sauce
2 tablespoons Savita
1/2 cup fresh mushrooms, chopped
4 cups water
Heat, stirring gently, then add:
1 tablespoon cornstarch, dissolved in a little cold water
Stir the sauce until thickened. Add the sauce to the steamed vegetables, heat to serving temperature and serve immediately.
Makes 6 servings

TOFU WITH TEMPURA VEGETABLES

This makes a good, change-of-pace meal.

Prepare:
Fresh Mushroom Sauce (page 16)
Add:
Chopped Chinese cabbage leaves to taste
Drain and cut into cubes:
Japanese-style bean curd (tofu)
Fold the tofu gently into the sauce, being careful it does not break up. On one end of a platter, put a mound of:
Steamed white rice
On the opposite end, place:
Tofu-sauce mixture
Between the mounds, pile rows of:
Tempura vegetables (following recipe)
Serve immediately with a decanter of soy sauce for those who wish to add it. What an adventure in texture and flavor is in store for you.

AMERICAN-STYLE TEMPURA VEGETABLES

I was asked to create recipes calling for the use of soy sauce and this is one of them. It is deceptively simple, and the end product is delicious in flavor and interesting in texture.

Prepare:

Cauliflower, broken into flowerets
Carrots, peeled and cut into 1/2-inch-wide strips
Green bell peppers, seeded and cut into 1/2-inch-thick strips
Onions, cut into 1/2-inch-thick slices
Yams or sweet potatoes, peeled and cut into 1/2-inch-thick slices
Zucchini, cut into 1/2-inch-thick slices

Put in a blender or food processor and whirl, or whip briskly, for 3 minutes:

2 eggs
1/4 cup water
1/4 cup soy sauce
3/4 cup all-purpose flour

(Whole-wheat flour may be used in place of the white for more interesting texture. If you do use it, add a very small amount more water.)

Heat in a deep skillet or wok to 375°F:

Peanut oil or vegetable oil for deep-frying

Deep-fry only one kind of vegetable at a time. Immerse the vegetables in the batter, coating well, then lift out with a strainer and drop into the hot oil. (Coat only enough vegetables at a time for one frying.) Fry the vegetables until golden brown. Zucchini and green peppers take the least amount of time; carrots and yams the longest. Cook the vegetables to suit your taste—soft or textured inside and crisp outside. Lift out with a slotted utensil and drain on paper toweling. Keep warm until all are cooked and serve immediately to retain crispness. If more batter is needed, whip up another batch. Accompany with:

Steamed rice or other cereal

AVOCADO LOAF

Mix together well:

1 egg, beaten
16 ounces fresh bean curd (tofu), pressed to remove excess liquid, then crumbled
2 tablespoons finely minced onion
2 tablespoons finely minced celery leaves
1/4 cup catsup
1-1/2 teaspoons salt
1 cup fresh bread crumbs
1 avocado, coarsely mashed
2 tablespoons chopped parsley

Grease a 12-hole muffin tin and divide the avocado mixture equally among the holes. Bake in a 400°F oven for 20 minutes. Do not overcook, as an acid taste will develop from the avocado.

While the loaves are baking, prepare the sauce. Cook until clear in:

1 tablespoon butter
1 tablespoon minced onion

In a separate dry skillet, lightly brown:

1/4 cup all-purpose flour

Be careful not to scorch or brown the flour too much. Add to the flour and mix well, then let cool:

2 tablespoons butter

Add and mix well, then cook over medium heat until thickened, stirring constantly:

Cooked onion
1 vegetable bouillon cube, dissolved in 1 cup hot water
1 tablespoon shredded cheddar cheese
Dash freshly ground black pepper
1/2 teaspoon Worcestershire sauce
Few drops fresh lime or lemon juice

When sauce has thickened, add:

1/2 avocado, coarsely mashed

(The sauce should be brown in color if the flour was browned properly.) Add:

Small amount chopped parsley (optional)

Do not overheat the sauce after adding the avocado, or an acid taste will develop. Serve the sauce over the loaves.
Makes 6 servings

FRESH MUSHROOM AND CHESNUT LOAF

Mix together well and put into a greased baking pan:

1 large onion, finely chopped
1 cup finely chopped celery, sautéed in butter
1/2 cup chopped parsley
1/4 pound walnuts, ground
1/2 cup wheat germ
1 cup old-fashioned rolled oats
5 slices dry white bread, crushed into crumbs
1-1/4 pounds chestnuts, roasted, peeled and coarsely cut
1/4 pound mushrooms, chopped and sautéed in butter
6 eggs, beaten

Mix together and heat but do not boil:

3/4 cup milk
3 vegetable bouillon cubes, crushed
1 teaspoon salt
1/4 teaspoon Savory Herb Blend
Pinch powdered sage

Combine the milk mixture with the vegetable mixture and bake in a 400°F oven for 1 hour.
Makes 8 servings

PECAN LOAF

Mix together well:

1-1/2 cups finely chopped celery
1-1/2 cups dry whole-wheat bread crumbs
1-1/2 cups ground pecans, or 6 ounces pecans, ground, reserving a few whole ones
3 tablespoons finely chopped onion
2-1/2 cups milk
3 tablespoons chopped parsley
1 teaspoon herb salt
3 eggs, well beaten
3 tablespoons butter, melted

(If a milder taste is desired, use white bread crumbs.) Let stand for 20 minutes, then turn into a buttered standard loaf pan and bake in a 375°F oven for 45 to 50 minutes until nicely browned.

While the loaf is baking, make the sauce. In a saucepan, melt:

4 tablespoons butter

Add and cook until thickened, stirring constantly:

2 cups milk, mixed with 1 egg yolk, beaten
1/2 cup minced parsley
Dash white pepper
1/2 bay leaf

When the sauce has thickened, remove the bay leaf. Spoon a generous amount of sauce over each loaf serving.
Makes 8 servings

Variation Add 1 cup sliced mushrooms, sautéed in butter, to the sauce.

ESSIE'S CHESTNUT LOAF

Make an X on the flat side of each, then roast for 20 minutes in a moderate oven:

1 pound Italian chestnuts

Cool the chestnuts until they can be easily handled, then remove the outside husk and the inside fibrous skin. Slice the nuts very thin and lay one-third of them in a well-buttered casserole. Top the chestnut layer with:

2 large onions, sliced

Top the onion layer with:

Shredded sharp cheddar cheese

Top the cheese layer with:

Half of the remaining sliced chestnuts

Top the chestnut layer with:

1 onion, thinly sliced

Top the onion layer with:

Shredded sharp cheddar cheese
The remaining sliced chestnuts

Pour over the layers:

1 (7-ounce) can evaporated milk

Bake in a 375°F oven for 45 minutes.

While the casserole is baking, make the sauce. In a saucepan melt:

4 tablespoons butter

Add and cook until tender:

1 cup sliced mushrooms
2 green onions, finely chopped
1/4 teaspoon herb salt

Add and cook, stirring constantly, for 2 minutes:

1 tablespoon all-purpose flour

Then add and stir in well:

2 cups sour cream

Heat just to serving temperature. Put a portion of the chestnut loaf on each serving plate and spoon some of the sauce over the top. Garnish each serving with:

Minced parsley
Paprika

Makes 6 servings

ALMOND-VEGETABLE LOAF

In a mixing bowl, combine:
1 cup dry bread crumbs
1 teaspoon salt
1 vegetable bouillon cube, crushed
1/3 cup hot water
In a blender or food processor, grind together:
1 cup almonds
3 carrots
5 parsley sprigs
6 green onions and tops
1 teaspoon fresh oregano leaves
1 teaspoon fresh basil leaves
1 teaspoon fresh marjoram leaves
Add vegetable mixture to mixing bowl and mix together well. Then add, mixing in well:
3 eggs, beaten
Put into a well-greased standard loaf pan, but do not pack tightly. Cover with foil and bake in a 375°F oven for 45 minutes or until firm.
Makes 6 servings

NUT AND LENTIL LOAF

Soak overnight in:
4 cups water
2 cups lentils
Cook the lentils in the soaking water in a pressure cooker for 20 minutes at 15 pounds pressure.
In a large saucepan, melt:
4 tablespoons butter
Add and cook over low heat for 15 minutes:
1/4 cup Bakon yeast, dissolved in a little water
12 stalks celery, finely minced
1 teaspoon Savory Herb Blend
4 cloves garlic, finely minced
1 teaspoon herb salt
4 teaspoons salt
Combine lentils and celery mixture and add:
4 cups finely minced onion
4 eggs, beaten
1 cup old-fashioned rolled oats
1 cup walnuts, coarsely chopped
1 cup almonds, coarsely chopped
Turn into 2 well-buttered standard loaf pans. Bake in a 400°F oven for at least 1 hour.
While the loaves are baking, make the sauce. In a saucepan, melt:
4 tablespoons butter
Add and cook very slowly for 30 minutes:
2 cups minced onion
2 vegetable bouillon cubes, crushed
Add and heat:
2 cups water
Then add and cook until thickened, stirring constantly:
2 tablespoons cornstarch, dissolved in a little water
2 tablespoons all-purpose flour, dissolved in a little water
When thickened, add:
2 tablespoons tomato catsup
Serve some of the sauce over each portion of loaf.
Makes 8 servings

Note This loaf can be cut into portions when cold, wrapped in foil, and then in a plastic bag, and frozen for future use. You need only defrost the number of slices you need. Put about 1/4 cup of water in a small skillet and lay the foil-wrapped slices in it, being careful that no water gets into the packages. Cover tightly and steam for about 3 minutes.

NUT LOAF

In a skillet or saucepan, melt:
4 tablespoons butter
Add and cook until just tender:
3 cups chopped celery
Remove from the heat. Mix together well and combine with the celery:
3 cups finely chopped onion
1 cup almonds, ground into flour in blender
2 cups chopped walnuts
2 cups toasted cashews, chopped
1/2 cup old-fashioned rolled oats
1/4 cup sesame meal
1/4 cup hulled sunflower seeds
2 pounds cottage cheese
1 cup cooked rice of choice
4 teaspoons salt
1/4 teaspoon freshly ground black pepper
1/2 teaspoon Savory Herb Blend
6 eggs, lightly beaten
Turn into a greased standard loaf pan and bake in a 400°F oven for at least 1 hour. If a firmer loaf is desired, bake an additional 30 minutes.
Makes 8 servings

SOYBEAN LOAF

Soak overnight in:
Water to cover
1 pound soybeans
The next day, cook the beans in their soaking water in a pressure cooker for 35 minutes at 15 pounds pressure. Drain the cooked beans, reserving the cooking liquid. Mash the beans and set aside. In a saucepan, cook until tender:
4 cups sliced celery
8 cloves garlic, minced
2 green bell peppers, sliced
1 cup minced parsley
1 tablespoon Vegetable Herb Blend
1 tablespoon Worcestershire sauce
1 tablespoon herb salt
Combine:
10 slices whole-wheat bread, finely cubed
Reserved soybean cooking liquid
Then combine:
Bread and liquid
Mashed beans
Celery mixture
2 pounds Monterey jack cheese, shredded
4 eggs, beaten
2 cups hulled sunflower seeds
1/4 cup soy sauce

Turn into a large shallow pan and bake in a 375°F oven for at least 1 hour, or until moisture has almost completely evaporated. Serve with:
Light Tomato Sauce (page 19)
Makes 8 to 10 servings

WALNUT CROQUETS

Grind in a blender or food processor, but not too fine:
1 cup walnuts
Mix together:
Ground walnuts
3 slices dry white bread, ground into crumbs
2 tablespoons sesame seeds
2 tablespoons wheat germ
1/2 cup grated sharp cheddar cheese
1 small zucchini, minced
2 green onions and tops, finely minced, or 1 small yellow onion, finely minced
Mix together and add to the walnut mixture:
2 eggs, beaten
1 teaspoon herb salt
1 teaspoon Savory Herb Blend, or 1/2 teaspoon each crumbled dried basil and marjoram
Make sure the mixtures are well combined or the patties will fall apart in the skillet. Make 6 patties, each 1/2 inch thick. In a skillet, brown the patties on both sides in:
Equal portions butter and vegetable oil
Serve, topped with:
Mornay Sauce (page 16) or Rich Cream Sauce (page 16), with chopped parsley added
1/4 cup parsley, minced
Makes 6 servings

CASHEW CALAVO

Mix together well:
1 cup whole raw cashews
1 cup whole raw pine nuts
1 cup cooked turmeric-flavored or plain rice
1 cup Ranch House Béchamel Sauce (page 15) or Rich Cream Sauce (page 16)
Divide this mixture evenly among:
6 avocado halves, peeled
Put the filled avocado halves close together in a shallow baking dish or in individual baking dishes.
Spoon over each half:
Mornay Sauce (page 16) or, any rich cheese sauce
Bake in a 350°F oven until the sauce begins to bubble. Serve very hot.
Makes 6 servings

ALMOND CROQUETS

Grind in a blender or food processor, but not too fine:
1 cup roasted almonds
Mix together:
Ground almonds
2 tablespoons sesame seeds
2 cloves garlic, finely minced
3 green onions and tops, finely minced
3 slices dry white bread, ground into crumbs
Mix together and stir into almond mixture:
2 eggs, beaten
1/2 cup sour cream
1/2 cup cottage cheese
1 teaspoon herb salt
1 teaspoon curry powder, or to taste
Make sure the mixtures are well combined or the patties will fall apart in the skillet. Make 6 patties, each 1/2 inch thick. In a skillet, brown the patties on both sides in:
Equal portions butter and vegetable oil
Serve, topped with:
Mornay Sauce (page 16) or Rich Cream Sauce (page 16)
Makes 6 servings

Variation Omit the curry powder and add to the sauce chopped parsley and minced chives to tate.

CHEESE ENCHILADAS

Here is the Ranch House way of making enchiladas.

Prepare:
8 heaping tablespoons chopped black olives
8 heaping tablespoons grated cheddar cheese
Put in a 12-inch skillet to a depth of 1 inch:
Equal portions peanut oil and margarine, or peanut oil only
Heat, but do not allow to get too hot.
Have ready:
8 corn tortillas
Using kitchen forceps, gently slide, separately, 4 tortillas into the oil, one under another so that the first one stays on top. This will prevent overheating, which would cause them to have bubbles and break apart when being rolled. They must be hot enough to bend easily, but should not start to cook. Remove each tortilla with forceps, allowing each to drip over the pan. Stack at the end of a rectangular (1-1/2-by-9-by-13-inch) glass or metal baking dish. Heat 4 more tortillas and add to stack.
On the tortilla at the top of the stack, put 1 heaping tablespoon of olives and 1 of cheese, spreading them in a long line so that the tortilla can be rolled around them as if it were a cigarette paper. (I ran into difficulty when I first tried this. I couldn't get the tortilla to wrap around the other ingredients in the neat roll—like little crêpes—and I went back to the grocer to complain. Fortunately, a Mexican woman was there, and helpfully told me that the thing to do was to put the tortilla in hot fat or oil before trying to roll it; and of course this was the proper thing to do to make them pliable.)

As the tortillas are rolled, lay them in a row crosswise along the dish. Each should have enough filling so that it is at least an inch in diameter when rolled. The 8 should just fill the baking dish, with a little room between each one.
Spoon over them, enough to cover:
Enchilada Sauce (following)
Bake in a 325°F oven only long enough to get them good and hot all the way through. They should bubble at the edges of the pan, but should not be cooked too much as the tortillas will become mushy and fall to pieces and the texture will be lost. They should be firm when served, so that the fork can be nicely pressed through them. Take up the enchiladas with a long, wide spatula aided by a large spoon. Usually, 2 is a serving.
Spoon over each serving:
Additional Enchilada Sauce
Garnish each serving with:
Grated cheddar cheese
1 green olive
Some people spear a small pickled yellow chili on a toothpick and stick it into each enchilada. This is for those who like very hot Mexican food and would think the meal incomplete without the extra hot relish. If desired serve in a relish dish to accompany the enchiladas:
Very finely chopped onions, mixed with a little chopped parsley
The onions are spooned over the enchiladas at the table. Some cooks prefer to roll the onions inside the enchiladas, but I think they lose their extra-fresh taste when they are used this way. This freshness is important, as it gives a lift to the rich and heavy nature of the enchiladas.
Makes 4 servings

ENCHILADA SAUCE

Put in a kettle and bring to a boil:

1 (28-ounce) can Ortega brand red chili sauce
3-1/2 cups water
2 vegetable bouillon cubes, crushed
1/2 teaspoon pulverized fresh oregano, or 1/4 teaspoon crumbled dried oregano
1 teaspoon minced fresh basil, or 1/2 teaspoon crumbled dried basil
1/6 teaspoon ground cumin
2 large sprigs coriander

Add and cook, stirring constantly, until thickened:

3 tablespoons cornstarch, dissolved in a little water

Remove from the heat and stir in just until beginning to melt:

3 tablespoons grated cheddar cheese

Makes approximately 5 cups

Note If a hotter sauce is desired, use only 2-3/4 cups water and reduce the cornstarch to 2 tablespoons.

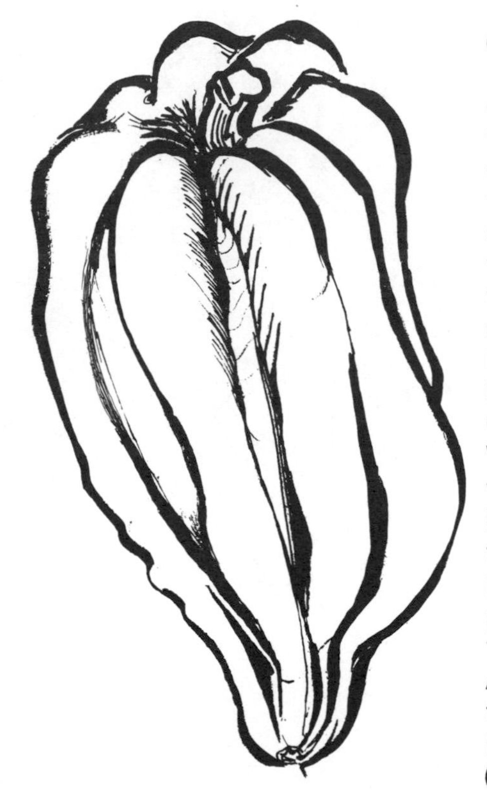

CHILI RELLENO

Bring to a boil and keep hot until needed:

1 (16-ounce) can tomato juice
1 bay leaf
1 vegetable bouillon cube, crushed
Dash onion salt
Dash garlic salt
2 sprigs coriander

Have ready for each person:

1 fresh or canned long green chili pepper

(If canned chili peppers are used, just remove the seeds, if desired. If seeds are left in, it will be a very hot dish. If fresh chili peppers are used, place them under the broiler until skin turns brown, remove and wrap in a cold wet cloth. Unwrap and peel off skins. Remove seeds, if desired.)

For each pepper, cut a 1-1/2-inch square, 1/2 inch thick, of:

Cheddar cheese

Wrap the cheese with the whole chili pepper if it has been seeded. If left whole with the seeds, stuff the cheese into the larger end of the pepper. Separate:

1 egg per chili pepper

Add to the bowl of whites and to the bowl of yolks:

Pinch salt for each egg used

(This will thicken the eggs and make the batter hold up.)

Measure:

1 tablespoon sifted all-purpose flour for each egg used

Beat the yolks until light yellow in color and thick. Beat the whites until stiff, glossy peaks form. Fold the yolks into the whites, then fold the flour into the egg mixture with a wire whisk. Do this folding very gently. Dip the filled chili peppers into the egg batter, then lift them out with a spoon, making sure there is sufficient batter to cover each pepper.

Fry in:

Hot peanut oil

As the chili peppers brown on the underside, baste them with the oil to keep them from coming apart and splattering. Then turn with a spoon and spatula and brown on the second side. They may have to be turned once again to cook completely. When light brown on all sides, remove with a slotted utensil and drain on paper toweling.

Just before serving, immerse the chili peppers in the hot tomato sauce and serve immediately with additional sauce, if desired. Garnish with:

Grated cheddar cheese
Minced parsley

PIMIENTO RELLENO

Drain:
Canned whole pimientos
Cut into wedges that will just fit into each pimiento:
Mild cheddar cheese
Lay the stuffed pimientos in a baking dish, allowing 2 per serving. In a blender or food processor, whip together, allowing for each 4 pimientos:
1 egg
1 tablespoon half-and-half cream
1 tablespoon all-purpose flour
Dash herb salt
1 green onion and top, chopped
Pour batter over stuffed pimientos and sprinkle with:
Raw pine nuts
Bake in a 400° oven until batter rises and is nicely browned, about 30 minutes. Serve with:
Light cheese sauce

FRENCH-FRIED PIMIENTO RELLENO

Prepare, as in preceding recipe:
8 canned pimientos, stuffed with mild cheddar cheese wedges
In a blender or food processor, whip together:
3 eggs
9 tablespoons all-purpose flour
3 tablespoons half-and-half cream
1/2 teaspoon herb salt
In a small skillet, heat to a depth of 1/2 inch:
Peanut oil
Dip stuffed pimientos into batter and slide them into the hot oil. Fry until golden brown on both sides. Do not have the oil so hot that the pimientos brown before the cheese melts. Serve on a platter with:
Light cheese sauce
Makes 4 servings

TAMALE PIE

Cook slowly for 15 minutes in:
1/3 cup olive oil
2 onions, chopped
2 cloves garlic, chopped
Add:
1 green bell pepper, chopped
1 (16-ounce) can tomatoes with juice
1-1/2 cups corn kernels
2 tablespoons chili powder
8 ounces fresh bean curd (tofu), pressed to remove excess liquid, then crumbled
Grind in a mortar, then add to tomato mixture and cook for 15 minutes:
1 teaspoon salt
1 large sprig oregano
1 large sprig thyme
1 large sprig basil
In a separate pan, cook until thick:
3 cups milk
1 cup yellow cornmeal
Add and stir in well:
4 eggs, beaten
In a casserole, mix together:
Tomato mixture
Mortar mixture
Cooked cornmeal
1-1/2 cups pitted ripe olives
Bake in a 350°F oven for 1 hour. Remove from the oven and sprinkle on top:
1/2 pound cheddar cheese, shredded
Return to the oven and bake until lightly browned, about 10 minutes.
Makes 8 servings

FROM PUERTO RICO

A friend of mine from Puerto Rico, Isabel Biascoechea, is a splendid cook of typical Puerto Rican—or rather, Spanish—food. She says Spanish food is never hot, but is very colorful.

Here are four of her recipes. One, Hallaca, is a bit difficult to prepare and is done in banana leaves. Isabel said it is traditional in Puerto Rico and is sold on street corners in every town, the way hamburgers are here.

The oil used in cooking the rice in this recipe is made with the seeds of the achiote tree, native to Puerto Rico. I understand that most of the yellow coloring used in foods is derived from the seeds of this tree. It is nutritionally very high in vitamin A.

The little chilis used are sweet but not hot. The culantro leaves are available, as far as I know, only in Puerto Rico, but if you are an enterprising herb gardener, you will have coriander growing in your herb garden, and it can be used as a substitute.

HALLACA
(Stuffed Banana Leaves)

Cook until tender, drain and reserve liquid:
1 cup water
1 potato, peeled and cubed
2 stalks celery, thinly sliced
2 carrots, finely diced
1 teaspoon salt
Cook until the corn leaves the sides of the pan in:
3 tablespoons achiote oil (page 140) or peanut oil
Corn kernels from 8 ears of corn
Liquid reserved from cooking vegetables
1 teaspoon salt
Add and remove from the heat:
2 cups lightly cooked green peas
In a separate skillet, sauté for 2 minutes in:
2 tablespoons peanut oil
1 green onion and top, minced
1 clove garlic, minced
Add and cook for 10 minutes:
1/2 green bell pepper, coarsely chopped
1/2 cup chopped canned tomato
1/4 teaspoon crumbled dried oregano
1 teaspoon tomato paste
6 pimiento-stuffed green olives, sliced
(I always add a little basil at this point, but Puerto Ricans are superstitious about this herb.) Combine all ingredients and mix well. Slit out the center vein, being careful not to tear the leaves, of:
Banana leaves
Cut leaves into 12-inch square sections, making 12 pieces in all, and wash well, being careful not to tear them. Lay each section flat and fill the center with 1/4 cup of the vegetable mixture. Pull the sides together and fold down from the top twice to make a snug fit over the vegetables; tuck the ends under. Using colored string (the Puerto Ricans like to make it colorful), tie from both sides, making a rectangular package. Drop the packages into boiling water and boil for 15 minutes. Remove from water, cut the string, and serve immediately so that when the leaves are opened the contents can be eaten while still hot.
Makes 6 servings

RED BEANS

Soak overnight in:
Water to cover
1 pound (2 cups) red beans
The next day, cover with fresh water and simmer until tender. If using a pressure cooker, cook at 15 pounds pressure for 30 minutes. In a skillet, cook until golden brown in:
2 tablespoons vegetable oil
1 cup finely chopped onion
Combine the beans and onion. Pound in a mortar to a pulp and add to the beans:
1 teaspoon salt
1 clove garlic, minced
1 green bell pepper, finely chopped
1 tablespoon Bakon yeast
1 teaspoon dried oregano
Then add:
1 tablespoon tomato paste
1/2 potato, peeled and grated
Mash part of the beans to thicken the liquid in the pot, then cook over very low heat (they will burn easily now) for 15 minutes, or until the potato is cooked.
Makes 6 servings

PUERTO RICAN RICE

In a small heavy saucepan, heat to a boil:

1 cup peanut or corn oil
2 heaping tablespoons achiote seeds, or large pinch ground turmeric

Boil the seeds for 1 minute (overcooking will destroy the color), then strain. Cool and pour into a heated glass jar. The oil is now ready to use in this and other recipes.

In a saucepan, place over medium heat:

2 tablespoons olive oil

Add and cook until clear:

1 large onion, minced

While onion is cooking, pound in a mortar to a pulp:

2-1/2 teaspoons salt
1 clove garlic
1/4 teaspoon dried oregano
2 fresh culantro or coriander leaves
2 fresh aji dulce (small Puerto Rican chili peppers)
1 green bell pepper, finely chopped
1/4 teaspoon dried basil (optional)

Add to the onion. Then add:

1 (28-ounce) can tomatoes and juice, chopped

Cook mixture down until much of the liquid is gone and add:

2 cups unwashed brown or white rice
5 pimiento-stuffed green olives, chopped

Cook over high heat until rice begins to stick to pan, then add and stir in thoroughly:

1/4 cup achiote oil

Add:

4 cups water, boiling

Stir once, cover immediately, turn heat to low and cook until rice is tender. Do not remove the cover until rice is done. (California brown rice will require about 1 hour cooking time; Louisiana or Texas brown, or white long grain, about 30 minutes.)

Makes 8 servings

GARBANZO BEANS

Soak overnight in:

Water to cover
1 pound garbanzo beans

The next day, cover with fresh water and simmer until tender. Do not finish with too much water or the beans will be mushy. If using a pressure cooker, cook at 15 pounds pressure for 35 minutes.

In a covered pan, cook until clear in:

2 tablespoons vegetable oil
1 large onion, minced

Grind in a mortar and add to onion:

1/2 teaspoon salt
1 clove garlic, minced
1/2 teaspoon dried oregano
1/2 teaspoon dried basil
2 fresh aji dulce (small Puerto Rican chili peppers)
2 fresh culantro or coriander leaves

Add:

1 cup chopped canned tomatoes with a little juice
1/2 cup chopped green bell pepper
1 cup grated banana squash (optional)
1 cup shredded Swiss chard
1 tablespoon olive oil
Cooked garbanzo beans

Cook over low heat for 15 minutes.

Makes 6 servings

A TYPICAL INDIAN CURRY

My introduction to real Indian curry was at the Theosophical Headquarters in Wheaton, Illinois. Betsan and John Coats, of the English Coats cotton family, had just returned from India where they had been living for some time. Betsan, who is a tremendously vital and inventive person (and incidentally had a very successful restaurant in Australia), decided she would prepare a genuine Indian dinner, complete with barefoot girls in saris to serve it.

In order to create as nearly as possible the atmosphere of an Indian restaurant, she cleared the cement-floored basement dining room of furniture and, with washable paint, decorated it with beautiful, typical designs of India. Diners sat on the floor and the food was served on leaves and was eaten with the fingers.

Those who could, sat in Padmasana, the traditional lotus posture. The others cracked their knee joints trying or just sat as comfortably as they could. The food was brought around in huge dishes by the serving girls and ladled out on our leaves. As no banana trees grow in Illinois, well-washed burdock leaves were substituted. The proper etiquette in India is to pick up the food using only the first two fingers of the right hand. You then flick it off these two fingers into the mouth—and that is quite a trick. When one drinks from a cup or other vessel in India, the lips are never allowed to touch the vessel. The head is tipped back and the liquid poured into the open mouth.

It was a lovely dinner and all went well until after the finger bowls had been passed, when around came a little box filled with a brown paste. Some of us assumed it to be a dessert and started to eat it, but found it didn't taste very good. It was sandalwood paste, and diners are supposed to rub some on their fingers to remove all traces of the odor of food.

There is no standard recipe for curry. Each cook prefers various combinations, using from a few to fifteen or twenty ingredients to make a single dish. Indians make curry using a "massala," which we call curry powder. Massala is an Indian word meaning a combination of herbs and/or spices that have been freshly ground together, to be added to onions and garlic that have been "cleared" in "ghee." Ghee is clarified butter. A massala may be used for flavoring many different dishes, each requiring a different combination of herbs and spices. The villagers in India, lacking refrigeration, clarify their butter to keep it from getting rancid. It is set aside in a warm place (or boiled in a pan) until all of the solids have precipitated, then the butter oil is poured off. Since it is free from the milk solids that fresh butter contains, this oil has less tendency to become rancid.

A little ghee is put into a saucepan and melted. Onions and garlic, chopped fine or coarse, are then added and simmered until well done. Then the massala, consisting of the dry, freshly ground herbs and spices, is added and this mixture is again simmered until it becomes a slightly thick paste. Heat must be kept low, lest it burn the spices. Fresh coconut milk is then added in the desired amount. A good curry is never thickened with such things as flour or starch. The

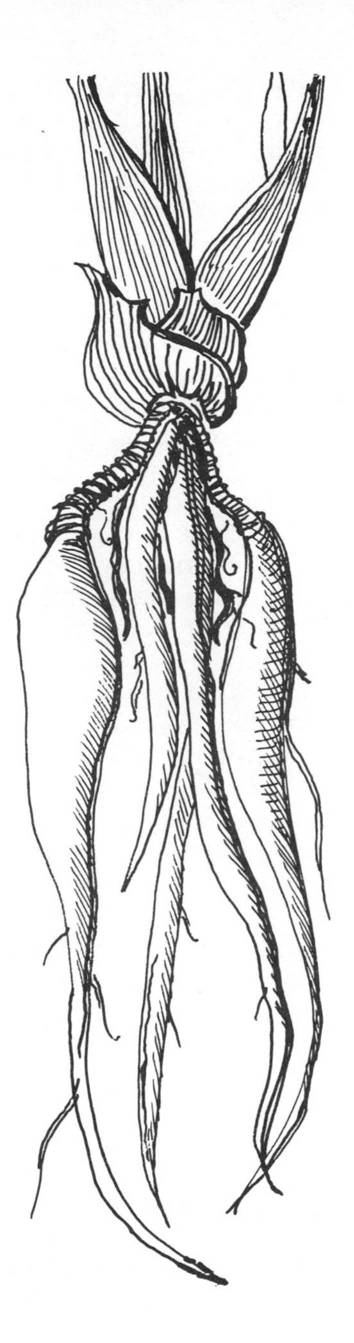

proportions are gauged so that, after the required number of hours of simmering, it has the correct consistency.

Cow's milk, substituted for coconut milk, doesn't have the same sweet flavor. If it is used in place of the coconut milk, a slight extra sweetening has to be added. A good curry is actually a sweet-sour sauce, combined with vegetables. Of course, there is elaborate preparation involved in the serving of a complete Indian curry dinner, and it always was—and still is for that matter— a major event at the Ranch House.

CURRY POWDER

Grind together in a blender or food processor for at least 5 minutes:
2 teaspoons coriander seeds
1/2 teaspoon cumin seeds
2 cardamom pods, halved
2 whole cloves
1/2 teaspoon ground mace
1/6 teaspoon ground allspice
1 bay leaf, broken up
3 sprigs thyme, or 1/6 teaspoon dried thyme
1 teaspoon fenugreek seeds
2 teaspoons ground turmeric
2 small dried red chili peppers (Japanese type)

VEGETABLE CURRY

Put into blender or food processor and run until a powder:
2 teaspoons coriander seeds
1-1/2 teaspoons ground turmeric
1/2 teaspoon cumin seeds
1/2 teaspoon mustard seeds
1/2 teaspoon ground ginger
1/2 teaspoon black peppercorns
2 small red chili peppers (Japanese type)
1/2 stick cinnamon, cut up
2 cardamom pods, halved
1/2 teaspoon fenugreek seeds
3 whole cloves
Fry slowly until clear, without browning, in:
2 tablespoons butter or ghee
2 cloves garlic, minced
1 cup minced onion
When onion mixture is clear, add prepared spice mixture. (This is the massala.) Cook for about 30 minutes, *very slowly* to avoid burning or sticking. When finished, it should be a thick paste. For a more lusty flavor, this spice and onion mixture may be doubled.

Add to the spice and onion mixture, and simmer again very slowly:
2 cups fresh coconut milk
(This can be purchased in many good food shops, frozen fresh, or it can be made by using 2 cups hot water and 2 cups grated coconut meat, running in the blender for 5 minutes, then straining.)

When all ingredients are cooked to a fragrant paste, thinned by the coconut milk and simmered again, add the following *cooked* vegetables:
1 cup cut-up green beans
1 cup lima beans
1 cup cut-up squash (zucchini, yellow crookneck or green summer)
1 cup coarsely cut celery
1/2 cup thinly sliced carrot
1/2 cup tiny caulifiowerets
Simmer again for about 15 minutes to blend flavors, then add:
1 cup uncooked fresh or frozen shelled green peas
3 canned pimientos, diced
3 or 4 tablespoons fresh lemon or lime juice, or to taste
4 or 5 tablespoons orange marmalade or flavor of choice
Simmer again for about 5 minutes to blend flavors.
Adjust seasonings with:
Salt
Add, if desired:
1/2 cup coarsely shredded, fresh coconut meat
1/2 cup sour cream (an American indulgence) or plain yogurt
The secret of this type of cooking is to do it slowly on very low heat. Fast cooking will destroy the texture as well as the flavor. Even with all of the cooking, if done properly the vegetables will still have body. Remember, this curry should be sweet-sour in taste, and spicy. For real curry lovers, double the red chilis and peppercorns in the curry powder mixture when preparing it.

Rice should always be served with the curry—plenty of it—preferably saffron flavored. Turmeric may be substituted to color and flavor the rice. For a simple curry dinner, a vegetable sauce or dahl should always be spooned over part of the rice. Small bowls of yogurt, chutney, peanuts, raisins, coconut (grated or shredded) and cashews should be passed to put on the plate to be delicately mixed with the curry. Cold buttermilk as a beverage is good to take down the heat if the pepper mixture is doubled.
Makes 6 servings

MUNG DAHL

Mung dahl, which are split dried mung beans, are available in many health food stores and in Indian markets.

Soak for 2 days in:
2 cups water
1 cup mung dahl
Then cook dahl in soaking water until just tender, about 15 minutes.
Grind together:
1 onion
3/4 teaspoon ground coriander
1/4 teaspoon chili powder
1/2 teaspoon salt
Add onion mixture to dahl along with:
1 potato, peeled and shredded
1 tomato, chopped
Simmer until potato is cooked, then add and simmer gently for 10 minutes:
1 teaspoon fresh lemon juice
Chopped fresh coriander to taste
1/2 cup shredded fresh coconut
Makes 4 servings

DAHL OF YELLOW SPLIT PEAS

In India, a legume is used to make dahl that is not readily available in this country, so I have substituted the nearest thing to it, which is yellow split peas. When finished, this dish should be a semithick gruel. In India, I am told, it is eaten in many homes three times a day over rice. This is their main source of protein. As many of the people in India do not eat flesh or even eggs, this is a dietary necessity.

Boil gently, uncovered, until tender but not mushy:
3/4 cup yellow split peas
2 cups water
1 teaspoon salt
In a pan with a tight-fitting cover, fry until clear but not brown in:
2 tablespoons butter or ghee
2 cups minced onion
Make a massala by grinding together:
1-1/2 teaspoons Curry Powder (page 142)
Pinch dry mustard
1/2 teaspoon granulated white sugar
1/2 teaspoon ground turmeric
Add to the cleared onions and slowly cook to a paste.
Add the onion and spice paste to the cooked peas, and cook for about 15 minutes. Remember, slow cooking is the secret. The dahl should be just thin enough to run down into the rice when spooned over it.
Serve, sprinkled with:
Minced parsley
Makes 6 servings

SAMBALS

Many countries on the other side of the world serve food that is similar to the curried foods of India, and most of them serve it accompanied with a variety of relish and condiment "sambals." These are fresh vegetables and fruits, sliced and marinated in a dressing of seasoned and thickened cold, fresh coconut milk. Also, a variety of nuts and raisins are passed as dry sambals to be mixed with the curry when it is eaten. It is of great importance that the fruits and vegetables be crisp and fresh before each is marinated in the dressing, and that each is marinated separately, never together.

Prepare:
Thinly sliced red and green bell peppers
Thinly sliced cucumber
Thinly sliced red cabbage
Small tomato wedges
Cooked shoestring beets
Hard-cooked eggs, sliced lengthwise and the slices cut in half
Peeled orange slices, cut in half
Marinate the above in:
Chilled Sambals Dressing (following)
Use just enough dressing to coat each piece, but not enough to make them soggy. Serve in a comparmentalized dish lined with:
Bronze lettuce leaves
To prepare the dry sambals, fry in:
Butter
Roasted whole almonds
Add:
Equal portion raisins
Put in a small dish. Make up other dishes of:
Roasted cashews
Roasted peanuts
Raw pine nuts
Raw pistachio nuts
Grated fresh coconut
Chutney
Yogurt

SAMBALS DRESSING

Frozen fresh or canned coconut milk from Hawaii and Southeast Asia is now available in many markets. If none is found near you, it can be made as follows.

Put into a blender or food processor:
2 cups grated coconut
2 cups hot water
Run the blender for at least 5 minutes to extract all the milk. Press out the milk through a sieve. You will have about 2 cups.

In a saucepan, heat together:
2 cups coconut milk, mixed with 2 tablespoons cornstarch
1-1/2 teaspoons onion salt
1/6 teaspoon garlic salt
Bring to a boil, stirring continually with a wire whisk. When thickened, add and stir in well:
1/4 cup fresh lemon or lime juice
Remove from the heat, cover and refrigerate immediately to keep a thick scum from forming on the top.

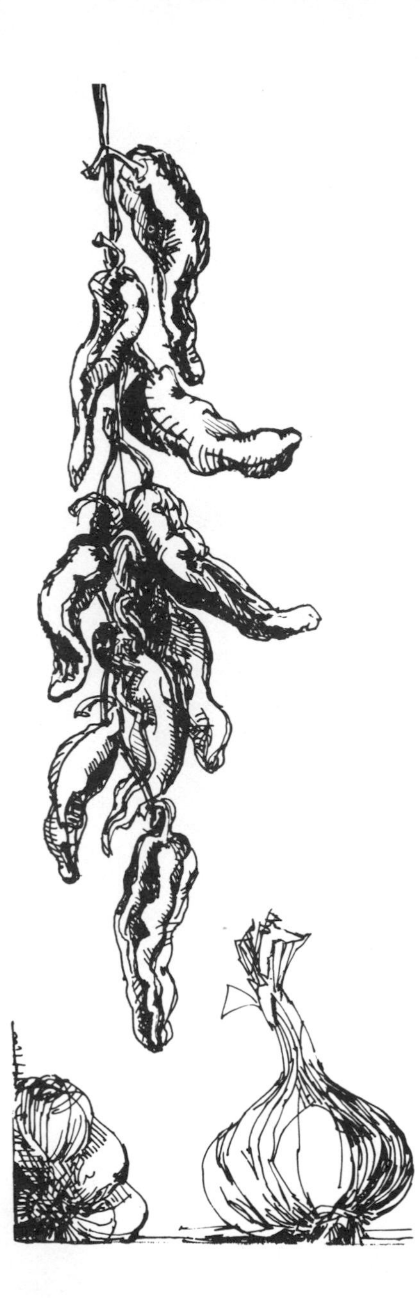

HOT SAUCES

To make a green and a red hot sauce to accompany a mild curry, prepare the following, then serve in small dishes.

GREEN HOT SAUCE

Put into a blender or food processor and run 1 minute:
5 drops green food coloring
6 long green chili peppers, blackened over an open flame and peeled (or substitute canned ones)
1/2 cup water
2 tablespoons cornstarch
1 teaspoon white vinegar
Put in a saucepan and cook over low heat just until thick. Refrigerate until ready to use.

RED HOT SAUCE

Put into a blender or food processor and run for 5 minutes, or until evenly powdered:
10 small red chili peppers (Japanese type)
Combine in a saucepan and cook over low heat until thick:
Powdered red chili peppers
1 cup water
10 drops red food coloring
1 tablespoon cornstarch
1 teaspoon white vinegar
Refrigerate until ready to use.

POPPADUMS

Poppadums are available in many gourmet food shops. They come packed in small boxes and are prepared by dropping them quickly in very hot oil and taking them out just as they finish curling and before they get a chance to burn, which they do easily. These are a very good accompaniment to curry and serve as bread.

Now you will have what is called an eighteen-boy curry. Traditionally each separate dish is carried by a small boy in a turban. You can create quite a festive atmosphere if you can find eighteen small boys to serve, and persuade them to wear turbans!

A friend of mine who traveled in the Far East some years ago tells me that in a large hotel in Java she remembers a seventy-boy curry.

PINEAPPLE GUAVA CHUTNEY

Many good chutney recipes are available and here is mine. The guavas used here are the California type. They have no seeds. The Florida type have to be whirled in a blender, then strained to remove the seeds before cooking. Cook very slowly to a nice, thick consistency:

3 pounds pineapple guavas, peeled and halved
3 pounds granulated white sugar
4 cloves garlic, minced
1 ounce dried red chili peppers, ground in a blender or food processor to a fine powder
4 ounces ginger root, peeled and sliced

Add and continue cooking for about 30 minutes:

2 cups white vinegar
1-1/2 pounds raisins
2 teaspoons salt
1 teaspoon ground cinnamon
1/6 teaspoon ground cloves
1/6 teaspoon ground cardamom
3/8 teaspoon cayenne pepper
1/2 cup fresh lemon or lime juice (optional, for added tartness)

Transfer to hot sterilized jars and seal.
Makes approximately 4 pints

SAFFRON RICE

When Beatrice Wood, a well-known ceramicist from Ojai, went on her first U.S. government-sponsored tour of India to give talks on art in the various cities, I asked her to buy me some saffron. It never occurred to me to tell her any certain amount, although I knew a little about the price of it from previous purchases. When it was convenient, she asked her hostess whether her cook could buy some for her. The hostess asked how much she wanted and she said, "Oh, about three pounds." This caused the hostess and the cook to gasp, as its price per *ounce* is extraordinarily high. She did bring back a small amount, however, for which I was extremely grateful. Indian saffron is richer, darker in its red-orange color than the Spanish or Italian, and gives a better flavor to rice. The saffron should always be steeped in hot water ahead of time and used as part of the liquid in a recipe. The following is a recipe prepared in the Indian manner.

In a skillet that can be tightly covered (preferably a copper-clad one 8 inches in diameter), melt:

2 tablespoons butter or ghee

Add:

1 cup unwashed long-grain white rice
1 teaspoon salt

Stir constantly with a wooden spoon until the rice begins to absorb the butter and turn opaque. Do not brown it.
Quickly add:

1-1/2 cups water, boiling
1/8 teaspoon powdered saffron, steeped in
1/2 cup boiling water

The secret of this method is in having the rice hot enough, so that when the boiling water is added it does not stop boiling—otherwise the rice will be sticky instead of fluffy. Cover immediately, reduce the heat to low and cook for about 20 minutes, or until all of the liquid is absorbed, and little craters appear on the surface. Do not remove the lid while the rice is cooking, and it is a good idea to put an asbestos pad under the pan to keep the heat low and even.
Makes 6 servings

INDONESIAN RIJSTTAFEL

These recipes may be of value if you are entertaining special friends and want to serve a buffet. Some years ago when I visited the Bali Restaurant in Amsterdam, I was served over twenty different dishes for their *rijsttafel,* which literally translated means "rice table." Here are recipes from a Javanese-born Dutch friend that you can use to create your own elaborate *rijsttafel.* Add Indonesian Rice (page 90) and other relishes as you desire.

MUSHROOMS AND TOFU

First, cook a large quantity of rice, white or brown, and mound it on a long platter. At one end of the platter spoon this dish, and on the other end, Triekadel, which follows.

In a skillet, cook until clear in:
2 tablespoons peanut oil
1 onion, minced
Add and cook until tender and flavors are well blended:
1 or more cups sliced mushrooms
1 cup crumbled fresh bean curd (tofu)
1/4 cup catsup, or to taste
1/4 teaspoon salt

TRIEKADEL

Mix together well:
1 (16-ounce) can whole kernel corn, drained
1/4 cup minced parsley
1/2 pound spinach leaves, chopped
1 cup grated Parmesan cheese
1 green pepper, chopped
3 eggs, beaten
1/2 cup chopped mushrooms
1/2 cup white sauce
1/8 teaspoon ground cloves
1/8 teaspoon ground nutmeg
Enough old-fashioned rolled oats to form a batter suitable for fritters
Grease a hot griddle or a large skillet and drop corn mixture by spoonfuls onto surface. Brown well on both sides and place on end of rice platter.

BOEME

Cook just until tender in:
Boiling salted water
1/2 pound dry thin noodles
Drain well and set aside.
In a skillet, cook just until tender in:
4 tablespoons butter
2 cups sliced mushrooms
2 green onions and tops, minced
1/4 teaspoon salt
Toss vegetable mixture with cooked noodles and add:
1-1/2 cups shelled green peas, or 1 (10-ounce) package frozen green peas, thawed
Heat to serving temperature.

GADO GADO

Blanch just to wilt, then drain well:
1 pound spinach, trimmed and leaves torn
1 pound bean sprouts
1 green onion, cut up
In a saucepan, combine and heat just until flavors are blended:
1/2 cup water
1/2 cup chunky-style peanut butter
1 teaspoon sugar
1/4 teaspoon grated ginger root
Let cool and pour over the blanched vegetables.

COLD VEGETABLES WITH PEANUT SAUCE

Steam until tender crisp as many different types of vegetables as desired, drain well and put each on a dish to cool. Prepare the following sauce, which is served in a separate bowl to be added by the diners according to taste. (The sauce recipe may be increased proportionately, depending on how many you are serving.)

In a saucepan, cook until clear in:

2 tablespoons peanut oil
2 onions, minced

Add and mix in well, then heat just until flavors are blended:

1 teaspoon firmly packed brown sugar
1 tablespoon fresh lime juice
1/4 cup chunky-style peanut butter
1 cup coconut milk (page 145)
Dash salt

Let cool before serving.

INDONESIAN LEMON JELLY DESSERT

Beat together for 1 minute:

2 eggs
2 egg yolks
1-1/2 cups granulated white sugar
Freshly grated peel of 4 lemons
2/3 cup fresh lemon juice
1/2 pound butter, melted (1 cup)

Pour the filling into:

Prebaked 9-inch pie crust

Cover the top with:

Rum-flavored whipped cream

This dessert must be served very cold.

Note Another excellent dessert is vanilla ice cream topped with Green Ginger Sauce (page 175) and shredded fresh coconut.

desserts

Cookbooks have so many wonderful desserts, one would think there is hardly a need for more; still, some of the recipes given here may titillate your palate. Many are my own creations, often made at the request of customers who have come to the Ranch House so frequently that they have become good friends, and I love nothing better than to try to find new things to delight them.

Most families have dessert recipes handed down to them or they originate ones that are made over and over again for the enjoyment of family and friends. Mothers are famous for creating these pleasures, and rightly so. In my family, many such treasures came from an old, coming-to-pieces little brown book kept by my grandmother from about 1860. Ingredients were called for in scant cups, heaping teaspoons, etc., as was the custom before the advent of Fannie Farmer of Boston Cooking School fame, who revolutionized the whole system of measures in recipes. Her insistence that all measures be level and exact has been a great boon, especially to those just learning the fine art of cooking.

My interest in food is due to an awareness of the opportunities it creates for an atmosphere of gentle good will. A kind of thankfulness for the blessings of good food and companionship enhance the early memories of my family life. We seemed always to have friends at our table, especially for Sunday dinner. Dad was the meat cook for these occasions and of course Mother did the pastries. My sister Dorothy took care of the table arrangements, and I had a hand in the salads and vegetables.

During the twenties, I was a pianist playing in jazz bands and away from home most of the time. On holidays and especially on my birthdays, Mother always remembered me by mailing one of her famous Imperial Sunshine cakes. She would get just the right-sized box, wrap the cake in waxed paper, put a small bunch of flowers in the center, and send the package off special delivery. It was amazing how it always arrived in such good condition. She would write on the package, "Handle with care—special birthday cake!" Perhaps this legend stayed the throwing hands of postal employees.

IMPERIAL SUNSHINE CAKE

Sift, then measure:
1 cup cake flour
Sift together 3 times, then set aside:
Sifted cake flour
3/4 teaspoon cream of tartar
Beat until stiff, glossy peaks form:
6 egg whites
1/4 teaspoon salt
In a saucepan, combine and bring to a boil, stirring to dissolve sugar:
1-1/2 cups granulated white sugar
1/2 cup water
When the boiling sugar-water mixture forms a thread from

the tip of a spoon, pour the hot syrup in a fine stream on the beaten egg whites, beating the mixture until it cools.
Add to the cooled mixture:
6 egg yolks, beaten
Fold the sifted flour mixture carefully into the egg mixture.
Then mix in:
1 teaspoon orange extract
Pour the batter into an ungreased 9-inch tube pan and bake in a 325°F oven for 50 to 60 minutes, or until a wooden pick inserted in the center comes out clean. Remove from the oven and invert to cool completely. Do not ice this cake! The flavor and texture are too marvelous to be diluted by anything.
Makes one 9-inch cake

APPLESAUCE SPICE CAKE (Old Wives' Tale Cake)

With an electric mixer, whip until creamy:
1/4 pound butter, at room temperature
Add and continue to whip:
1/2 cup granulated white sugar
1/2 cup firmly packed brown sugar
When sugars are well incorporated, add and whip until well blended:
1 egg
Sift together:
1-3/4 cups sifted white pastry flour
1/2 teaspoon salt
1 teaspoon baking soda
1 teaspoon ground cinnamon
1/4 teaspoon ground cardamom
1/2 teaspoon ground cloves
Dredge with some of the flour mixture:
1/2 cup seedless raisins
1/2 cup dried currants
Add remaining flour mixture to butter-sugar mixture and mix in well. Then add, incorporating well:

1 cup lightly sweetened applesauce, strained and warmed slightly
Add and mix in well:
Dredged fruit
1 cup chopped walnuts
Turn into a greased 9-inch tube pan and bake in a 350°F oven for 50 minutes, or until a wooden pick inserted in the center comes out clean. Remove from the oven and invert to cool completely. Ice with:
Brandy Cheese Icing (following)
Makes one 9-inch cake

BRANDY CHEESE ICING

Whip together until very creamy, about 5 minutes:
1/4 cup cream cheese
1-1/2 tablespoons half-and-half cream
2 cups powdered sugar
1/4 teaspoon vanilla extract
2 tablespoons good-quality brandy

ANGEL CAKE MIT SCHLAG

The phrase, *mit schlag,* used in the name of this recipe means whipped cream in Austrian. This dessert was developed after my first trip to Vienna, where I was served whipped cream on nearly every dessert I ate—especially the tortes. Fresh strawberries, hulled and halved, can be used to decorate the top of this cake.

Sift together 3 times:
1 cup sifted white pastry flour
1/2 cup granulated white sugar
Sift twice:
1 cup granulated white sugar
Whip until frothy:
11 ounces egg whites, at room temperature
1 tablespoon water
1 tablespoon fresh lemon juice
(A wire whisk and large bowl work well for this task. An electric mixer can be used, but must be watched carefully as it tends to overmix.) When good and frothy, add and whip to form stiff, glossy peaks:
1 teaspoon cream of tartar
1/2 teaspoon salt

Fold into the egg whites until completely dissolved:
Sifted sugar
This is an important step, for unless all of the sugar dissolves, the texture is porous. Overmixing tends to make it heavy. Sift in:
Flour-sugar mixture
Fold the flour-sugar mixture in thoroughly, and then fold in:
1/2 teaspoon vanilla extract
Turn the batter into an ungreased 9-inch tube pan, evenly distribute it, then run a long knife through the batter to release any large air bubbles that may exist. Bake in a 400°F oven for 25 minutes. Remove from the oven and invert to cool. Refrigerate until ready to ice, then cut into layers and ice with the following whipped cream topping.

To make the topping, put into a chilled mixing bowl and whip until just stiff:
2 cups whipping cream
Add and whip just enough to incorporate:
1/4 cup powdered sugar
1/2 teaspoon vanilla extract
1/2 teaspoon rum, brandy, or Curacao
Once cake is iced, refrigerate until ready to serve.
Makes one 9-inch cake

Note This cake may be iced with icing of choice, in which case it need not be refrigerated before serving.

VIENNESE HAZELNUT CAKE

Sift together:
21/2 cups sifted white pastry flour
4 teaspoons double-acting baking powder
3/4 teaspoon salt
Mix together:
1/2 cup plus 1 tablespoon cold milk
3-1/2 tablespoons hot water
3/4 teaspoon vanilla extract
Beat together well:
1-1/3 cups granulated white sugar
5 eggs
6 tablespoons vegetable shortening
Combine the flour mixture and egg mixture, then beat in half of the milk mixture until well combined. Add the remaining milk mixture and beat in well. Blend in:
1-1/3 cups filberts, ground in a blender to a powder
Line a shallow 10-by-14-inch baking pan with waxed paper and spread the cake mixture in it evenly. Bake in a 350°F oven for 25 minutes, or until lightly browned. Remove from the oven and cool completely. It is best to put it in the refrigerator for a short time so that it will not crumble when cut. Invert pan to remove cake, then remove waxed paper. Split cake into 2 layers, then cut each layer into 3 lengthwise pieces.

To make the icing, beat together well:
1/2 pound butter, at room temperature
1 pound plus 5 ounces powdered sugar
2 tablespoons plus 2 teaspoons cocoa powder
2 tablespoons instant coffee powder
7 tablespoons half-and-half cream
Ice each layer, then the top of the cake with the icing. Decorate top, placing one on each portion, with:
Whole filberts
If desired, accompany each serving with a thin slice of:
Coffee ice cream
Makes 1 cake

Note This cake will keep well in the freezer for 1 month if tightly wrapped in aluminum foil or plastic wrap.

RANCH HOUSE RUM TRIFLE

Arrange upside down on the bottom of a 9-inch glass casserole that can be tightly covered:
Almond macaroons
Spoon over the macaroons, distributing evenly:
1 tablespoon good-quality dark rum
(Myer's Planter's Punch is excellent.) Set aside.
Split in half to form 2 layers:
8-inch sponge cake
Lay the bottom layer of the cake on the macaroons and spread on its surface a thin layer of:
Seedless raspberry jam
Place upside down on top of the raspberry jam layer to completely cover:
Almond macaroons
Place the second layer of sponge cake on top of the macaroons and set aside.

To make the custard sauce, mix together in the top pan of a double boiler placed over simmering water:
4 egg yolks, beaten
1/4 cup granulated white sugar
Pinch salt
1 teaspoon vanilla extract
Add:
2 cups milk, scalded
Heat, stirring constantly until the custard coats a spoon. Spoon over the top layer of sponge cake, distributing evenly:
2 tablespoons good-quality dark rum
Then immediately pour the hot custard sauce over the top. To do this, use a spoon and pour directly into its bowl so that the pouring stream does not make a hole in the cake top. Gently lift up the sides of the cake so the custard flows to the bottom and soaks the first layer of macaroons. Cover and refrigerate for at least 24 hours. The finished product should be neither too soggy nor too dry, and the top should be lightly glazed with the custard.
Makes 8 servings

CALIFORNIA ORANGE-RAISIN CAKE

Squeeze the juice from:
2 oranges
Grind together:
Orange peel from the 2 oranges
1 cup seedless raisins
In a mixing bowl, combine and mix well:
Reserved orange juice
Ground mixture
1/4 pound butter, at room temperature
1-1/4 cups granulated white sugar
2 eggs
1 teaspoon salt
2/3 cup buttermilk
2 cups sifted white pastry flour
1 teaspoon baking soda
Turn into a greased standard loaf pan or an 8-inch tube pan and bake in a 350°F oven for 45 minutes, or until a wooden pick inserted in the center comes out clean.

While the cake is baking, mix together well:
3/4 cup fresh orange juice
1/4 cup granulated white sugar
1/4 teaspoon Curacao (optional)
Remove the cake from the oven and spoon the orange juice mixture over it immediately, distributing evenly.
Makes 1 loaf cake

SOFT GINGERBREAD

Cream together:
1/2 pound butter
1 cup granulated white sugar
Mix together well, then add to creamed mixture, blending in thoroughly:

2 teaspoons baking soda, dissolved in
1 cup boiling water
1 cup molasses
1 teaspoon salt
1 teaspoon ground ginger
1 teaspoon ground cinnamon
2-3/4 cups all-purpose flour
Then add and beat in:
2 eggs
Turn into a greased 9-by-13 inch shallow baking pan ar bake in a 350°F oven for about 45 minutes, or until a wooden pick inserted in the center comes out clean. Remove from the oven and, while hot, ice with a thin mixture of:
Powdered sugar and hot milk
Makes 12 servings

Note When cool, this gingerbread can be sealed in a plastic bag and frozen. To thaw, remove from the bag and put in a slow oven for about 20 minutes. It will be as good as when freshly baked. A wonderful idea for the busy working cook.

GERMAN ALMOND KUCHEN

Dissolve in:
1/4 cup lukewarm water (85°F)
1 cake yeast, crumbled
1 teaspoon granulated white sugar
Add to yeast mixture:
1 cup lukewarm milk (98°F)
Let stand for about 10 minutes until bubbly. In a large bowl, mix together:
1/2 pound butter, at room temperature
Peel of 1 lemon, grated
1/2 cup granulated white sugar
Pinch salt
Add and mix in well:
4 egg yolks, beaten
When yeast mixture is bubbly, add to it:
1 cup white bread flour, sifted

Combine the yeast mixture with the butter mixture, mix well and then add:
2-1/2 cups white bread flour, sifted
Beat well to develop the gluten. Form into a ball, put in a bowl, cover and refrigerate overnight.

The next day, make the filling. Whip until soft peaks form:
4 egg whites
Pinch salt
Gradually add, mixing gently to incorporate:
3/4 cup all-purpose flour, sifted
Gradually add, mixing gently to incorporate:
1 cup ground almonds
Turn refrigerated dough out on a lightly floured board and, with a floured rolling pin, roll out into a 1/2-inch-thick rectangle. Spread the almond filling evenly over the rectangle and roll up from a long side jelly-roll fashion. Put into a greased 9-inch tube pan, bringing ends together to meet and form a ring. Cover and let rise in a warm place until double in bulk. Bake in a 350°F oven for about 1 hour.
Makes one 9-inch cake

PEASANT BAZAAR COFFEE CAKE

Mix together well:
2 cups firmly packed brown sugar
1/4 pound butter, at room temperature
2 cups all-purpose flour
Set one-third of this mixture aside to be used for topping. To the remaining two-thirds, add and mix well:
1 egg
1 cup buttermilk
1 teaspoon salt
1 teaspoon baking soda
1 teaspoon ground cinnamon
1 teaspoon ground nutmeg
1/2 teaspoon ground mace
Turn into a 9-inch square pan that has been lined with oiled waxed paper and spread evenly. Sprinkle the reserved flour mixture over the top. Then sprinkle over the top:
Chopped nuts of choice
Shredded coconut
Bake in a 325°F oven for 35 minutes, or until browned and wooden pick inserted in the center comes out clean. Remove from the oven and serve warm or at room temperature.
Makes 1 cake

DARK FRUIT CAKE

This recipe, which makes six cakes, is perfect for holiday season gift-giving.

Steam for 5 minutes over boiling water:
3 pounds seedless raisins
1/2 pound dried currants
With an electric mixer, cream with whip attachment:
1 pound butter, at room temperature
Add and whip until fluffy:
2 cups firmly packed light brown sugar
Add and whip well:
6 eggs, at room temperature
Add and whip well:
1/4 cup molasses
1/4 cup orange juice
1/4 cup sherry
2 tablespoons vanilla extract
1/4 cup white corn syrup
Sift together, then whip into butter mixture:
5 cups white bread flour
1-1/2 teaspoons ground cinnamon
1/2 teaspoon ground cloves
1/2 teaspoon ground nutmeg
1/2 teaspoon ground allspice
1/2 teaspoon ground mace
1/2 teaspoon baking soda
1 teaspoon double-acting baking powder
1/2 teaspoon salt
Put into a large bowl while still warm:
Steamed raisins and currants
Add and mix together well:
3 pounds mixed candied fruit, diced
1 pound candied cherries
1/4 pound pitted dates, chopped
Add and mix well:
1 cup white bread flour
(The flour will keep the fruit from settling to the bottom of the cake batter.) Combine the fruit mixture and the batter, then mix in:
1 pound walnut meats, chopped
1/2 pound pecan meats, chopped
Divide batter among six 8-by-4-1/2-inch foil loaf pans. Decorate tops with:
Candied pineapple pieces
Candied cherries
Whole almonds
Walnut halves
Bake in a 250°F oven for about 2 hours. Be sure the tops rise and crack slightly for then the cakes are done. Remove from the oven and glaze with:
3/4 cup white corn syrup, mixed with 2 teaspoons water
When cool, bend the sides of the foil pans away from the cakes and pour along each long side:
1 tablespoon brandy
Replace foil sides, cover tightly and store. It is best to let them age for a good while before eating.
Makes 6 loaf cakes

CRISP DATE-WALNUT TORTE

Beat together lightly:
2 eggs
1/2 cup firmly packed brown sugar
1/4 teaspoon vanilla extract
Sift together, then beat into egg mixture:
2 tablespoons all-purpose flour
1 teaspoon baking powder
1/8 teaspoon salt
Fold in:
1/2 cup walnuts, coarsely chopped
1/2 cup pitted dates, coarsely chopped
Turn into a 8-inch cake pan and bake in a 325°F oven for 40 to 45 minutes. Remove from the oven, let cool, then break into pieces in size desired. Put into stemmed glasses and serve with a garnish of:
Whipped cream
Candied cherry
Makes 6 to 8 servings

PERSIMMON CAKE

Sift together:
2 cups all-purpose flour
1 teaspoon baking soda
3/4 teaspoon salt
1 teaspoon double-acting baking powder
1/2 teaspoon ground cinnamon
1/2 teaspoon ground nutmeg
1/2 teaspoon ground allspice
Cream together:
1/4 pound (1/2 cup) butter or shortening of choice, at room temperature
1-1/2 cups granulated white sugar
Combine flour and butter mixtures and then add, one at a time, beating well after each addition:
2 eggs
Add and mix in thoroughly:
1-1/2 cups persimmon pulp
1 tablespoon fresh lemon juice
1 cup chopped pitted dates
1/2 cup raisins
3/4 cup chopped nuts
Turn into 1 standard loaf pan or 2 small ones and bake in a 325°F oven for 1 hour. This is a very heavy mixture, so it takes time to bake completely. Be sure the top has risen before removing from the oven. This indicates that the inside is dry enough to have evaporated the moisture and thus produced the steam necessary for it to rise.
Makes 1 large or 2 small loaf cakes

CHERRY NUT CAKE

Sift together:
5-1/2 cups white bread flour
1 teaspoon double-acting baking powder
1/2 teaspoon baking soda
1/2 teaspoon salt
1/2 teaspoon ground cardamom
1-1/2 teaspoons ground mace
With an electric mixer, cream with whip attachment:
1 pound butter, at room temperature
Add and whip until fluffy:
2 cups granulated white sugar
Add and whip well:
6 eggs, at room temperature
Add and continue to whip:
3/4 cup sherry
1/4 cup light corn syrup
2 tablespoons vanilla extract
Add and continue to whip until well mixed:
Sifted flour mixture
Mix together:
3 pounds cherries, pitted
1/2 cup white bread flour
Add:
1 pound walnut halves
Fold cherry-walnut mixture into cake batter. Be sure all of the ingredients are well incorporated, then divide into 5 greased standard loaf pans.
Decorate the tops with:
Candied cherries
Walnut halves
Bake in a 250°F oven for 2 hours and 10 minutes. The tops should rise slightly and crack when done. Remove from the oven and glaze while hot with a mixture of:
3/4 cup light corn syrup
2 tablespoons water
Makes 5 loaf cakes

CHEESE CAKE

Mix together well:
16 graham crackers, finely crushed
4 tablespoons butter, melted and kept warm
1/4 cup firmly packed brown sugar
1/8 teaspoon ground cinnamon
While mixture is still warm, line a 10-inch glass pie dish with it, pressing it on firmly and reserving 2 tablespoons for use later.
With an electric mixer, whip until smooth and fluffy:
8 ounces cream cheese
4 ounces hoop cheese (dry baker's cheese)

Add and whip until well blended:

4 eggs

Add and whip again:

2 tablespoons fresh lemon or lime juice

1/2 teaspoon freshly grated lemon or lime peel

Add and whip until thoroughly mixed:

1/2 cup granulated white sugar

1/4 cup sour cream

Turn mixture into crumb-lined pie dish and bake in a 350°F oven for 20 minutes. Remove from the oven and sprinkle on top:

Reserved graham cracker mixture

Return cake to oven and bake 6 minutes more—no longer as it will dry out. It should jiggle a little when removed from the oven, but not be too soft in the middle. This cake is soft when cut, but not runny.

Makes 12 servings

CREAM MERINGUE TORTE

Cream:

4 tablespoons butter

Sift, then beat into butter:

1/2 cup granulated sugar

Beat the butter-sugar mixture until fluffy. Then beat in:

4 egg yolks

1/2 teaspoon vanilla extract

Sift together:

1 cup cake flour

2 teaspoons double-acting baking powder

1/4 teaspoon salt

Add sifted ingredients to butter mixture alternately with:

5 tablespoons heavy cream

Beat batter unil smooth, then spread into 2 greased 9-inch cake pans.

Whip until stiff peaks form:

4 egg whites

1/8 teaspoon salt

Gradually add while continuing to beat:

1 cup granulated white sugar

1/2 teaspoon vanilla

Carefully spread egg-white mixture over batter in the 2 pans.

Stud one egg-white layer with:

1/3 cup slivered blanched almonds

Bake in a 350°F oven for about 40 minutes. Remove from the oven and cool in the pans.

Shortly before serving, place the layer without the almonds on a cake plate. Spread on it, reserving 1/4 cup:

1 recipe Cream Filling for Pies (page 166), or

1-1/2 cups whipped cream

Place almond-studded layer, meringue side up, on filling and spread over it:

Reserved cream filling or whipped cream

Garnish with:

Strawberries, apricots, cherries or other fruit

Makes one 9-inch cake

FUDGE PIE

Joanne Woodward once laughingly told me that her success as a Beverly Hills hostess was based on serving this delicious pie for dessert. The temperature of the ingredients is the secret to the success.

With an electric mixer, beat together until blended but not fluffy:

1/4 pound butter, at room temperature
1 cup granulated white sugar
1 teaspoon vanilla extract

(Be careful not to overbeat this!) In a saucepan, or the top pan of a double boiler placed over simmering water, melt and then cool:

2 squares (2 ounces) Baker's baking (bitter) chocolate

Pour the cooled chocolate into the butter-sugar mixture, then add and beat again:

2 egg yolks, at room temperature

Add and beat enough to smooth out the batter:

1/3 cup sifted all-purpose flour

Turn mixture into a wide mixing bowl. In another bowl, beat until stiff, glossy peaks form:

2 egg whites
1/8 teaspoon salt

Add and beat in until dissolved:

1 tablespoon granulated white sugar

Stir one-fourth of the beaten whites into the chocolate mixture to lighten it, then fold in the remaining whites until no streaks of white show. If at any stage this mixture is *too light* and fluffy, it will rise in the baking and then fall when cool, creating a crust that is separate from the pie itself. Pour the batter into a 9-inch cake pan that has a built-in cutter, for this pie is extremely difficult to remove from the pan when cold. Bake in a 325°F oven for 30 minutes. Remove from the oven and cool completely before serving. On top of each serving, lay a thin slice of:

Vanilla, coffee or peppermint stick ice cream

Makes 10 servings

Idiot's Delight Top the ice cream slice with some fudge sauce and then Crème de Menthe Sauce (page 174).

MERINGUES

Whip with an electric mixer set on high speed until stiff peaks form:

1-1/4 cups egg whites (about 10), at room temperature
3/8 teaspoon salt

Gradually add while whipping at lowest speed:

2-1/2 cups plus 1 tablespoon granulated white sugar

When whipping in the sugar be sure it is thoroughly dissolved. If it is not, the meringues will weep, won't get crisp and will be tough on the bottom. When all the sugar is incorporated, add and fold in gently:

3/4 teaspoon vanilla extract

Drop by spoonfuls on a brown-paper–lined baking sheet. Spread each into a circle with a rubber spatula—not too thick for they rise a little in the baking. About 1/2 inch thick is best. If a pastry bag is used for forming the egg whites, they may be made into meringue cups by coiling the egg whites up at the edge of each flat circle until the desired height is reached.

A baker told me that if one lets the meringues set for a couple of hours before baking they

will be whiter in color after they are baked. Slow baking is essential. Bake in a 275°F oven for 55 minutes. Remove from the oven and, just when they are cool, lift them from the brown paper. If they stand too long, they are hard to loosen from the paper.
Makes approximately twenty-four 3-inch meringues

MERINGUE FOR CREAM PIES

The secret of a good meringue is to have the egg whites at room temperature. This recipe makes meringue for one nine-inch pie.

Beat until stiff peaks form:
3 egg whites, at room temperature
Large pinch salt
Gradually add while continuing to beat:
6 tablespoons granulated white sugar
Fold in:
Few drops vanilla extract
Spread meringue on pie and bake in a 450°F oven until browned, about 6 or 7 minutes. This high heat makes a tender meringue without drying it out.
Makes meringue for one 9-inch pie

FRUIT-TART SHELLS

Combine:
2 cups white bread flour
1/2 cup stone-ground whole-wheat flour
3 tablespoons brown sugar
3 tablespoons raw or turbinado sugar
1 teaspoon salt
Cut in with a pastry blender or 2 knives until a crumbly consistency:
7/8 cup vegetable shortening
Add and mix to form a smooth dough:
1/4 cup plus 2 tablespoons cold water, or as needed
Roll out dough on a lightly floured board into a very thin sheet. Cut into circles that just fit over inverted tart tins; lay the circles over the tins. (The size varies, though 3-inch tins are popular.) Bake in a 375°F oven for 15 minutes. Watch carefully to prevent burning, and be sure the shells are nice and brown before removing them. Remove from the oven, then lift shells from tins immediately while they are flexible.
Makes approximately twenty-four 3-inch tart shells

PIE CRUST

Follow the directions given here carefully, and you will be assured success.

In a mixing bowl, combine:
2-1/2 cups white bread flour
1 teaspoon salt

With 2 knives or a pastry blender, cut into flour to form a coarse mixture the size of marbles:
1 cup vegetable shortening
Now, using your hands and rubbing them together in a back-and-forth motion, sheet the mixture into flat pieces of shortening with a thick coating of flour. Do not overmix! Stop before you think you should. Make a hole in the center of the mixture and pour in:
1/2 cup water
Quickly mix together with a spoon, only enough to enable you to handle the dough. Again, stop mixing before you think you should. Turn the dough out onto a lightly floured board and divide in half. Press out 1 of the halves gently, very gently, then roll out into a circle 1/8-inch thick or less. The circle should be about 2 inches greater in diameter than the pie pan you will be using, most often a 9-inch one. (If for a fruit pie, be sure to use a deep pan.) Fold the circle in half and lift carefully onto the pan. Then unfold and ease the pastry into place, firmly shaping it against the pan. Bounce the pan once on a countertop to "seat" the crust and thereby prevent shrinking. Trim off any

rough edges even with pan rim. Use the second half of dough to form a top crust or a second single-crust pie.

If mixed correctly, this dough will make a particularly good thick top crust for fruit pies without being tough. The very thin layers of shortening, all of them coated with flour and moistened with water, will fry in the oven, making crisp flakes that will not readily soak up the juice from a fruit pie or the cream from a soft pie. The secret is never to overmix. Rather, try to undermix to the extent that the dough is almost impossible to handle on the floured board.

If a recipe calls for a prebaked crust, the simplest method to use is this one. Lightly dust the pie crust with flour and place a second pie tin on top. Sandwiching the pie crust between the tins prevents it from bubbling. Bake in a 375°F oven for about 30 minutes, or until lightly browned and tender. The top pan can be lifted slightly so you can see if the crust is completely baked. Remove from the oven and remove the top tin. Crusts can be baked in this manner and stored without refrigeration for at least one week. Refrigeration will make them sweat and become soggy.

RASPBERRY SUPREME PIE

Mix together well:
24 graham crackers, finely crushed
6 tablespoons butter, melted and kept warm
6 tablespoons firmly packed brown sugar
While mixture is still warm, line two 8-inch pie plates with it, pressing it on firmly. Bake in a 350°F oven for about 10 minutes. Let cool before filling.

Beat together until light and very smooth:
2 ounces cream cheese
1/2 cup sour cream
3 tablespoons finely chopped candied ginger
1 teaspoon freshly grated orange peel
10 tablespoons powdered sugar
Drain, reserving juice:
1 (12-ounce) package frozen raspberries, thawed
Thicken reserved juice with:
2 tablespoons cornstarch, dissolved in a little water
Chill juice in refrigerator and then stir in berries. Whip until stiff:
1 cup whipping cream
Add and fold in well:
3 tablespoons powdered sugar
Fold raspberry mixture into cream. Divide raspberry-cream mixture between:
Prebaked graham-cracker crusts
Refrigerate until serving time.
Makes two 8-inch pies

FRESH RHUBARB PIE

In a kettle, combine and bring to a boil:
1 cup water
2 drops red food coloring
Pinch salt
Add and cook, stirring constantly, until very thick:
1/4 cup cornstarch, dissolved in a little water
Add and stir until completely dissolved:
2 cups granulated white sugar
Remove from the heat and mix in:
2-1/2 pounds rhubarb, cut into 1-inch pieces
Turn rhubarb mixture into:
Unbaked 9-inch pie crust
Cover with:
Latticework top or complete top crust
Bake in a 450°F oven for about 25 minutes, or until nicely browned.
Makes one 9-inch pie

LEMON MERINGUE PIE

During the time I managed a pie bakery in Columbus, Ohio, the establishment turned out over two million pies. The following recipe was one of our standards. If the method is followed exactly, the results are truly delicious.

In a saucepan, bring to a boil, stirring to dissolve sugar:
2 cups water
1/8 teaspoon salt
1 cup granulated white sugar
2 teaspoons freshly grated lemon rind
6 tablespoons cornstarch, dissolved in a little of the water
Cook until clear and thick. Remove from the heat and quickly stir in:
3 egg yolks, lightly beaten
Beat in very, very lightly:
1/3 cup fresh lemon juice
Then beat in lightly:
3 tablespoons butter, cut into very thin slices
Do not attempt to add the last 3 ingredients all at once, because a starchy taste will develop. By following this procedure exactly, the pie will have a delicious fresh lemon flavor. Turn the lemon mixture into:
Prebaked 9-inch pie crust
Top with:
Meringue (page 161)
Makes one 9-inch pie

FRESH APRICOT PIE

In a saucepan, combine and bring to a boil, stirring constantly:
1/2 cup apricot pulp
2 cups water
1/8 teaspoon salt
1/2 cup cornstarch
Add and bring again to a boil, stirring to dissolve sugar:
2 cups granulated white sugar
Juice of 2-1/2 lemons
Pinch ground nutmeg
Pinch ground cinnamon
Remove from the heat and mix in:
2-1/2 pounds apricots, peeled, halved and pitted
Turn apricot mixture into:
Unbaked 9-inch pie crust
Cover with:
Latticework top or complete top crust
Bake in a 450°F oven for about 25 minutes, or until nicely browned.
Makes one 9-inch pie

PECAN PIE

Mix together well:
2 tablespoons butter, melted
1 cup firmly packed light brown sugar
2 tablespoons all-purpose flour
Add and beat in well:
2 eggs
1 teaspoon vanilla extract
1/4 teaspoon salt
Add and beat lightly:
1 cup white corn syrup
Turn mixture into:
Unbaked 9-inch pie crust
Arrange on top:
1/2 cup pecan halves
Bake in a 375°F oven for 35 minutes, or until set.
Makes one 9-inch pie

GREEN TOMATO MINCE FILLING

In the Midwest, this is an autumn recipe, usually made when the first frost catches the green tomatoes on the vine before they have had time to ripen. Of course, it can be made any time firm, green tomatoes are available.

In a large kettle, mix together:
2-1/2 pounds green tomatoes, cubed

2-1/8 pounds tart apples, peeled and cubed
6 ounces dried currants
1-1/4 pounds seedless raisins
4-1/4 cups firmly packed brown sugar
1-1/4 cups cider vinegar
1-1/2 tablespoons ground cinnamon
1-1/2 teaspoons ground cloves
1-1/4 teaspoons ground allspice
1-1/4 teaspoons ground black pepper
1 tablespoon salt
1 pound mixed candied fruit, diced
1-1/4 teaspoon powdered mace

Simmer *gently* for about 3 hours, or until apples and tomatoes are very soft. Then remove from the heat and mix in:

1/2 pound butter, thinly sliced

Store in a tightly covered crock, until ready to use. When you are ready to make the pies, mix into the filling:

1/2 cup brandy
1/2 cup sherry

Makes filling for three 9-inch pies

Note This pie filling will keep without refrigeration for many months.

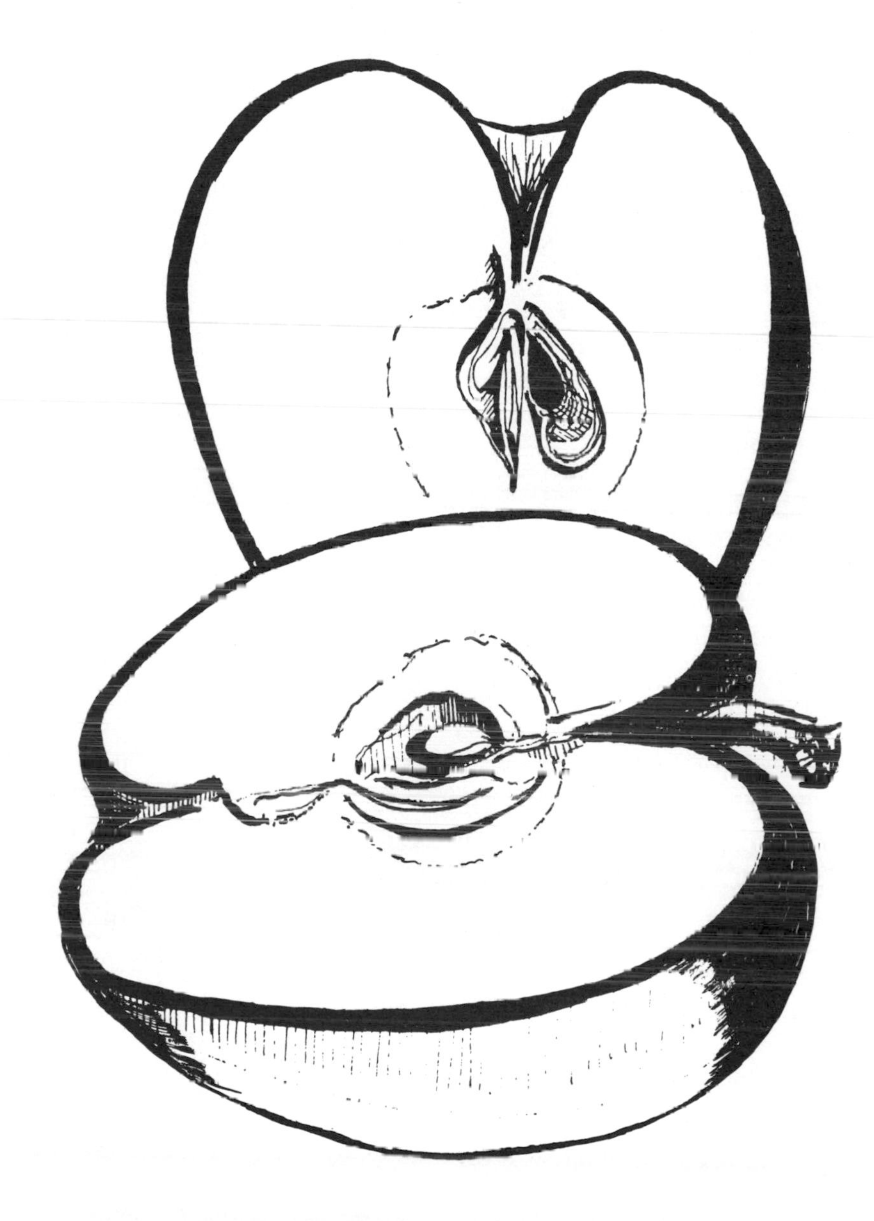

CREAM FILLING FOR PIES

In a saucepan, combine:
2 cups milk
3/4 cup granulated white sugar
Bring to a boil, stirring to dissolve sugar. Mix together with a wire whip, then add to hot milk and stir vigorously until mixture thickens:
1/2 cup milk
3-1/2 tablespoons cornstarch
3 egg yolks
1/8 teaspoon salt
1 teaspoon vanilla extract
When thickened, remove from the heat, add and stir in:
1 tablespoon butter
Any fruit may be added to this cream filling. It may be fresh or canned and well-drained, such as:
Sliced peaches and apricots, seedless grapes, chopped figs
Mix into the filling-fruit mixture:
1-1/2 teaspoons cornstarch
Any lightly toasted nuts may also be added, such as:
Pecans, English or black walnuts, macadamias, cashews
Makes cream filling for one 9-inch pie

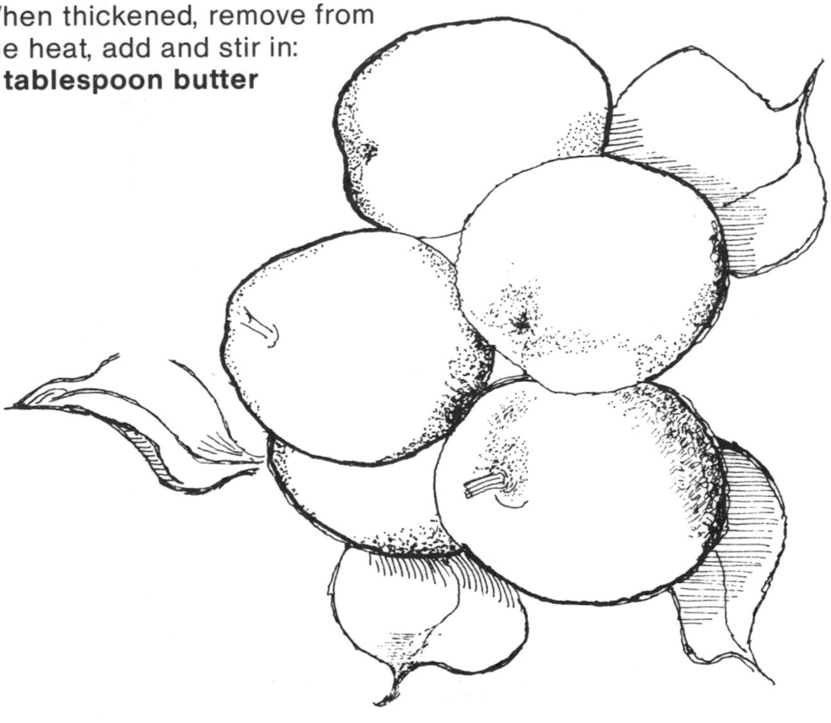

FRESH PERSIMMON CREAM PIE

Prepare:
1 recipe Cream Filling for Pies (preceding)
Prebaked 9-inch pie crust
Peel and slice into pieces resembling orange segments, preparing enough to form a single layer on the pie crust:
Persimmons
Arrange the segments on the pie crust and pour hot cream filling over the top. Cover and refrigerate immediately just until filling is completely cool. Remove from the refrigerator and top with:
Whipped cream
Makes one 9-inch pie

FRESH BANANA CREAM PIE

Prepare:
1 recipe Cream Filling for Pies (preceding)
Prebaked 9-inch pie crust
Slice, enough to form a single layer on the pie crust:
Bananas
Arrange the banana slices on the pie crust and pour hot cream filling over the top. Cover and refrigerate immediately, just until filling is completely cool. Remove from the refrigerator and top with:

Whipped cream or meringue (page 161)
(If meringue is used, bake at 450°F until browned.)
Makes one 9-inch pie

TOASTED PECAN CREAM PIE

In a saucepan, combine and bring to a boil:
2 cups milk
3/4 cup granulated white sugar
Beat with a wire whip, then add to hot milk mixture and cook, stirring constantly, until thickened:
1/2 cup milk
3-1/2 tablespoons cornstarch
3 egg yolks
1/8 teaspoon salt
1 teaspoon vanilla extract
Remove from the heat and stir in:
1/2 cup toasted pecan halves
Turn pecan mixture into:
Prebaked 9-inch pie crust
Cover and refrigerate immediately just until filling is completely cool. Remove from the refrigerator and top with:
Whipped cream or meringue (page 161)
(If meringue is used, bake at 450°F until browned.)
Makes one 9-inch pie

CHOCOLATE MOUSSE PECAN PIE

To make the crust, grind to a powder in a blender:
2 cups pecans
Combine the pecans with:
1/3 cup granulated white sugar
3 tablespoons butter, melted
Press this mixture into a *well-greased* 9-inch pie pan and chill for 30 minutes, then bake in a 350°F oven for 12 to 15 minutes. Remove from the oven and let cool.
To make the filling, combine in the top pan of a double boiler placed over simmering water:
4 egg yolks
1/2 cup granulated white sugar
Dash salt
Heat until thickened, stirring constantly. Add and mix in well:
1 cup whipping cream
3 squares (3 ounces) semi-sweet chocolate, melted
3 tablespoons crème de cacao
Remove from the heat, let cool and pour into baked crust. Refrigerate until set. Just before serving, whip until stiff:
1 cup whipping cream
Add and fold in:
2 tablespoons powdered sugar
1 teaspoon dark rum
Cover the pie with the whipped cream and serve.
Makes one 9-inch pie

FRESH COCONUT CREAM PIE

In a saucepan, combine and bring to a boil, stirring constantly to dissolve sugar:
2 cups milk
3/4 cup granulated white sugar
1/2 cup shredded fresh coconut
Mix together with a wire whip, then add to hot milk and stir vigorously until mixture thickens:
1/2 cup milk
3-1/2 tablespoons cornstarch
3 egg yolks
1/8 teaspoon salt
1 teaspoon vanilla extract
When thickened, remove from the heat, add and stir in:
1 tablespoon butter
Turn mixture into:
Prebaked 9-inch pie crust
Cover and refrigerate immediately just until filling is completely cool. Remove from the refrigerator and top with:
Whipped cream or meringue (page 161)
(If meringue is used, bake at 450°F until browned.)
Decorate top with:
Grated fresh coconut
Makes one 9-inch pie

FRESH FRUIT COMPOTE

Combine whatever you find fresh in the market for this compote. The fruits given here are only suggestions.

Prepare:

1 pound peaches, peeled, pitted and sliced
1 pound seedless grapes
1 pound apricots, peeled, halved and pitted
1 pound pears, peeled, cored and sliced
2 cups melon balls, such as casaba, crenshaw, honeydew and/or watermelon

If you do not have the syrup reserved from making Follies Bergère Peach Melba, following, make the following syrup. In a saucepan, combine:

1 cup water
2 cups granulated white sugar

Bring to a boil, stirring to dissolve sugar, cover and simmer 5 minutes. Then add and stir in well:

1/2 teaspoon vanilla extract

Poach the peaches in the syrup for 1 minute, or until soft. Lift peaches out with a slotted utensil. Chill the syrup. When the syrup has chilled, mix together:

1/2 cup cointreau
1/2 cup brandy
2 cups of the reserved chilled syrup
Toss the poached peaches and all of the other fruits in the brandy sauce and refrigerate for at least 1 hour.

A nice way to serve this compote is to hollow out completely a watermelon half reserved from making melon balls. Chill it while the fruit is chilling. When you are ready to serve the compote, pour the fruit into the chilled melon shell and garnish with:
Whipped cream
Green and red cherries in syrup
Makes 12 to 16 servings

PEACH DUMPLINGS

In a good-sized kettle that can be tightly covered, put:
1 (28-ounce) can sliced cling peaches and syrup
Mix together:
4 cups white pastry flour
1 teaspoon salt
8 teaspoons Royal (tartrate) baking powder
(It is important that this type of baking powder, rather than the double-acting type, be used in this recipe, for tartrate powder begins to rise immediately upon being moistened.) Add and cut in with a pastry blender or 2 knives until the dough is the consistency of coarse cornmeal:
1/3 cup vegetable shortening
In a 2-cup measuring cup, break:
1 egg
Add to make 1-1/2 cups liquid:
Milk
Beat the milk and egg together and add to dry ingredients, mixing only enough to incorporate. Do not overmix. Bring peaches and their syrup to a boil. To make the dumplings, dip a tablespoon into the boiling liquid, then dip it into the batter and lift a spoonful of the batter out. Drop the batter into the pot of boiling syrup and repeat until all of the batter has been added to the pot. This must be done *very quickly.* Cover the pot immediately and do not remove the cover while the dumplings are cooking. The dumplings should be ready in about 15 minutes. Ladle the peach slices, dumplings and some of the syrup into large soup bowls. Serve with:
Half-and-half cream
Diners may add as much cream to their bowls as desired.
Makes 8 servings

FOLLIES BERGERE PEACH MELBA

In a saucepan, combine:
1 cup water
2 cups granulated white sugar
Bring to a boil, stirring to dissolve sugar, cover and simmer 5 minutes to form a syrup. Then add and stir in well:
1/4 teaspoon vanilla extract
Poach for 1 minute in the syrup:
3 pounds ripe peaches, peeled, halved and pitted
Lift peach halves from syrup with a slotted spoon, let cool, then chill.

With an electric mixer, whip well:
2 cups seedless black cap raspberry jam
1/4 cup brandy
2 teaspoons commercial chocolate syrup
1 tablespoon port wine
For each serving, put in a dessert dish:
1 scoop vanilla ice cream
Top the ice cream with:
1 peach half, pit side down
Spoon over ice cream:
Approximately 2 tablespoons raspberry syrup
Top with:
Dollop of whipped cream
Makes 12 to 14 servings

FROZEN CHEESE WITH FIGS

Force through a sieve:
1-1/2 cups (3/4 pound) cottage cheese
Mix together and add to cottage cheese:
2 cups sour cream
1/2 teaspoon salt
1/8 teaspoon ground nutmeg
1/2 cup granulated white sugar
1 teaspoon lemon extract
Turn into a refrigerator tray and freeze.

To serve, have ready:
8 dried figs
Cut frozen cheese mixture into 8 squares, place 1 square on each dessert plate and arrange a fig in the center of each square.
Makes 8 servings

BAKED PRUNE WHIP

Put through a ricer:
2/3 cup cooked pitted prunes
Add and mix together well:
1/2 cup granulated white sugar
1 teaspoon fresh lemon juice
Beat until stiff, glossy peaks form:
2 egg whites
1/8 teaspoon salt
Fold the egg whites into the prune mixture and turn into a greased 1-quart baking dish. Put the dish in a pan with hot water to a depth of 1 inch and bake in a 350°F oven for about 45 minutes, or until set. Serve at once, topped with:
Whipped cream
Makes 4 to 6 servings

CHEESE PASKHA

This Easter sweet from Russia is pressed in a wooden mold and usually bears the sign of the cross or the initials XB, meaning "Christ is Risen."

Mix together well:
12 ounces cream cheese
1/2 cup sour cream
1/4 pound sweet butter, at room temperature
1/4 pound granulated white sugar
1/4 pound almonds, chopped
1/4 pound mixed candied orange and citron peel
1/2 pound seedless white raisins
If you have no mold, put the mixture in a cheesecloth bag and let it hang for at least 24 hours. If you have a mold, it should remain in it 24 hours. Slice to serve.
Makes 8 servings

MRS. BERGENGREN'S INDIAN PUDDING

In the top pan of a double boiler placed over simmering water, heat, stirring constantly, until thickened like cereal:

4 cups milk
3 tablespoons fine yellow cornmeal
2 tablespoons pearl tapioca, soaked in water until softened

Add and mix in well:

1 cup light molasses
1 teaspoon ground cinnamon
1 egg, beaten

Turn into a buttered 1-1/2-quart baking dish. Cover and bake in a 275°F oven for 2 hours. Serve warm with:

Vanilla ice cream

Makes 8 servings

TIPSY PUDDING

And it really is! Some years ago an English friend who had a store where I traded gave me this recipe. She said it was a great favorite with her family, and so it may be with yours.

Break (do not cut) into pieces and put in a 1-quart glass casserole to fill three-quarters full:

Very stale cake (an 8-inch one should do)

The cake must be dry and rather hard. Pour over the cake:

1 cup sherry

Let stand to soak in well for 1 hour.

In the top pan of a double boiler placed over simmering water, heat together until thick enough to coat a spoon well:

2 cups milk
3 egg yolks, lightly beaten
1 cup granulated white sugar
1/8 teaspoon salt
1/2 teaspoon vanilla extract

Do not overcook or the mixture will curdle. Pour custard over soaked cake. Top with:

Sweetened whipped cream, generously flavored with rum

Makes 4 to 6 servings

CHERRY PUDDING

Drain and reserve the juice from:

1 No. 2 can pitted sour cherries

Butter a 9-inch tube pan and cover the bottom with the cherries.

Cream with an electric mixer, using the beater:

4 tablespoons butter
1/2 cup granulated white sugar

Add and beat again:

2 eggs

Sift together, then beat into butter mixture:

2 cups white pastry flour
1/2 teaspoon salt
1 tablespoon Royal (tartrate) baking powder

(It is important that this type of baking powder, rather than the double-acting type, be used in this recipe, for tartrate powder begins to rise immediately upon being moistened.)

Add and mix again, but do not overmix:

1/4 cup milk

Spread the mixture over the cherries and bake in a 375°F oven for 40 minutes. Turn out onto a heated plate, cut into wedges, and serve with the following sauce.

While the pudding is baking, combine and bring to a boil:

1 No. 2 can pitted sour cherries with juice
Juice reserved from first can

Add and cook until clear and thick, stirring constantly.

1/4 cup cornstarch, mixed with 1 cup granulated white sugar

When thickened, add and stir in well:

1/2 cup water

Heat to serving temperature and spoon over the pudding at the table.

Makes 10 servings

PERSIMMON CREAM

Audye Reynolds Tuttle, who contributed to the original Ranch House cookbook, gives us another of her wonderful inventions—beautifully simple and delicious.

In a blender or food processor, mix for at least 4 minutes:

2 cups peeled persimmons
1 cup whipping cream
1/2 cup coffee cream

When smooth and thick, divide among 6 sherbet glasses and chill for at least 1 hour.
Garnish each serving with:

Whipped cream, tinted with red food coloring if desired
1 teaspoon coarsely chopped pecans

Makes 6 servings

COFFEE MOUSSE

In the top pan of a double boiler placed over simmering water, heat:

1-1/2 cups brewed strong coffee
1/2 cup milk
1/3 cup granulated white sugar
1 tablespoon gelatin, softened in a little of the milk

In a mixing bowl, beat well with a spoon:

3 egg yolks

Pour hot mixture over beaten yolks, stirring constantly. Add and beat in only until dissolved, then let cool:

1/3 cup granulated white sugar
1/2 teaspoon vanilla extract

Beat until light and fluffy, then fold into coffee mixture:

3 egg whites
1/4 teaspoon salt

Divide among 6 sherbet glasses and chill. Serve, topped with:

Whipped cream

Makes 6 servings

ERICA SQUARES

While visiting Carmel some time ago, I contacted a friend of many years, Erica Weston, granddaughter of the famous photographer, Edward Weston. This charming woman, now living in Big Sur, invited my wife and me to tea, at which she served a very sweet concoction that was so delicious I told her I had to have the recipe. Here it is, named "Erica Squares" for her, though she is far from "square."

Cream together and press firmly and evenly into a well-greased, shallow, 9-by-12-inch baking dish:

12 tablespoons (3/4 cup) butter
3 tablespoons granulated white sugar
3 cups cups all-purpose flour

Bake in a 350°F oven for 20 minutes. While this layer is baking, mix together well:

2 cups firmly packed brown sugar
3 eggs, beaten
3 tablespoons all-purpose white flour
3/4 teaspoon baking powder
1-1/2 tablespoons vanilla extract
1-1/2 cups chopped walnuts
3/4 cup shredded coconut

Remove first layer from the oven and immediately top it with the brown sugar mixture. Return it to the oven and bake for 20 minutes more. Remove from the oven and let cool.
Mix together well:

1/4 pound butter, softened
1-1/2 tablespoons vanilla extract
1-1/2 cups powdered sugar

If this mixture seems too dry to spread, add just to moisten slightly:

Heavy cream

When the base is cool, spread the powdered sugar mixture over the top. To serve, cut into squares.
Makes approximately 48 squares

CHOCOLATE-WALNUT SQUARES

Cream together:
1/4 pound butter, at room temperature
2/3 cup firmly packed light brown sugar
Add and mix until crumbly:
2 cups sifted all-purpose flour
Pat this mixture evenly into a shallow 8-by-12-inch baking pan.
Beat together:
2 eggs
2 cups firmly packed brown sugar
1 teaspoon vanilla extract
Add and mix in:
1/2 cup all-purpose flour
1 teaspoon double-acting baking powder
Add and mix in:
1-1/4 cups chopped walnuts
1 (6-ounce) package semi sweet chocolate chips
Spread this mixture over butter mixture in pan and bake in a 375°F oven for 25 minutes, or until golden brown. Remove from the oven and let cool. Cut into small squares to serve.
Makes approximately 30 squares

PRALINES

In a saucepan, combine and heat, stirring well to dissolve sugar:
4 cups firmly packed brown sugar
1/2 cup coffee cream
2 tablespoons butter
Using a candy thermometer, cook for 3 minutes at 240°F. Remove from the heat and immediately stir in:
1/2 pound pecan halves
Wait until the mixture has begun to cool slightly, then put a spoonful on a sheet of waxed paper to see if the mixture has cooled enough to begin to set. It should crystallize when cold. If it is spooned out too soon, the first few will stay sticky and you will be unable to remove them from the paper. When it is the proper temperature, drop by spoonfuls onto waxed paper.
Makes approximately 2-1/2 pounds

MRS. REEVES' ROCKS

Cream together:
2 cups granulated white sugar
1/2 pound butter, at room temperature
Mix together:
1 cup sour milk or buttermilk
3/4 teaspoon baking soda
3/4 teaspoon cream of tartar
Mix lightly into butter mixture:
Sour milk mixture
4 eggs
Then add and mix in:
4 cups all-purpose flour
Fold in:
1/2 pound pitted dates, chopped
1/2 pound raisins, chopped
1 cup coarsely cut English walnuts
1 teaspoon vanilla extract
Spoon mounds (in size desired) of mixture onto greased baking sheets, then spread each mound out slightly. Bake in a 400°F oven for 10 to 12 minutes, or until brown. Remove from the oven, place on waxed paper and let cool.

TOPPING FOR FRESH STRAWBERRIES

This easy-to-prepare dessert is quite delicious.

Mix together well:
2 cups sour cream
1/2 cup Dundee ginger marmalade
Hull:
3 baskets strawberries
Set 8 of the largest berries aside for garnish. Mound the remaining berries in 8 stemmed glasses. Spoon about 1/4 cup topping over each glass of berries and garnish each with 1 of the reserved berries. Decorate each serving with:
A few fresh mint leaves
Makes 8 servings

RANCH HOUSE SPUMONI ICE CREAM

Mix together:
1/2 gallon vanilla ice cream, softened
1-1/2 pounds mixed candied fruit, chopped
6 ounces pecans, coarsely chopped
Add, pouring very slowly down the side of the mixing bowl so that it will not splash, and mix in well:
1 cup brandy
Refreeze until hard, making certain that the ice cream has not begun to melt before returning it to the freezer. Spoon into attractive dishes to serve.
Makes 12 to 16 servings

AVOCADO SHERBET

Mix together well, then freeze:
1 large avocado, mashed
Fresh lime juice to taste
Fresh lemon juice to taste
Grated tangerine peel to taste
3 egg whites, beaten until stiff
1-1/2 cups granulated white sugar
2 cups water
1 tablespoon unflavored gelatin, softened in a little of the water

CREME DE MENTHE SAUCE

In a saucepan, combine:
2-3/4 cups granulated white sugar
1-1/2 cups water
3/4 cup white corn syrup
5 drops green food coloring
Bring to a boil, stirring constantly to dissolve sugar, cover and boil for 5 minutes. Remove from the heat and let cool. When cool, but not cold, stir in well:
3/4 cup green crème de menthe
2 tablespoons dry sauterne
This sauce does not need to be refrigerated. If you do refrigerate it, it will crystalize.
Makes approximately 2-1/2 cups

GREEN GINGER SAUCE

Delicious over vanilla ice cream and topped with grated coconut.

Soak overnight in water to cover:
1/2 pound ginger root
The next day, peel and slice 1/8 inch thick, then cut into 1/8-inch cubes.

In a saucepan, combine:
2 cups granulated white sugar
7/8 cup water
1/4 cup white corn syrup
Bring to a boil, stirring to dissolve sugar, cover and boil for 5 minutes. Uncover and add the ginger, then cover again and boil gently for 30 minutes. The syrup must boil very slowly so that it does not evaporate. When done, stir in:
2 or 3 drops green food coloring
Makes approximately 2 cups

RUSSIAN CREAM SAUCE

Serve over strawberries, peaches or other fresh fruit.

Beat together until thick and lemon colored:
2 egg yolks
3 tablespons granulated white sugar
Add and beat until light and fluffy:
1 cup heavy cream
Stir in:
1/4 cup rum
Beat until stiff, glossy peaks form:
2 egg whites
Fold the egg whites into the cream mixture.
Makes approximately 2 cups

CHOCOLATE SAUCE FOR ICE CREAM

Place in a saucepan:
3/4 cup water, boiling
4 squares (4 ounces) Baker's baking (bitter) chocolate
Heat slowly until completely dissolved and thick, stirring constantly to prevent burning and sticking. Add and bring to a boil, stirring to dissolve sugar:
2-1/4 cups granulated white sugar
3/4 cup evaporated milk
Boil for 2 minutes, then remove from the heat and add:
1 tablespoon butter
Let cool to lukewarm, then stir in:
1/2 teaspoon vanilla extract
Cover and store in the refrigerator.
Makes approximately 3 cups

PRALINE SAUCE

In a saucepan, combine:
2 cups firmly packed brown sugar
1/2 cup white corn syrup
2 tablespoons butter
3/4 cup coffee cream
2 teaspoons light molasses
1/8 teaspoon maple-flavored extract
Bring to a boil, stirring constantly to dissolve sugar, and boil until mixture reaches 220°F on a candy thermometer. Remove from the heat and cool. Do not overcook, or the sauce will crystallize.
Makes approximately 2 cups

NEW ORLEANS DELIGHT

One of the most popular desserts at the Ranch House is this very simple but deliciously rich concoction.

On an individual serving dish, place:
3-inch meringue (page 160)
Top meringue with scoop of:
Coffee ice cream
Spoon over ice cream:
Praline Sauce (preceding)
Arrange on top:
6 pecan halves
Makes 1 serving

talk of many things

"The time has come,
the walrus said . . ."
—L. Carroll

There are some things too good to leave out, that seemingly have no specific place in a book like this.

KITCHEN EQUIPMENT

Pressure cooker So many recipes in this book call for the use of a pressure cooker, a friend said that something should be written about one so that the person unfamiliar with its use might be able to use one easily. There are many types on the market—some aluminum and some made of stainless steel. The former are completely satisfactory, but if the price is not too high the stainless variety is easier to clean.

There is little danger in using these pressure pots because the simplest ones have a weighted pressure cap that will quickly tell if the pressure is too high. All that could happen is that the little cap would be knocked off it it weren't attended to in time. (I use them *without the cap* for many vegetables. This way there is still a little pressure built up because of the slowness of the escaping steam.)

If the vegetables are to be served with a sauce added later, then place a trivet in the bottom of the cooker and use about a half cup of water in the pot. If they are to be served in their own juice, then do not use the trivet—just add the seasoning and butter or olive oil later, after the vegetables are cooked. Remember—one of the secrets of well-flavored vegetables is to use as little liquid as possible in cooking them to prevent the dilution of their own juices.

Gricer A cone-shaped device with cutting holes in it, it either bolts to the table or has a rubber suction cup that holds fast to a smooth surface. There are usually three cones accompanying it: one that makes tiny threads, one that makes shoestringlike threads and one that makes thin slices. It can be used for shredding cheese, coconut, vegetables, etc.

Rotary slicer This is a very handy tool, though not essential. It consists of a wheel with very sharp blades that rotate against the food to be sliced. It is excellent for slicing cabbage, potatoes, beets, carrots, etc.

Mixing machines Many kinds of mixers are now on the market. One of them, the KitchenAid, is a heavy-duty model with many different attachments. All of the attachments are useful for their particular work. It is especially handy to have two wire beaters when doing baking to avoid the necessity of constantly having to wash a single one.

VEGETARIAN FOOD PRODUCTS

Bakon yeast This product is very good in the normal vegetarian diet and a real flavor boon in the restricted diet, for it contains no starch, sugar, meat or salt. It is 100 percent hickory-smoked torula yeast and can be added to anything when a bacon or rich nutty flavor is desired.

Gravy Quick As its name suggests, this is a commercial product of good quality, used chiefly to make gravy. It is low in calories and made of wheat flour, yeast extract, soy and other vegetable proteins.

Savita A thick paste made of vegetable protein and spices for flavoring vegetarian dishes; used for years by vegetarian cooks.

Marmite is a European product that can be used in place of Savita. It can be found in health-food stores.

Vegeburger, choplets Meat substitutes canned under the Loma Linda brand name, well known to most vegetarians.

Hoop cheese, or soft baker's cheese, is obtainable at most dairies. It is actually cottage cheese with a good deal of the moisture removed. Too strong in flavor for serving alone but excellent used in cooking.

YOGURT

You can start making your own yogurt simply by taking a small portion from a carton of any reliable commercial yogurt or, better still, obtain a live culture from your health food store. What you are going to do is to provide a situation in which this culture can grow. To do this, you put it in milk and keep the milk at a constant body-heat temperature. It can be put on an asbestos pad over the pilot light of your stove or, if you are dedicated to making your own yogurt you can buy, through your health food or hardware store, an electrical device made to keep the mixture at the correct and constant temperature. If you can get TB certified raw milk from your dairy, this is the best to use to assure top quality. Start with a quart of warm milk. Stir in a half cup of the culture. Cover the container with a solid cover, not a cloth, and put it in the warm place. Within 24 hours it should be set, and you can take a half cup of it and start the whole process over again. It is that simple.

Yogurt is not just sour milk. Wonderful bacteria live in it and they help to keep established in the intestines the necessary flora that make digestion possible in the human body. People in Europe and especially of the Near East have eaten yogurt for centuries. Mix it with a little brown or raw sugar and put it over fresh fruit; use it in place of sour cream or with a little jam mixed in or just cool, plain yogurt is delicious.

AMERICAN SYSTEM OF LIQUID MEASURES

Since so many of my friends in England and in Europe have said they want copies of this book, perhaps this little table will be helpful to them:

3 teaspoons	= 1 tablespoon
2 tablespoons	= 1 ounce
8 ounces	= 1 cup
2 cups	= 1 pound
	= 1 pint
4 cups	= 2 pounds
	= 1 quart
8 pounds	= 4 quarts
	= 1 gallon

SUNDAY BRUNCH ON THE HILL

When the Ranch House was still in its original location, and people came in the back way because the front porch was in no condition to hold them up, Sunday brunch was an event that friends brought outsiders to as a special treat. People would come by on their Sunday morning horseback rides, park their mounts under the trees in the backyard, and come in to sit at the kitchen table so they could have sour cream pancakes hot off the griddle.

SOUR CREAM PANCAKES

With an electric mixer, beat until combined, but do not overmix:
1/2 cup milk
4 eggs (7 ounces)
1/2 cup all-purpose flour
2 tablespoons wheat germ
1/4 cup stone-ground whole-wheat flour
1/4 cup old-fashioned rolled oats
1 teaspoon baking soda
1/2 teaspoon salt
1-1/2 cups sour whipping cream
(Commercial sour cream can be used, but it will not work as well in this recipe.) Heat an ungreased griddle until hot enough to sizzle when a bit of butter is dropped on it. Unless the griddle is hot enough, the cakes will not rise quickly and therefore do not attain their true lightness. If it is too hot, they will burn before they can be turned. The frying is the most difficult part, as it is hard to keep the griddle the correct temperature. You may make the pancakes any size you wish, though smaller ones, about 2 to 3 inches across, are easier to turn. When small bubbles appear on the top, lift up a corner to see if the pancake can be turned. They cook rapidly, and usually are ready to turn before they seem done. They must be handled carefully to avoid splashing the batter when they are turned. When nicely browned on the second side, remove from the griddle and serve.

Because these pancakes are very tender, they should never be served with cold butter or syrup. Many people prefer hot maple syrup and hot butter over them, but others, who do not want so much sweetness, like easy-to-prepare Maple Butter (following).

Makes approximately twelve 3-inch pancakes

Note An electric griddle set on the highest temperature works well for making these pancakes.

MAPLE BUTTER

With an electric mixer, whip until light and the consistency of whipped cream, scraping down the sides of the bowl as you whip:
12 tablespoons (3/4 cup) butter, at room temperature
Add in a thin, steady stream, whipping mixture until light and fluffy:
2 cups maple syrup, at room temperature

NANCY'S SEVILLE ORANGE MARMALADE

This is the best recipe I have found to make English-style orange marmalade. Wonderful for Christmas gifts.

Select:
Bitter wild oranges
Wash the fruit thoroughly and cut each orange in half lengthwise. Lay the orange halves, cut sides down, in a shallow dish and slice very thin, beginning at the stem end of the

half. Transfer the fruit and juice to a large kettle and tie the seeds, which contain the pectin necessary to make the mixture jell, in a muslin bag. (The muslin bag should be large enough to allow the seeds to swell as they cook.) For each pound of fruit in the kettle, add:

5 cups water

Then add the bag holding the seeds and bring the mixture to a boil. Boil for 10 minutes, then let the mixture stand for a full 24 hours. Bring to a boil again and boil for 10 minutes, then let the mixture stand for another 24 hours. Remove the seed bag, squeezing it to release all of the pectin into the oranges. For each 2 cups of fruit and juice in the kettle, add:

2-1/4 cups granulated white sugar

Bring to a boil and boil for at least 25 minutes, or until good and thick. Ladle into hot, sterilized jars and seal immediately.

CLOTTED OR CORNISH CREAM

Having lived briefly in both Devonshire and Cornwall, I think you might like to try this recipe for their famous clotted cream.

Place a pan of very rich unpasteurized milk on an asbestos pad on the stove. The pan should be large and shallow to allow the cream to rise. The slower the milk is heated, the better. Small rings and undulations on the surface of the milk indicate when it is sufficiently scalded. When the process of scalding is complete, remove the pan from the heat and place it in the refrigerator until the following day. Then skim the cream off into a storage vessel and refrigerate it until ready to use. Bring it out and let it come to room temperature before serving. This will ensure a light texture.

ENGLISH TEA

You are now ready to have a "proper tea" according to English tradition. Prepare the Scotch Scones on page 79. Place a large bowl of clotted cream on the table, along with some strawberry jam and Nancy's Seville Orange Marmalade, preceding, or any jam you desire. While the scones are hot, split them open, spread plenty of clotted cream on the cut sides, and then some jam. You should have a pot of strong, hot English tea, the Earl Grey type is good, at the table. The tea must be good and strong so that milk and sugar can be added.

BEIGNETS

This recipe for the French Quarter version of doughnuts comes from the Cafe du Monde, which I visited every afternoon when I lived in New Orleans. Delicious with foamy *café au lait.*

In a heavy saucepan, combine and bring to a boil:

1/4 pound butter
1 cup water
2 teaspoons granulated white sugar

Add all at once, stirring vigorously until mixture leaves sides of pan:

1 cup all-purpose flour

Cool mixture slightly, then beat in, one at a time, until batter is smooth and shiny.

2 eggs
1 egg yolk

Heat to 375°F:

Fat for deep-frying

Drop batter by heaping teaspoonfuls into hot fat and fry until golden brown. Lift out with slotted utensil and drain on paper toweling.

Sift over the top:

Powdered sugar

Makes 24

A SLIMMING MEAL

Sometimes it happens that one person in a family needs to lose weight, and what to serve becomes a problem. Here is a very simple meal that takes little time, is delicious and does not have many calories.

In a small skillet, place:
1 small pat butter
1 small onion, sliced
4 or 5 medium to large mushrooms, sliced
Sprinkle on top:
Herb salt
Vegetable Herb Blend
Cover and cook until onion is nearly done. Smooth mixture to cover skillet bottom and break into skillet:
1 egg
Cover and cook slowly until egg is done to your liking. Slip out of skillet onto heated plate.
Garnish with:
Minced parsley
Serve with the following salad.

Prepare a dressing by mixing together:
1 teaspoon Dijon mustard
2 tablespoons water
Arrange on a salad plate:
Tomatoes and green bell pepper slices, or raw vegetable of choice
Torn lettuce leaves
Pour the dressing over the vegetables and sprinkle with:
Herb salt
This is so simple it hardly seems like it would be good, but it is.
Makes 1 serving

AN ELEGANT PARTY

This assortment of food will satisfy your vegetarian and meat-eating friends alike.

Prepare:
Wassail Bowl (page 185)
Welsh Rarebit (page 101) with toasted bread fingers for dipping
Ginger and Nut Dip (page 182) with white melba toast for dipping
Artichoke and Mushroom Canapes (page 181)
Olive and Cheese Sandwich Spread (page 183), omitting the 1/4 cup cream cheese so spread can serve as dip
Grandmother's Spiced Nuts (page 182)
Artichoke Dip (page 181) with an assortment of raw vegetables for dipping
Arrange all of these foods on the front third of a long table, leaving room for the very important centerpiece I am about to describe.

Find a long board of light-colored wood. Pine is quite suitable. Sand it well and apply a good waterproof finish. Then make a visit to a good-quality cheese store and purchase as many small pieces of imported cheeses as you can afford; twenty or so varieties would be good. Place the sanded board down the center of the table, put the pieces of cheese on it and stick a flag indicating the name and country of origin in each piece of cheese. Provide a variety of crackers and/or breads for eating with the cheese.

Directly behind the cheese "board" arrange a large display of seasonal fruits and vegetables; some bouquets of fresh flowers would be nice, too. There should also be a good supply of wines nearby.

ARTICHOKE AND MUSHROOM CANAPES

Slice 1/4 inch thick:
Large mushooms
Drain:
Marinated artichoke hearts
Mix together well, using a blender or food processor, until mixture thickens slightly:
2 parts olive oil
1 part wine vinegar
Salt to taste
Pour marinade over mushrooms and artichokes in a bowl and let stand for at least 1 hour before serving.
Place mushroom-artichoke mixture on:
Lettuce leaves
Garnish with:
Halved cherry tomatoes
Sliced canned pimientos
Fresh herb sprigs of choice

ARTICHOKE DIP

Whirl in a blender or food processor until smooth:
2 (7-ounce) jars marinated artichoke hearts, drained
Add and blend until smooth:
2 cups sour cream
6 ounces (3/4 cup) cream cheese
2 tablespoons commercial cocktail sauce
Herb salt to taste
Put this dip into a medium-sized bowl and place in the center of a very large dish. Surround the bowl with a variety of vegetables, all of which have been washed, dried and chilled.

ALMOND-MUSHROOM PATE

Cook until clear in:
4 tablespoons butter
2 large onions, minced
6 cloves garlic, minced
1 cup celery leaves, minced
Add and cook until all moisture evaporates:
1-1/2 pounds mushrooms, thinly sliced
1/4 cup dry sherry
Remove from the heat, add and mix in well:
1 tablespoon crumbled dried basil
1 teaspoon crumbled dried marjoram
1/2 teaspoon crumbled dried sage
1/4 teaspoon freshly ground black pepper
2 teaspoons Bakon yeast (optional)
1 tablespoon fresh lime juice
1/4 cup sour cream
1-1/2 cups ground toasted blanched almonds
Then stir in:
1 cup grated Swiss cheese
This mixture may be spread on toast rounds or stuffed into Broiled Mushrooms (page 115) or cooked pasta shells. Whichever of these methods you choose, put under the broiler before serving. When piping hot, remove and top with:
Salted sliced almonds

EGG-STUFFED CELERY APPETIZER

In a skillet, cook slowly for 10 minutes, being careful not to brown, in:
2 tablespoons butter
3 cloves garlic, minced
1 large onion, minced
4 teaspoons curry powder
1/2 teaspoon herb salt
Remove from the heat, let cool and mix with:
6 hard-cooked eggs, finely chopped
1/2 cup mayonnaise
2 teaspoons prepared mustard
1 teaspoon finely minced mango chutney or chutney of choice
Stuff this mixture into 2-inch-long pieces of celery. Refrigerate until ready to serve. Just before serving, sprinkle with:
Paprika

GINGER AND NUT DIP

Whip together until very smooth:
1 pound cream cheese
1/2 cup sour cream
1/2 cup soft candied ginger (taken from Dundee ginger marmalade)
1/2 cup chopped walnuts or nuts of choice
Grated peel of 2 oranges, reserving a little for garnish
Chill mixture so that it will become firm before serving. Serve with:
White bread toast, or bread or crackers of choice

DATE-NUT HORS D'OEUVRE

Whirl in a blender or food processor until smooth:
8 ounces cream cheese
2 tablespoons strawberry preserves
1/4 cup strawberry-flavored yogurt
Spread this mixture on:
12 slices Date-Nut Bread (page 77)
Arrange the slices in stacks of 3, spread side up, making 4 stacks in all. With a sharp knife, cut each stack in quarters, forming 4 squares. On one of the quarters place:
1 strawberry
On each of the remaining 3 squares, place 1 of the following:
1 grape
1 black cherry
1 peach slice
(You may, of course, select any fresh fruit that is in season.) These make very interesting finger food. They both look appetizing and taste excellent.
Makes 16 canapes

GRANDMOTHER'S SPICED NUTS

Once when I went to a ranch to buy walnuts, the man in charge asked if I would like to taste some spiced walnuts he had just prepared. Naturally I did, and they were a delicious concoction. He said the recipe had been given to him by his grandmother. Other nuts are good prepared this way, but walnuts are best.

In a 2-quart saucepan, combine:
1 cup granulated white sugar
1/4 teaspoon salt
1 teaspoon ground cinnamon
6 tablespoons milk
Heat until mixture reaches the soft ball stage—236°F on a candy thermometer. Remove from the heat and quickly stir in:
1 teaspoon vanilla extract
Add and mix in well:
3 cups walnut halves
Quickly turn mixture out onto a sheet of waxed paper. You must work quickly so that the nuts can be separated before they crystallize into a hard ball.
Makes 3 cups

WATERCRESS SANDWICH SPREAD

Sprinkle lightly with:
Herb salt
6 hard-cooked eggs
Finely chop the eggs and set aside. Prepare:
3 cups watercress leaves
Sprinkle watercress lightly with:
Salt
Mix together well:
1/2 cup mayonnaise
1/2 teaspoon Dijon-style mustard
Combine the eggs, watercress and mayonnaise mixture and mix until smooth. This mixture makes excellent open-faced sandwiches, as well as the more traditional type. Serve the sandwiches garnished with:
Pickle slices
Olives
Carrot and celery sticks
Makes approximately 4 cups

OLIVE AND CHEESE SANDWICH SPREAD

This sandwich spread uses a common convenience food, but don't be dissuaded from preparing it because of this. The taste of the combination is quite extraordinary and it has great eye appeal.

Whip together until smooth:
2 cups (1 pint) sour cream
1/4 cup cream cheese
Add and mix in well:
1 package Lipton onion soup mix
2 cups well-drained chopped black olives
Let the mixture stand for at least 2 hours to reconstitute the soup mix, then spread on bread of choice to make open-face sandwiches. Arrange over the spread:
Uncooked fresh or frozen and thawed green peas
Makes approximately 5 cups

NUT SANDWICH SPREAD

Whip until smooth:
1 pound cream cheese
Add and mix together well:
1/2 cup well-drained chopped pineapple
1 banana (not too ripe), mashed
1/2 teaspoon ground nutmeg
1 teaspoon freshly grated orange peel
Spread cream-cheese mixture on:
Thinly sliced Oatmeal Bread (page 76)
Sprinkle on top:
Chopped nuts of choice
A few currants
Makes approximately 3-1/2 cups

Variation Make a triple-decker sandwich. Take 3 slices of the oatmeal bread, spread filling on 2 of them and top each with a *very thin* orange slice with peel. Stack these 2 slices and top with the third one. Secure with toothpicks until ready to serve. Serve, garnishing each plate with fresh strawberries or other fresh fruit.

AVOCADO AND EGG OPEN-FACE SANDWICH

Mix together:
2 hard-cooked eggs, chopped
1 avocado, diced
1 green bell pepper, minced
2 tablespoons mayonnaise
2 teaspoons fresh lime or lemon juice
1 teaspoon soy sauce
Grind in a mortar:
1/2 teaspoon herb salt
1/2 teaspoon Omelet Herb Blend
Combine the mortar mixture and egg mixture and mix well.
Spread mixture on:
Whole-wheat bread slices
Serve with garnishes as desired.
Makes approximately 2-1/2 cups

GREEN CRUNCH SANDWICH FILLING

Whip until very smooth:
1 pound cream cheese
Mix together and let stand so moisture drains off thoroughly:
4 green onions and tops, finely chopped
1 green bell pepper, finely chopped
2 canned pimientos, finely chopped
2 tablespoons finely chopped celery
1 teaspoon herb salt

When the vegetable mixture has released all of its moisture, transfer with a slotted utensil to the cream cheese. Mix with the cream cheese until just blended, but not enough to make the mixture mushy. This filling is excellent to take along on a picnic. Spread it thickly on bread of choice to make open-face sandwiches, or use for making traditional closed sandwiches.
Makes approximately 3-1/2 cups

RACLETTE

This well-known Swiss dish is often served after a skiing party, with everyone sitting around a great fireplace, glass of white wine in hand and spicy conversation flowing. You really need a fireplace for this.

Set close to the fire in a heatproof dish so that it will keep warm and soft on one side:
1 large square Emmentaler or raclette cheese
Have warmed plates at hand. Take from the soft side of the cheese a very thin slice and place it flat on the plate.
Have ready in a large wooden bowl:
Small new potatoes, boiled in jackets and kept warm
(The potatoes can be kept warm by wrapping them in a cloth.) Each guest should have a three-tined fork, the kind on which the tines are very sharp and in a triangle so the potatoes can be speared without crumbling, and a small knife for peeling the potatoes. The diner peels a potato, cuts off a bite of it, wraps it in the slice of cheese, pops it into his mouth and washes it down with wine! The Swiss potatoes are small, sweet and flavorful, so let this be your buying guide.

ASHA LEE'S MINT CHUTNEY

Shred in blender:
1 coconut, husk removed
Set coconut aside. Almost fill a standard blender container with:
Well-packed fresh mint leaves
Add and whirl until well mixed:
Juice of 1 lemon or lime
1 teaspoon salt
1 tablespoon honey
1 onion, cut up
1/4 cup coriander leaves
1 tablespoon grated ginger root
Combine the mint mixture with the shredded coconut and let stand to blend flavors. This is excellent served with any curry dish or as a garnish for open-faced sandwiches.
Makes approximately 2-1/2 cups

CHAYOTE SQUASH OR ZUCCHINI PICKLES

In a large pan, place:
4 quarts thinly sliced unpeeled chayote squash or zucchini
1 large onion, thinly sliced
2 red or green bell peppers, thinly sliced
Sprinkle over the top:
1/2 cup salt
Cover with:
Ice cubes
Cover pan and refrigerate overnight. The next day drain well.
In a large pan, combine:
5 cups white vinegar
5 cups granulated white sugar
1-1/2 teaspoons ground turmeric
1 tablespoon mustard seeds
1 tablespoon celery seeds
1 teaspoon ground cloves
Bring mixture to a boil and, stirring constantly, boil until it forms a syrup. Add the vegetables and reduce to medium heat. Bring mixture to scalding, but do not boil. Ladle into hot, sterilized jars and seal.
Makes 8 pints (4 quarts)

QUINCE HONEY

Peel and grate:
5 large quince
In a saucepan, combine:
2 cups water
5 pounds (10 cups) granulated white sugar
Heat but do not boil, stirring constantly until sugar dissolves and a syrup is formed. Then add the quince, bring to a boil and boil for 15 to 20 minutes. If quince is overripe, add, after boiling 20 minutes:
1 teaspoon fresh lemon juice
Ladle into hot, sterilized jars and seal immediately.
Makes approximately 4 cups

WHOLE CRANBERRY SAUCE

In a saucepan, combine and bring to a boil, stirring to dissolve sugar:

2 cups granulated white sugar
2 cups water

Add and simmer without stirring for 5 minutes:

1 pound (4 cups) cranberries, well washed and picked over

(If you wish a firmer sauce, cook longer than 5 minutes.) Cranberries will usually pop within 5 minutes. They must all pop before removing from the heat, for this allows the sugar to penetrate them.

Makes approximately 4 cups

GRAPPLE

This drink is excellent for serving to people who drink neither coffee nor tea. Especially good for a luncheon on a hot day.

Mix together:

2 parts unsweetened apple juice
1 part unsweetened grape juice

Serve over:

Ice

Garnish with:

Mint sprig

WASSAIL BOWL FOR CHRISTMAS

In a saucepan, combine and boil for 10 minutes, stirring to dissolve sugar:

2 cups water
2 cups granulated white sugar
1/2 teaspoon freshly grated nutmeg
2 teaspoons ground ginger
2-inch-stick cinnamon
6 whole cloves
6 allspice berries, or 1/4 teaspoon ground allspice
4 whole cardamom pods, halved
4 coriander seeds

Let cool and strain into a large kettle. Add:

2 quarts ale or good-quality stale beer
2 fifths sherry

Beat until very thick:

12 egg yolks
1 tablespoon granulated white sugar

Beat until stiff, glossy peaks form:

12 egg whites
1 tablespoon granulated white sugar

Fold whites into yolks, then fold in half of ale mixture. Heat remaining half of ale mixture, but do not boil. Pour the egg mixture into a large punch bowl that can be kept warm, then add reheated ale mixture. Add and stir in:

1 or 2 cups cognac or good-quality brandy

This is the best holiday punch I have ever tasted. It is guaranteed to delight all your guests. One batch serves 15 guests

INTERESTING HOT CHOCOLATE

In a saucepan or the top pan of a double boiler placed over simmering water, melt:

1 square (1 ounce) Baker's baking (bitter) chocolate

Add:

1/2 cup hot water

Mix together and add:

6 tablespoons granulated white sugar
2 tablespoons cocoa powder
1 teaspoon instant coffee powder

Stir in well, then add:

Few drops almond extract or a little almond paste

Heat nearly to boiling point and add:

4 cups milk

Reheat to serving temperature and whip well with a wire whisk. Serve, topped with:

Whipped cream or miniature mashmallows

Makes 4 servings

index

ALAN HOOKER

Alan Hooker, owner of the distinguished Ranch House restaurant in Ojai, California, has been a vegetarian since 1932. The recipes in this book are based upon his extensive foreign travels and constant experimentation over three decades to develop the Ranch House's repertoire of over 600 dishes. His nonconformist approach to cooking has brought the restaurant wide acclaim: a string of annual *Holiday* magazine awards since 1973 and four stars in the *Mobil Guide*. "The Ranch House is a true original," pronounced *Gourmet* magazine, "the restaurant of a man who understands flavors and foods in a fundamental way." And fellow vegetarian Joanne Woodward, a frequent Ranch House visitor and noted as a fine cook herself, confesses, "Some of my best recipes come from Alan Hooker."

Hooker's interest in food dates back to his childhood when his family lived next door to a retired chef from the Waldorf Astoria. At Beloit College he majored in chemistry, learning laboratory disciplines that were later helpful in formulating recipes and understanding the chemistry of food. After college he joined a traveling jazz band as a pianist and played at many of the great hotels and clubs in the United States and Europe; when not at the piano, he was likely to be in the kitchen observing the chef.

In 1937, he left the entertainment world to live in Ohio, on a commune engaged in the serious study of Eastern philosophy. While in Columbus he managed a bakery, developing numerous pie crusts and fillings. When the bakery made plans to expand into a chain, Alan left and with his wife, Helen, moved to Ojai, where they opened a vegetarian boarding house. Alan's cooking became so popular with friends of the boarders that the Hookers eventually expanded into a restaurant.

In 1970, Alan Hooker published the best of his meatless recipes from the Ranch House in the first edition of *Vegetarian Gourmet Cookery*. The following year a companion volume of his non-vegetarian recipes, *Herb Cookery*, won the R. T. French Tastemakers Award as the best paperback cookbook published in America. In the past decade, both books have sold over 275,000 copies in North America, while separate editions of each were published in England and Australia.

SARA RAFFETTO

Sara Raffetto studied painting at the University of California at Berkeley and later with Rico LeBrun in Los Angeles. In 1961 she received a Fulbright grant to study painting in Italy. She has illustrated several other 101 Productions books, including *The Art of Cooking for Two*, *The Wine Bibbers Bible* and *The Tea Lovers Treasury*.